REMNANTS OF EMPIRE IN ALGERIA AND VIETNAM

After the Empire:
The Francophone World and Postcolonial France

Series Editor
Valérie Orlando, Illinois Wesleyan University

Advisory Board
Robert Bernasconi, Memphis University
Alec Hargreaves, Florida State University
Chima Korieh, Central Michigan University
Françoise Lionnet, UCLA
Obioma Nnaemeka, Indiana University
Kamal Salhi, University of Leeds
Tracy D. Sharpley-Whiting, Hamilton College
Frank Ukadike, Tulane University

Dedicated to the promotion of intellectual thought on and about the Francophone world, *After the Empire* publishes original works that explore the arts, politics, history, and culture that have developed in complex negotiations with the French colonial influence. The series also looks at the Hexagon and its borders, and at the transgressions of those borders that problematize notions of French identity and expression.

Of Suffocated Hearts and Tortured Souls: Seeking Subjecthood through Madness in Francophone Women's Writing of Africa and the Caribbean, by Valérie Orlando

Francophone Post-Colonial Cultures: Critical Essays, edited by Kamal Salhi

In Search of Shelter: Subjectivity and Spaces of Loss in the Fiction of Paule Constant, by Margot Miller

French Civilization and Its Discontents: Nationalism, Colonialism, Race, edited by Tyler Stovall and Georges Van Den Abbeele

After the Deluge: New Perspectives on Postwar French Intellectual and Cultural History, edited by Julian Bourg with an Afterword by François Dosse

Remnants of Empire in Algeria and Vietnam: Women, Words, and War, by Pamela A. Pears

Packaging Post/Coloniality: The Manufacture of Literary Identity in the Francophone World, by Richard Watts

REMNANTS OF EMPIRE IN ALGERIA AND VIETNAM

Women, Words, and War

Pamela A. Pears

LEXINGTON BOOKS
Lanham • Boulder • New York • Toronto • Oxford

LEXINGTON BOOKS

Published in the United States of America
by Lexington Books
An imprint of The Rowman & Littlefield Publishing Group, Inc.
4501 Forbes Boulevard, Suite 200, Lanham, Maryland 20706

PO Box 317
Oxford
OX2 9RU, UK

British Library Cataloguing in Publication Information Available

Library of Congress Cataloging-in-Publication Data

Pears, Pamela A., 1971–
  Remnants of empire in Algeria and Vietnam : women, words, and war / Pamela A.
Pears.
    p. cm. — (After the empire)
  Includes bibliographical references and index.
  ISBN 0-7391-0831-X (cloth : alk. paper)
  1. Algerian fiction (French)—Women authors—History and criticism. 2.
Vietnamese fiction (French)—Women authors—History and criticism. 3.
Postcolonialism in literature. 4. Women in literature. 5.
Postcolonialism—Algeria. 6. Postcolonialism—Vietnam. 7. Women and
literature—Algeria. 8. Women and literature—Vietnam. I. Title. II. Series.
PQ3988.5.A5P43 2004
843'.91409358—dc22

                                                    2004012216

Printed in the United States of America

♾™ The paper used in this publication meets the minimum requirements of
American National Standard for Information Sciences—Permanence of Paper
for Printed Library Materials, ANSI/NISO Z39.48-1992.

For Florence Lucille Welton

CONTENTS

ACKNOWLEDGMENTS

Writing this book has been a long journey and has left me beholden to many people, whom I am happy to finally acknowledge.

To my professors at the University of Pittsburgh, I am indebted. It is to Phil Watts that I owe the greatest thanks. I have been incredibly lucky to attend his intellectually stimulating classes, receive his scholarly advice, and call him my mentor. Without his encouragement and constant support, this manuscript would probably not exist. Yves Citton inspired me to critically think about literature more than I ever had before. He, along with Giuseppina Mecchia, Dennis Looney, and Mounira Charrad, also read this manuscript in its earlier incarnation as my doctoral dissertation. I thank all of them for their insightful comments and critical perspectives. Others at the university whom I wish to thank include Ben Hicks, whose guidance has always been valuable, and Diana Meriz, whose work ethic inspires and awes me. I thank both of them for their continued friendship and professional advice. At Millersville University of Pennsylvania, Byron Detwiler taught me to work hard and aim high. I will forever be grateful to him for those precious lessons.

While I was working on this project many of my friends willingly agreed to read parts of the manuscript or listen to my thoughts on different ideas. Literally hours were spent discussing parts of this manuscript with Kim Middleton, whose intellectual acumen and perceptiveness enabled me to construct some of the book's most fundamental arguments. Carol Wilson spurred me on with objective comments and fresh ideas. Amy Reinsel's patient and constructive readings helped shape at least two of these chapters. Aparna Nayak-Guercio has been a sounding board for my ideas for as long as I've been doing this research. Charles Davidson and Claudia Esposito provided me with inspiration, suggestions, and laughter throughout the entire writing process. Special thanks go to Marilou Valdez who introduced me to the work of Kim Lefèvre. Monika Losagio was also an invaluable resource, whose kind heart is unequalled.

It is also essential that I acknowledge Jack Yeager, who, while I was conducting research on the book, willingly answered questions and provided me with the France 2 interview of Kim Lefèvre. Mimi Mortimer gave me professional advice and a forum in which to present my work on several occasions. Rob Mortimer generously gave me a copy of his article, which has helped me to prove my argument linking Algeria and Vietnam.

I am grateful to Valérie Orlando for suggesting I submit the manuscript for publication and for providing valuable commentary on it. At Rowman and Littlefield and Lexington, I thank Robert Carley for his assistance and Serena Krombach for ushering the manuscript into publication.

I also wish to thank my friends and colleagues at Washington College and in Chestertown, Maryland, who have created a caring and supportive environment in which to work: Andrea Motyka, Tamara Smith, John Kluttz, Kelly Meyer, Kitty Maynard, Louise Amick, Beverly Wolff, Colin Dickson, George Shivers, and Cindy Licata.

Above all, I need to thank my parents, Tish and Gerald Pears, whose love and encouragement have always served to remind me that goals can be achieved. My sister, Tammy, was my first French teacher—for that and so much more I am forever grateful. I thank my brother, Mark, for his forthright questions and his dear friendship. To my parents-in-law, Connie and John Costrini, I am thankful for their support and understanding over all these years.

My one regret is that my grandmother, Florence Welton, did not live to see the publication of this book. She was the first to tell me I would be either a writer or a teacher. I think she would be proud to know I have more or less become both.

Finally, my husband, David Costrini, has listened to me discuss this book for the past five years, sometimes when I am sure he had lost interest. However, his patience and solid support have provided me with the strength to complete it. For his selflessness I am forever grateful.

Part of chapter two appeared previously as "Kateb Yacine's Journey Beyond Algeria and Back" in *Research in African Literatures* 34, no. 3 (fall 2003). I thank the editors and editorial staff for their valuable advice and for their kind permission to reprint it here.

1

FRAMING, DEFINING, AND QUESTIONING

According to Françoise Lionnet, in her collection of essays on women's writing, entitled *Postcolonial Representations: Women, Literature, Identity*:

> Women writing in postcolonial contexts show us precisely how the subject is "multiply organized" across cultural boundaries, since this subject speaks several different languages (male and female, colonial and indigenous, global and local, among others). The postcolonial subject thus becomes quite adept at braiding all the traditions at its disposal, using the fragments that constitute it in order to participate fully in a dynamic process of transformation. (Lionnet 1995: 5)

Lionnet suggests that through transforming traditions, regardless of their origin (in either the colonizing tradition or in the indigenous culture), the woman writer is creating a hybrid text that puts into question the binary opposition of *self* verses *other*. In other words, these women incorporate all of their experiences in order to produce a literary output that serves as a solution for divisive problems of difference. The universal message found in their writing stems from the fact that, as Lionnet explains, "métissage is 'universal' even if, in each specific context, power relations produce widely varying configurations, hierarchies, dissymmetries, and contradictions" (1995: 4). For, as she states, *all* cultures have to some degree been influenced by or incorporated aspects of other cultures with which they have come into contact.

This notion of hybridity is in great part derived from the work of philosophers Gilles Deleuze and Félix Guattari in their text, *A Thousand*

Plateaus.[1] In their chapter entitled "Becoming-Intense, Becoming-Animal
. . .," they discuss the ways in which a person's or an object's contact with
another being will create what they call "a becoming." This phenomenon,
according to them, does not allow for an individual or article to imitate or
identify with someone or something (1987: 272). Instead, it creates a space
that is "in-between, the border or line of flight or descent running perpendicular to both" (1987: 293). In other words, "a becoming" represents
a moment of métissage or hybridity. If we apply this line of thinking to literature, the writer who is a product of colonization and writes in the colonizer's language is separate from the colonizing power (there is no assimilation). Instead, the contamination of one field (colonized) by another
(colonizer) creates "a block of coexistence" (Deleuze and Guattari 1987:
292). The written product, which is the end result of this coexistence, manifests characteristics of *all* cultures that have impacted the writer. In effect,
a hybrid space is created, in which identity is not determined by one of two
cultures. For Deleuze and Guattari, systems of knowledge and learning
should not follow a linear, what they call arborescent, trajectory; rather,
they should be rhizomorphous, thus producing clusters of "stems and fila-
ments" which connect and overlap with one another (1987: 15). Rhizomorphous or rhizomatic thought enables one to think outside of defined
categories and allows one to envision affiliative relationships that create
new systems of thought.

Another equally useful theoretical framework, and one that challenges
aspects of the aforementioned school of thought, can be found in the
work of Christopher Miller, specifically in *Nationalists and Nomads*.
Miller argues that the concept of hybridity as a model of cultural and literary analysis actually has its roots in colonial literature (1998: 4).
Miller's quotation of Léopold Sédar Senghor's comments on René Maran
is very telling in this respect. He cites Senghor's following description of
Maran:

> [He was] the first man in the Francophone world to be called upon to choose
> between "French writer" and "black man." Out of *integrity*, he was the first to
> refuse to choose; instead, he chose to take on both responsibilities, wholly and
> simultaneously. Such was the attitude dictated to him by the search for truth:
> *dialectically* to go beyond the contradictions of his situation not by *transcend-
> ing* them, ignoring them but, rather, by *integrating* each of the two realities into
> the other and into itself. (cited in Miller 1998: 127)

Furthermore, Miller mentions in his introduction that critics who fail
to permit valid notions of particularism, when interpreting texts, are in-

deed participating in a binary opposition themselves (1998: 6–7). In Miller's analysis, the advocating of one method of interpretation (hybridity) over another (binarism) participates perhaps unwittingly in the very exclusionary tactics it condemns. While Miller does not invalidate Lionnet's work, he does caution us to "maintain inasmuch as it is possible a visible distinction between description and prescription and, therefore, to describe what [we have] read without projecting desiderata onto it. Prescriptive programs based on such work can then be all the more persuasive" (1998: 7).

Throughout this book my approach will involve close readings of four novels and will focus partly upon theories of hybridity and literary fragmentation presented by scholars such as Françoise Lionnet, based upon the philosophical underpinnings of Deleuze and Guattari; however, I have aimed to keep in mind the warnings of Miller and not lose sight of the idea that "each culture needs its 'others' in order to define itself; since self and other are inseparable, the study of a culture should not attempt to enshrine its essence but rather should examine the ways in which inside and outside affect each other" (Miller 1998: 5). In the works I examine we will indeed uncover instances where it is clear that two cultures (French and either Algerian or Vietnamese) manifestly affect one another because they are binary opposites. Thus, although I have relied heavily upon the theories of nomadism and hybridity set forth in Deleuze and Guattari's A Thousand Plateaus and elaborated upon in Françoise Lionnet's Postcolonial Representations, I have also tried to demonstrate the moments in which these theories do not function productively in the narratives. There are occasions where the model of hybridity does indeed break down, indicating a regression to self versus other dichotomies.

The strength of this body of literature can be found in both its lack of clear-cut solutions and its embodiment of the ongoing struggles brought about by colonialism and its aftermath. For this reason, I frequently discuss the fragmentation of the various female subjects. By this I mean the splits that appear within the works themselves, whether they are formal or thematic. This fragmentation takes on various forms: literal sentence fragments; snippets of dialogue; multiple characters and narrative voices; psychological divisions; confrontations with transforming societal roles; scattered memory. For the female subjects presented in the four novels we will scrutinize, fragmentation is not a positive effect of postcolonialism. On the contrary, it is quite the opposite. However, while these characters, as depicted by the novelists, live out very conflicted and difficult, sometimes traumatic, existences that do not serve as models of nomadic perfection, they also reconcile the fragmentation to a new vision of their lives and futures. In other words, they manifest the possible positive effects of fragmentation by reappropriating it and rendering it constructive rather than entirely destructive.

The narrative strategy of fragmentation has been used, especially throughout twentieth-century French-language literature, to create a polyvocal work. Educated in the same system as many metropolitan French writers of the time, Yamina Mechakra, Ly Thu Ho, Malika Mokeddem, and Kim Lefèvre employ and illustrate similar techniques of fragmentation. In chapter three, I examine revolutionary wars in Algeria and Vietnam, demonstrating how fragmentation serves as both the result of (*La Grotte éclatée*) and the solution to (*Le Mirage de la paix*) women's confrontation of changing roles. In Yamina Mechakra's *La Grotte éclatée*, narrative voices and interpretations overlap, giving way to a new form of textual analysis. Ly Thu Ho's characters in *Le Mirage de la paix* fail to unite the fragmentary parts of their lives in an expected manner, yet they strive to allow various, and often conflicting, traditions to coexist. In the subsequent chapter, we examine fragmentation as it is used in *L'Interdite* and *Retour à la saison des pluies*. In particular, Malika Mokeddem creates a polyvocal text through her use of dual narrators in *L'Interdite*. Additionally, Kim Lefèvre demonstrates both literary and identity dispersion by way of repeated use of sentence fragments in *Retour à la saison des pluies*.

Throughout the twentieth century, the idea of a univocal text has become more and more contested, due in great part to the predominance of post-structuralist theory. In his theoretical text *S/Z*, Roland Barthes elucidates his theory of the modern text as an inherently polyvocal work (1970: 37). In postmodern works of fiction, authors develop various techniques to demonstrate this plurality; nevertheless, in spite of the specific techniques employed, the effect is predominantly one of scattering. Writers want to "demonstrate its [literature's] dispersal and fragmentation" (Eagleton 1983: 139). Barthes sees literature as shifting from a fixed representational group of decipherable signs to an "irreducibly plural, an endless play of signifiers which can never be finally nailed down to a single centre, essence, or meaning" (Eagleton 1983: 138). For Barthes the lone meaning of a text does not exist; rather, it is in a constant state of flux. In order to appreciate a literary text one must come to understand "de quel pluriel il est fait" [by what plural it is made] (Barthes 1970: 11). Consequently, literature is composed of fragmentary parts that are not necessarily united to form a whole. One manifestation of this desire to translate plurality during the twentieth century is the frequent and varied use of the technique of fragmentation. Since the

French colonial system ultimately creates the postcolonial female subject we see in the following four works, it is important to understand the way in which fragmentation as a literary technique has been used in metropolitan France. From this we will be able to see how Francophone writers from outside the hexagon have appropriated, then altered, the same technique, which will ultimately lead us to question the differences between *Francophone* writing and *French* writing.

In the French literary tradition, modernism and postmodernism have sought to distance themselves significantly from nineteenth-century realism; thus, these movements have done away with linear plots, character development, and traditional narrative. As Susan Rubin Suleiman points out in her study on the avant-garde, *Subversive Intent*, the fragment as a stylistic tool becomes a key instrument in defying

> the traditional criteria of narrative intelligibility, and correlatively the reader's sense-making ability: where the reader expects logical and temporal development, avant-garde fiction offers repetition or else the juxtaposition of apparently random events; where the reader expects consistency, it offers contradiction; where the reader expects characters, it offers disembodied voices; where the reader expects the sense of an ending, it offers merely a stop. Even typographically, it may assault the reader . . . by offering fragments with no indication of the order in which to read them. (1990: 36)

In post–World War II France, authors such as Marguerite Duras, Nathalie Sarraute, and Barthes have utilized fragmentation in order to question the very nature of language, discourse, and our conception of literature. As Suleiman indicates, we as readers search for a unity within any fragmented text in spite of the literary project inscribed therein (1990: 41). However, often the narrative is broken down to the point that only language is left, therefore implying on a psychological level that the subject of this narrative (if she is discernible) is irreversibly fragmented and alienated from herself. This type of fragmentation is evident in *L'Amant* by Duras, for example. Her semiautobiographical novel utilizes the technique in a way that completely depersonalizes and alienates her from her own *self*. The distance between author and narrator is apparent in her frequent vacillation between first and third person. Take, for example, the following: "L'enfant sait que ce qu'elle fait, elle, c'est ce que la mère aurait choisi que fasse son enfant, si elle avait osé, si elle en avait la force, si le mal que faisait la pensée n'était pas là chaque jour exténuant" (Duras 1984: 34). [The child knows that what she does is what the mother would have chosen that her child do, if she had dared, if she had the strength, if the exhausting evil that the thought made was not there every day.] Here, the author describes the child from a distance, as the omniscient, third-person narrator. However, in the ensuing paragraph, the narrator suddenly becomes a first-person, autobiographical voice: "Dans les histoires de mes livres qui se rapportent à mon enfance, je ne sais plus tout à coup ce que j'ai évité de dire, ce que j'ai dit" (Duras 1984: 34). [In the stories of my books that relate to my childhood, I suddenly no longer know what I avoided saying, what I said.] In this quotation we see the author as narrator discussing her own process of writing in the first person.

Temporal factors also reduce the continuity of the story—if we assume the story centers around her love affair as a young girl, or her childhood in Indochina, then how do we explain references to the Paris of her adult life? Immediately and without any visible transition, after describing her ongoing love affair with the Chinese man, through a first-person narrator, she launches into descriptions of women she met in Paris in the 1940s—Marie-Claude Carpenter and Betty Fernandez (Duras 1984: 79–85). Then, the third-person narrator returns abruptly to continue the story of the young girl's life with her Chinese lover in colonial Vietnam (Duras 1984: 86). Obviously the incongruity of the Parisian fragments represents an attempt to detemporalize our reading.

Another way that twentieth-century French narratives use the technique of fragmentation surfaces with Sarraute's *Enfance*. Her book is a 277-page dialogue between her *selves*, the author and her double. She disembodies her own voice by speaking to herself as both participants in a dialogue. On the opening page of the text, she discusses her plan to write her memoirs. The conversation with herself is filled with ellipses, incomplete sentences, and familiar language (Sarraute 1983: 7). The dialogue takes place inside her mind; she is both self and other. The conversational aspect of the work allows her to pass through a stream-of-consciousness construct that denies the boundaries of time and memory. Each conversation with her "double" will lead to discussions of her writing as well as memories of her childhood. It is through fragmented selves and fragmented dialogues (repeated ellipses occur at the end of her sentences, indicating incomplete thoughts and/or interruptions) that she communicates. She bases the book on impressions of her memories; thus, rather than trying to reconstruct an autobiography, Sarraute merely recounts episodes that resurface in fragments.

The preceding writers utilize the technique of fragmentation to question boundaries: Duras tests the limits of both autobiography and time. Likewise, Sarraute employs fragments to transgress the barriers of autobiographical voice. In the end, they are destroying preconceived notions about literary genres and language. The various usage of fragmentation points to a desire to *deconstruct* in order to *re-create* literature. This is exactly the same process that Mechakra, Ly, Mokeddem, and Lefèvre undertake in their writings. They are (re)appropriating literature; (re)forming it to suit their own experiences and messages; and (re)organizing it through fragmentation. As a literary device, fragmentation allows for multiplicity. In other words, a unique definition of the text, of narrative, or of voice, is no longer possible. It is through the destruction of unity, through the breakdown of straightforward narrative, or through the invocation of multiple voices that fragmentation makes way for new ways of thinking. Furthermore, these four women reach beyond literary barriers in order to confront cultural barriers imposed upon them by the French colonial tradition. Is it not another act of colonial dominance to label their literature as *Francophone*? The literary patterns they are following or contesting are similar, if not identical, to those of Duras and Sarraute, revolutionary French authors of the twentieth century, whose contribution to literary history has been an altering of both the narrative as a genre and critical interpretations of it.[2] The four authors and works we will study herein continue in that tradition of change and questioning. While one model does not suffice for all Francophone literature written by women, or even for all four of the novels examined here, common threads do exist.

Algerian author Yamina Mechakra's 1979 novel, *La Grotte éclatée*, depicts one woman's experience as a member of the National Liberation Front in Algeria during the war for independence. Mechakra, though too young to have participated in the war, did witness the devastating effects and the havoc wrought upon Algeria in the years that followed. Her translation of the tragedy of war comes in the form of this narrative, which does not follow an entirely linear pattern and is primarily constructed through fragments of memory.

Ly Thu Ho's *Le Mirage de la paix* was published almost a decade later, in 1986, in Paris. A Southern Vietnamese woman who lived in self-imposed exile in France until her death in 1989, Ly published three books dealing with Vietnam and its struggles during the latter half of the twentieth century. This, her last novel, takes place during the final years of the "American war" and ends with Reunification in 1975. While her narrative strategy is quite different from that of Mechakra, the contrast leads to a productive dialogic understanding of the representation of women's wartime roles in both Algeria and Vietnam.

Algerian author Malika Mokeddem provides us with an interesting example of coexisting cultures in her 1993 novel, *L'Interdite*. Written with dual narrators representing binary opposites, an Algerian woman and a French man, this novel actually explains how the juxtaposition of these two cultures is not anathema to identity reconciliation.

Finally, as the autobiographical narrator of *Retour à la saison des pluies*, (1990), Kim Lefèvre presents us with a privileged viewpoint from which we will witness the predicament inherent in joining together Vietnamese and French cultures. Lefèvre is, in fact, the daughter of a Vietnamese woman and a French man. Her case is particularly interesting in a study such as this, because she demonstrates the postcolonial female subject who is not merely caught between two worlds, but more importantly, embodying them.

One of the primary difficulties in doing a study such as this lies in the utilization of contested terms. The polemic surrounding the use of the term *postcolonial* has been widely noted.[3] In my use of this term I am indicating neither a static historical situation nor a particularly political one. I do not believe that Algeria and Vietnam need to be examined solely based upon the French colonial era, but my justification for using the term comes from my conviction that the authors are illustrating characters who are precisely affected by the French colonial heritage, more so than any other factor in their lives. The term postcolonial has been reproached for its linear reading of history (McClintock 1994: 292–93); nevertheless, I find it extremely useful for my purposes, because in the four novels I am studying, history *is* perceived in a linear fashion. All four authors describe characters whose existences undergo substantial transformations due to specific encounters with the French. In *La Grotte éclatée* the protagonist is facing war because of French domination of her country; in *Le Mirage de la paix* the French colonial era is seen as having paved the way for the "American war"; in *L'Interdite* the main character is completely transformed by her French education in Algeria; and finally, in *Retour à la saison des pluies* the narrator's mere existence embodies the encounter between a French soldier and a Vietnamese woman. Thus, there is an implied pre-French period, which, although not idealized, does exist in these novels, further emphasizing the linear progression from a colonial period to a *postcolonial* period.

For both nations, the end of World War II served as the catalyst to nationalist movements; therefore, I consider this to be the beginning of the *postcolonial* era, a period in which the colonial powers were beginning to crumble, and in which a firm nationalist sentiment began to take hold. In both Algeria and Vietnam, the events immediately following World War II were decisive. From North Africa to Southeast Asia there exists a wide span of land and water that, at first glance, appears to make it highly improbable to find links between the two. However, in both the nineteenth and twentieth centuries, France conquered and appropriated both areas of the world, attempted to assimilate the people living there, and desperately clung to both regions, forever linking them through a common colonial history. Not only do the two currently independent nations share a French colonial history, but they also possess a common connection through "two prolonged and large-scale [French military] campaigns" (Clayton 1994: 12), waged to stave off the inevitable process of decolonization. Both Algeria and Vietnam suffered under French rule for long periods of time, but with the end of World War II, the process now referred to as decolonization began. Since its colonization by the French in 1830, Algeria had not willingly accepted French rule; however, the uprising that occurred in Sétif on VE Day 1945 demonstrated a new insistence that the French were compelled to notice. With the repression of the uprising, an Algerian nationalist movement was born that would lead to a long and grueling war for independence that lasted from 1954 to 1962.

As for Vietnam, the French had conquered the southern area of Cochinchina a mere thirty years after Algeria, and later, in the 1880s, the empire added the northern parts of Vietnam: Tonkin and Annam. Along with Cambodia and Laos, which became protectorates of France in 1873 and 1893, respectively, France created Indochina. Just as the war in Europe was coming to a close (1944–1945), Vietnam was suffering one of its greatest famines ever. The Communist Viet Minh party, led by Ho Chi Minh, alleviated the worst of the famine by distributing rice to the people and businesses. With the prestige that he gained through his humanitarian efforts, Ho Chi Minh only had to wait until the capitulation of Japan in 1945 to proclaim the Democratic Republic of Vietnam. The emperor abdicated and what ensued was a seven-and-a-half-year war between the Viet Minh and France, with the French finally losing in 1954 at Dien Bien Phu. This led to the division of the country at the seventeenth parallel.

When the French were finally forced out of both countries, crippling divisions remained due to France's particularly zealous fight to maintain control in both nations. History and literature both show that the French empire held on especially tightly to Algeria and Vietnam. In Indochina, both Cambodia and Laos were granted independence prior to Vietnam's long fight with the French, and in North Africa, Morocco and Tunisia, had also managed to gain independence prior to the drawn-out battle for Algeria.[4] As a result, the two countries struggled to rediscover their identities by both denying the past and accepting it.[5] Historical parallels between Algeria and Vietnam abound and will be further explored in chapter 2.

Due to the sheer length of time that the French remained in both Algeria and Vietnam, a French linguistic legacy left its traces upon the populations, especially those who were taught through the colonial system of education. Future writers learned to read, write, and speak in an adopted tongue that they did not forget with independence. When the French left Vietnam and Algeria, these writers began the process of negotiating the coexistence of two cultures: their own and their former oppressor's.

Obviously these writers compose their works in French; these are not translations. Therefore, due to the lack of a better term I have chosen to refer to this literature as Francophone. Recently scholars have discussed possibilities for renaming this literature, and I argue through this study that perhaps the solution is not to delineate it at all.[6] In the end, the particularism and difference inherent in the act of naming serves to undermine the gesture of incorporating this literature into French departments at universities and colleges across the United States. My understanding and use of the term Francophone in the following chapters is therefore a momentary compromise. I employ it to refer to literature written in French by those not considered to be of French national origin. Inevitably, from the moment that a writer, who is considered to be non-French, begins to write in the French language, an internal separation is taking place. Arguably this ambiguous situation may be one of the most significant factors in determining that author's self-perception.

On the surface, the most apparent symbol of the remains of the French imperial project is the language itself. In *Imagined Communities*, Benedict Anderson demonstrates how language is one of the elements often present in uniting an otherwise diverse community. Through a lengthy examination of the rise of nationalism in Europe, Anderson analyzes the various developing stages of this nationalism and its impact upon the Western European colonies abroad. One factor that Anderson notes as extremely important to the creation of communities is what he calls the "lexicographic revolution in Europe," the advent of print capitalism and the unification of a literate population. This "created, and gradually spread, the conviction that languages . . . were . . . the personal property of quite specific groups—their daily speakers and readers—and moreover that these groups, imagined as communities, were entitled to their autonomous place in a fraternity of equals" (Anderson 1991: 84). Eventually, Anderson ties this directly to the colonies and their community formations. Colonial systems of education created elite French-speaking intelligentsias who paved the way for nationalism. They formed nationalist groups and advocated independence, often based upon principles learned from the French.[7] Anderson points to the importance of the intelligentsias in both the onset of nationalism and the creation of future nations (1991: 116).

Thus, the function of language is twofold. On the one hand, it serves as a unifier among diverse peoples and therefore joins together a community. On the other, in the case of colonized peoples, the mastery of the colonizer's language, in this case European, enabled revolutionary groups to gain access to popular European models of nationalism. Consequently, the bilingualism of the intelligentsia played a significant role in nation formation. The intelligentsia facilitated communication between colonial powers and the indigenous population, and many members of the revolutionary forces in both Algeria and Vietnam felt quite comfortable using the French language.[8] Inevitably, following the revolutions, the question of national language arose. Newly (re)formed nations wanted to disregard the French language that had been imposed upon them for more than a century; however, this proved to be more difficult than originally anticipated, since so many of the most well-educated nationalists were better trained in French than in Arabic or Vietnamese. As we will see through the study of *La Grotte éclatée, Le Mirage de la Paix, L'Interdite,* and *Retour à la saison des pluies,* due to the vastness of European empires, borders erected between nations have not necessarily meant linguistic boundaries. Language has been shared and imposed across limits, therefore creating a linguistic community that is ill prepared to define itself as one entity. Homi Bhabha invites us to consider the nation as a creation that

> fills the void left in the *uprooting* of communities and kin, and turns that *loss* into the language of metaphor. Metaphor, as the etymology of the word suggests, transfers the meaning of home and belonging, across the "middle passage," or the central European steppes, across those distances, and cultural differences, that span the imagined community of the nation-people. (1990: 291)[9]

Bhabha emphasizes the creation of the nation that comes out of the destruction of a community or particular kinship. In other words, like Anderson, Bhabha sees nationhood as an imagined community, which will from this point on replace the *uprooted* community of the past. The linear root structure, reviled by Deleuze and Guattari, is dismantled, which leaves a feeling of loss that is eventually replaced thanks to the language of metaphor. Here, Bhabha describes, in particular, the reality of exile. For formerly colonized nations Bhabha's interpretation seems largely pertinent because of the importance he places upon metaphorical language. For him, the transference of meaning is uniquely brought about through exile. Note that Bhabha's metaphor reaches across the *middle passage* (a reference to the slave trade, a product of imperial conquests), *or the central European steppes* (found specifically in Siberia and Southeastern Europe and described as vast, empty plains), thus from East to West, across expanses of earth and water. The metaphor here describes the figuratively or literally exiled individual: the postcolonial writer using European languages to render her message in the form of literature. This writer must transgress cultural difference, however impossible that project may initially appear.

It is within this milieu that minority writing becomes an important concept. Bhabha explains, in the context of the minority's discourses within a nation: "Minority discourse sets the act of emergence in the antagonistic *inbetween* of image and sign, the accumulative and the adjunct, presence and proxy. It contests genealogies of 'origin' that lead to claims for cultural supremacy and historical priority" (1990: 307). Hence, the minority writer's work refuses to accept hegemonic standards. As Edward Saïd demonstrates throughout his work, Western literary authority has always harkened back to a set of celebrated texts, the origins of Western literary tradition.[10] This practice has in fact led to institutionalized, unquestioned knowledge about, most often, the *Other*. When the *Other* takes the pen, however, so-called authoritative texts can be reevaluated. The relationship between a modern author and her predecessors is something that Saïd refers to as *filial*, where the son inherits from the father. Condemned by Saïd, as well as by Gilles Deleuze and Félix Guattari in *A Thousand Plateaus*, this relationship is not an alternative for the minority writer, who although schooled in the Western literary tradition does not necessarily inherit it.[11] Rather, the minority writer incorporates the tradition, learns from it, adapts it to her own project, and creates what Saïd, Deleuze, and Guattari would all agree is an *affiliative* relationship.

I have been discussing minority writing in the terms used by Bhabha, in particular, but for a clearer explanation of what it means to be a writer of *minor literature,* I turn specifically to Deleuze and Guattari's study of Franz Kafka, entitled *Kafka: Pour une littérature mineure.*[12] Kafka, a Czech Jew, wrote in German, and presents an interesting case study for Deleuze and Guattari's development of a theory of minor literature. They devote a chapter to answering the question of what indeed it is. Here, then, let us just summarize the main characteristics: (1) a minor literature is written in a major language (for our purposes, read *European* here); (2) everything in a minor literature is political; and (3) everything in a minor literature "takes on a collective value" (1986: 16–17). Minority writing does not have to take place within the "major" nation; rather, minority literature indicates writing done in the "major" language throughout the regions where that language is used. In an analysis of both the study done by Deleuze and Guattari, and a development of the theory of minor literature, Réda Bensmaia describes the concept of minor literature, as exemplified in the case of Franz Kafka, "as the result of an exigency" and therefore not a matter of choice. The minor writer cannot call upon a single heritage of any kind (linguistic, ethnic, or cultural) (1994: 215). Bensmaia's emphasis on the lack of singularity calls to mind the frequent treatment of fragmentation and multiplicity in the works of Mechakra, Ly, Mokeddem, and Lefèvre. All four of these writers demonstrate the desire to manifest the multiplicity of their experiences. They are somewhere between and among notions of singularity. This is precisely the reason they cannot merely adopt the Western literary traditions— the origins—mentioned earlier. While a Western writer may gain authority from the traditions of Western literature, a non-Western writer using that same language must take into account *multiple* origins, *multiple* authorities, and *multiple* identities.

These multiplicities vary from author to author; therefore, it is impossible to propose that there exists but one Francophone voice. I would, however, argue that the French linguistic, as well as literary, heritage present inherently in works written in the French language tends to bind these writers together. As Mary Jean Green points out, there is an understood linguistic bond that links literatures that might otherwise be extremely foreign to one another (Green et al. 1996: xi).

In addition to the common bond of French as a language of expression in their works, the four authors I study, Mechakra, Ly, Mokeddem, and Lefèvre, also share a desire to "de-exoticize the non-West, indicating the centrality of their concerns to the self-understanding of people everywhere. They insist on the relational nature of identity and difference" (Green et al. 1996: xi).[13] Within all four novels, both France itself and its literary traditions are redefined. Take, for example, Mechakra's novel, *La Grotte éclatée*, whose first edition was published in 1979. Among several references to metropolitan French literature are verses from Ronsard, prose from Gide, and echoes of structuralist theories prevalent in French literary criticism from the 1970s. Mechakra utilizes all of these references to canonical French literature and theory in order to reappropriate the French literary tradition. In a slightly different way, Ly's characters struggle with the Western influence upon their culture and question the role of tradition in their lives. Ultimately, the women in *Le Mirage de la paix* must make a decision as to how to incorporate Western ideals, Communism, and traditional Vietnamese culture into their lives in a positive, constructive way. Vietnam does not serve as an exotic backdrop to a purely anthropological study; rather, Ly forces the reader (presumably Western or at least literate in French) to see parallels between her own life and that of the women in this book. Mokeddem, in a text that condemns the role left to women in contemporary Algeria, does not promote France as a bastion of liberty contradicting Algerian realities. France does not serve as the ideal solution to Algerian problems in *L'Interdite*. She shows the ambiguity of her protagonist's choices; the impossibility of complete happiness with one's final decision; and the redefinition of the legacy of French colonialism as seen through her main character's eyes and the eyes of the young visionary, Dalila. Finally, Lefèvre's Vietnam in *Retour à la saison des pluies* works to undo both the narrator's own nostalgic memories of her childhood, and the reader's preconceived notions of the Vietnamese landscape. Furthermore, Lefèvre's Paris evokes the Asian quarters of the city, which might be unfamiliar to the Western reader or to someone who has read only French metropolitan accounts of the capital.

These four works stand in opposition, therefore, to both the clichéd exoticism and the ambivalent attitude toward colonial ideology present in much of the prose written in French during and since the colonial period. In his study, *Phantasmatic Indochina*, Panivong Norindr discusses the perpetuating of exotic stereotypes and colonial ideology through the invention or creation of an imaginary space, Indochina. According to Norindr, "At issue is not simply the fictional or real existence of Indochina but, perhaps even more important, the question of how factual truths have been used and manipulated to construct an identity for Indochina" (1996: 2). It is precisely this act of identity construction that the Vietnamese writers Ly Thu Ho and Kim Lefèvre are problematizing in their fiction. Instead of working to define a whole, unique identity for their characters, they show the parts that attempt to constitute a whole, but which often result in a group of fragments, and remain simply parts. One of the myriad pieces of their identities is constituted through memory. However, in their memories, the landscape of Indochina is not depicted as a location of desire or of nostalgia. If it initially is, this notion is later discounted as false.[14] In his introduction, Norindr notes that for Western writers using Southeast Asia as a backdrop, "Its [Indochina's] luminous aura sustains memories of erotic fantasies and perpetuates exotic adventures of a bygone era" (1996: 1). Unlike Ly and Lefèvre, for example, Marguerite Duras takes an ambiguous stand on the colonial history of Indochina. In a chapter dedicated to what he calls the "Indochinese trilogy" of Duras (*Un Barrage contre le pacifique*, *L'Amant*, and *L'Amant de la Chine du Nord*) Norindr demonstrates instances where

Duras subverts Western stereotypes—in particular, he writes that Duras's depiction of the Chinese lover in *L'Amant* "seems to subvert the type of sterile masculinity associated with Western clichéd notions of virility" (1996: 126). However, Norindr concedes that Duras's nostalgic Indochinese setting and refusal to admit political ideology into her work (in spite of the fact that it does surface by way of architectural and urban allusions) lead to an ambivalence: "One cannot look to Duras's Indochinese trilogy for a radical critique of the colonial situation. Like the protagonists of her novels, Duras negotiates the physical and symbolic geographies of Indochina in too ambivalent a fashion to support and sustain a coherent critical position" (1996: 130).

Robert Templer, like Norindr, points out the nostalgic fantasies of colonialism that continue to pervade Western notions of *Indochine*. Templer notes, in particular, that the West has acquired two different images of Vietnam: *Indochine* and *Nam*, both of which are nostalgic fantasies (1999: 11). Where *Indochine* implies the French colonial era, *Nam* makes reference to the television coverage of the American war in Vietnam. Templer emphasizes the disappointment of nostalgia-seeking tourists who discover, instead of these colonial visions, a poverty-stricken nation, suffering from failed Communism and struggling with a new form of Socialist capitalism.[15] Given these Western notions of Vietnam, writing for a Western audience about Vietnam could easily present an impasse for Vietnamese Francophone writers. Herein lies a major difference among the works of Duras, postcolonial *French* subject, and Ly and Lefèvre, postcolonial *Francophone* subjects. Both Ly and Lefèvre aim to "de-exoticize the non-West"; they do not allow for ambivalence regarding colonialism or its effects. Rather, they depict characters who need to negotiate the ambiguities caused by the link between the East and the West. Whereas Duras's three books fluctuate between subversion and acceptance of colonial ideology, *Le Mirage de la paix* and *Retour à la saison des pluies* seem to bypass the problem of colonialism altogether and instead deal with the issues facing the *post*colonial female subject, who is a product of the French *Indochine* as well as the American war in Vietnam. Consequently, they avoid the impasse of ideology and manage to debunk myths through their own descriptions of the landscape.

Similarly, the backdrop of Algeria has allowed "erotic fantasies" and "exotic adventures" to permeate all levels of French literature and art since the colonial era to the present. In describing the emergence of the Francophone novel in Algeria, Zahia Smail Salhi begins by surveying literature produced by French writers of the mid-nineteenth century about Algeria: "These writers created a literature of exoticism in which the central features were the desert, the palm tree and the camel. As for the native population, they were either presented as just another decorative element in the exotic background, or completely ignored" (Z. Salhi 1999: 16).

Later generations of French writers continued either consciously or sub-consciously to repeat the gesture of exoticizing and eroticizing the Algerian landscape. In his seminal text, *Culture and Imperialism*, Edward Saïd re-minds us that throughout much of the twentieth century Algeria is often treated as "an exotic locale in which [European protagonists'] spiritual problems . . . can be addressed and therapeutically treated" (1994: 183). As a primary example, Saïd discusses Albert Camus's short story, *La Femme adultère*, in which the main female character, Janine, suffers from emo-tional and psychological difficulties. She turns to the Algerian earth as a source of solace and pleasure. In the final scene of the novella, Janine com-munes with nature in a highly erotic passage that simulates sexual climax. The attachment to the earth provides one of the most literal examples of *pied-noir* appropriation of Algerian soil.[16] Beyond that, the erotic nature of her possession of the earth emphasizes a European preoccupation with the mysterious eroticism of the "Orient."

Likewise, Malek Alloula resurrects colonial postcards from the early twentieth century in his study, *The Colonial Harem*, in order to reveal the exotic and erotic objectification of Algeria and Algerians. Alloula's work aims to give the power of voice and *gaze* back to the models of these post-cards: "A reading of [this] sort . . . would be entirely superfluous if there ex-isted photographic traces of the gaze of the colonized upon the colonizer. In . . . the absence of a confrontation of opposed gazes, I attempt here, lag-ging far behind History, to return this immense postcard to its sender" (1986: 5). Through Alloula's collection of pictorial representations the reader bears witness to the process of *exoticizing* Algerian culture. Inherent in this exoticism, carried across the Mediterranean to France, is an element of eroticism, which is, Alloula notes, essential to phantasm: "There is no phantasm . . . without sex" (1986: 3). The creation of this notion of Algeria left an indelible mark especially upon those who had never been to the colony.

In both Yamina Mechakra's *La Grotte éclatée* and Malika Mokeddem's *L'Interdite*, the female protagonists do not fit any of the ready-made molds crafted by French writers, photographers, or artists. Rather than painting the portrait of an erotic, exotic landscape, Mechakra roughly sketches the daily toil and torture of war as seen through a woman's eyes. Our narrator is not only de-exoticized because of her role in the war, but she is also the pure contradiction to Alloula's postcards. Whereas the colonial postcards demonstrate the imbalance of power between photographer and subject, colonizer and colonized, man and woman, *La Grotte éclatée* metaphorically depicts the subject turning her gaze upon the photographer, the formerly colonized wresting power away from the former colonizer, and the woman as the primary lens through which we see the world. By the same token, Mokeddem's protagonist, Sultana, avoids immediate identification with both Algeria and France. As a doctor, a single woman, and an immigrant to France, she flatly refutes all the stereotypes of Algerian women that have been perpetuated since colonial times.

In addition to refuting Western stereotypical portrayals of Algerian and Vietnamese women, these authors implicitly (and in certain instances, explicitly) raise the question of nationality as a marker for identity. The problem of labeling them as either Algerian or Vietnamese forces one to confront the difficult question of nationality. Is an Algerian someone who is born in the country, someone who resides there, someone whose parents were either born or lived there, or is there some other defining factor of nationality? Does it merely reflect what appears on one's passport? Exceptional cases abound. Take, for example, the poet Jean Sénac. A *pied-noir*, therefore of European descent, Sénac chose to become an Algerian citizen and moved permanently there in 1962 following Algerian independence. Is he therefore Algerian? Contrast this to Albert Camus, who, although born in Algeria, later moved to France, and is cited now as a French writer, not as an Algerian one. Furthermore, let us consider the case of Kim Lefèvre, who has resided in France since the 1970s and has maintained (until recently) limited contact with Vietnam. Her father was French; however, she speaks poignantly of the difficulties she encounters when as a Vietnamese-French woman, she attempts to obtain a visa for travel to Vietnam. Her passport is French, but the Vietnamese embassy employees still see her as Vietnamese, not French.

As we can see, labeling the novelists and literature I will examine appears dubious and inevitably erroneous. In order to render the analysis coherent, I have chosen to employ these questionable national distinctions only when necessary, because I agree with Jack Yeager, who in the context of Francophone Vietnamese literature, speaks of the impossibility of categorizing it as either French or Vietnamese. He says that more than a national literature per se, it is an anomaly and a response to colonialism (1987: 7). None of the novels I examine can really be read as purely national works, that is, works belonging to one nation. Even *La Grotte éclatée*, arguably a nationalist novel, which uses the war for independence as the setting for the text, appears to distance itself from a reading that would tend to classify it in purely national terms. Since Mechakra did not in fact write the novel until the 1970s, it is impossible to view this as simply a nationalist work. Her goal could not be solely to promote the Algerian call for independence, because by the time she wrote the book, Algeria was already independent. Far from falling in line with a nationalist reading, *La Grotte éclatée* questions and attempts to answer its own questions on national identity.

The Maghreb and Indochina share a unique perspective on the phenomenon and predicament of Francophonie, which, in turn, enables us to examine certain parallels between the literatures of both regions. Yeager confirms this and expands on the question of language in Vietnamese writing and intellectual life: "Certainly the Vietnamese who were capable of writing creatively in French had spent years studying and to some degree being propagandized by the French-regulated educational system" (1987: 51). In addition, their choice to write in French did not constitute a great departure from the norms of intellectual life: "Among intellectuals . . . creating in another language was perfectly ordinary, in line with the imitation of the past so revered by Confucians. That the language was French rather than Chinese was merely a variation on an old familiar theme" (Yeager 1987: 53). However, Gail Kelly points out that the reformed script of the Vietnamese alphabet, Quoc-Ngu, instituted by the French, effectively separated ensuing generations of Vietnamese students from their own national literature, because they could no longer read it (1991: 25). The ultimate result of Vietnamese written with a Roman alphabet was ignorance of Vietnamese literature.

Similarly, in Algeria, according to Elisabeth Schemla,

[t]he written culture . . . has always been in the language of the colonizer: Saint Augustine, whose native tongue was Berber, wrote in Latin, the language of the region's Roman colonizers; Ibn Khaldoun . . . wrote in the language of the Arab colonizers; and contemporary authors like Kateb Yacine write in French, the language inherited from Algeria's last colonial era. (1998: 159–60)[17]

Heggoy indicates also that writing in French meant writing to a foreign audience, but that writing in standard Arabic would still not have alleviated this problem: "Had they been able to write in Arabic, they would still be caught in an impossible dilemma: their readers would be Egyptians and Syrians, for example, but only a few were Algerians" (1991: 107).

Beyond the psychologically ambiguous implications of choice, forced and free, of one language, that of the colonizer's, over another, that which is native, comes the political question of such a choice. And yet, as Serge Gavronsky indicates, French is not really a choice for most of these writers. Although Gavronsky's analysis deals primarily with sub-Saharan African writers and their experiences with French, his findings with regard to the educational use of French can be applied to both Algeria and Vietnam as well. According to him,

> French, from his earliest school experiences, was assimilated to the future [colonized] writer's vision of culture. French assumed the function of a linguistic code within which his literary self could and did naturally, find expression, in contrast to a native code which his parents, the priest, and the professor all systematically degraded. (1978: 845)

The French language becomes the unique tool for expression due to the devaluation of native culture and lauding of the colonizer's history and literature. All of the models serving as reference for the future writer will come from a French background, relegating the child's own civilization to an inferior position that is virtually ignored to the point of degradation by its own people. As soon as a language is used as the means for education, an ideological framework is created. The schoolchild will no longer hold his or her own culture in the same esteem. Frantz Fanon supports this notion of the implicit ties between culture and language: "Parler, c'est être à même d'employer une certaine syntaxe, posséder la morphologie de telle ou telle langue, *mais c'est surtout assumer une culture, supporter le poids d'une civilisation*" (1952: 14).[18] [To speak is to be able to use a certain syntax, possess the morphology of this or that language, *but it is especially to assume a culture, support the weight of a civilization.*]

This is especially problematic for the minority of young women who were educated in the French-language tradition at school, but expected to maintain traditional positions at home and in their society. Among the many consequences of the forced adoption of French in both countries, some women were suddenly sent to French schools. This new and separate path began to slowly transform selected parts of the female population in both Algeria and Vietnam. Although the French government initially expressed hesitation about educating colonized girls, opportunities were made available.[19] These girls were introduced to French notions of culture and civilization along with the traditional literary canon. Undoubtedly the French *mission civilisatrice* was not altruistic, but it did provide women with a new avenue for learning. While women's education did exist in both countries prior to the French system, it was certainly neither common nor compulsory.

My research is limited in scope to Francophone literature although literature written by women in both Arabic and Vietnamese has become more and more readily available. Initially, issues of publication may have prevented women's production in Arabic and Vietnamese, but in addition to that practical reality, we must not forget the educational background of the first novelists to emerge from both Algeria and Vietnam. These women are members of the bourgeoisie, educated in the French system, thus both familiar with the European literary tradition and literate in French.

Due to the exclusionary nature of the colonial educational system, the majority of women continued to remain outside educational structures. Often, only the urban middle-class population was affected by the French educational system, while rural women, as well as men, received much less attention from the French government. The Vietnamese author Mai Thu Vân points this out: "Pendant la colonisation, seule une minorité de citadines bénéficiaient de ce privilège; elles allaient faire leurs études en France" (1983: 47–48).[20] [During colorization only a minority of townswomen benefited from this privilege; they went to do their studies in France.] The majority of Francophone writers to come out of both Algeria and Vietnam represent an extremely narrow sample of the population. This is important to remember when considering the question of choosing to write in French: For many of these authors, there was/is no choice. The language in which they were educated is the language in which they will produce their own work.

Some women turned to writing in the colonizer's language as an alternative through which to reconcile the two opposing worlds they had to face daily. It is not without bitterness that these women began to search for a forum in which to express their thoughts. Ahmed Lanasri explains that the literature born out of this forced marriage between colonized subjects and the colonizer's language is a "produit hybride, . . . dès sa naissance, marquée par l'équivocité du sens. Conçue d'un croisement placé sous le signe de la violence physique et morale, cette production porte en elle les stigmates de la résignation et de la révolte" [hybird product, . . . from its birth, marked by ambiguity of meaning. Conceived from a meeting replete with physical and moral violence, this production carries within it the stigmas of resignation and revolt] (1995: 177). From its very inception this body of writing will be confrontational, and for women it will be even more so. Unlike men who had been writing earlier in Arabic, Latin, Vietnamese, or Chinese, most Algerian and Vietnamese women had never had the opportunity to write. The French language and educational system allowed for this new avenue of expression to emerge.

Not only did education play a key role in the language of expression for most authors, but publication practices have also influenced the emergence of works written in French. While both Algeria and Vietnam have had and continue to have their own publishing houses, during the wars and immediately following them, the government supervised all material to be published. In other words, a certain amount of censorship pervaded the publishing process. If a text was written in French, it could be sent for publication in France where the rules governing content would have been much less strict. In the climate of 1950s Vietnam, for example, regardless of the language used, a text would not be published unless it "served the Revolution and the masses" (Templer 1999: 179). The situation in Algeria bears some resemblance in that "Algerian literature . . . has become fairly well known simply because, being written in French, it could be published in France, and thus had no trouble reaching an international public. Algerians who write in Arabic, however, must be ever on the lookout for new ways to promote their work" (Voogd 1985: 92).

Today the widespread availability of Algerian texts, art, and music in France seems to be in great part due to the large Maghrebian immigrant population now living in the metropole. Additionally, former pieds-noirs who moved to France in 1962 provide an audience for this body of North African work.[21] Publishing houses have begun to capitalize upon this and several years ago the large multimedia chain FNAC featured books by Algerian writers, CDs by various "beurs,"[22] and magazines focusing on contemporary Algeria. Television features, such as the popular *Bouillon de Culture*, animated by Bernard Pivot, have helped to bring recognition to a variety of Algerian writers, including novelists, sociologists, and political activists.[23]

Although the audience for Vietnamese literature is much less evident to discern, Kim Lefèvre did enjoy success in France thanks to Bernard Pivot's previous television program, *Apostrophes,* in 1989, and to the subsequent growth of interest in the French role in Vietnam. The sudden revisiting of colonial Indochina in film and television sparked this interest.[24] Moreover, recent critical attention has been paid to the author Linda Lê, who was born in Vietnam in 1962 but moved to France in 1975, where she has lived ever since. Like Lefèvre, she has been featured on television programs and in French magazines.

No longer underrepresented in principle, but often used as tools for the translation of feminist values, these women writers merit the focus of my work because they are speaking for themselves and not allowing "[m]iddle-class Western feminists [to claim] political representation of all women—the right to speak for them—by constructing the image of a universal womanhood that privilege[s] categories of gender and erase[s] those of race and class" (Amireh 1997: 185). Their roles as writers give them the opportunity to express their own concerns—their own feminism as it applies specifically to their own circumstances. They are rendering obsolete "discussions about the essence of women [that] have usually taken as that essence the experience of white, heterosexual, middle-class women" (Mariniello 1998: 4). They are in effect enacting part of the gesture of subaltern speech, to use Gayatari Spivak's terms. For Spivak, the subaltern cannot in the end speak, because she is always *spoken for or about*. Systems of knowledge do not allow for subaltern women to truly speak through the written word. However, although to define these women as the pure subaltern would be misleading—they are after all from a privileged class and writing in a language that might not be accessible to all other women—they are nonetheless representing themselves and thereby taking possession of power and voice. Mechakra, Ly, Mokeddem, and Lefèvre all believe that the reader of French novels has much to learn from them. As Amal Amireh states, in speaking of Arab women writers, these women refute the notion that the subaltern woman "can only learn from her rescuer, but she herself does not have anything to teach" (1997: 189). None of these women sees herself as the rescuer of other Algerian or Vietnamese women; rather, each writer creates a narrative with which various types of women—not *a* monolithic Algerian or Vietnamese *woman*—can identify. Most importantly, the narratives reach across boundaries to a French audience, who will grasp new nonuniversalist concepts of women's issues.[25]

Women writers from Algeria and Vietnam present interesting works for analysis, since they not only have to overcome cultural biases that have only recently allowed them to write, but because they also have to come to terms with the new position that women have in their societies. Unlike men in their societies, these women have more "fragments" to join together, due to their expected roles within their society and their perceived roles from outside. Of the four novels that we will analyze in chapters 3 and 4, three of them are fictional narratives, while one is autobiographical. I have chosen to emphasize fiction because, as Françoise Lionnet says, "[F]ictional works make concretely visible the networks of influence and the questions of identity that are central to the debates over authenticity and postcolonial culture. The ambiguities and indeterminacies inherent in the literary text prevent the articulation of rigid or universalizing theoretical conclusions" (1995: 187).

In this book I will address primarily the questions of Algerian and Vietnamese women's literary representations of themselves. In order to do this, I first show the historical and literary links connecting the two nations of Algeria and Vietnam. I then analyze representation of women's wartime roles, as depicted in *La Grotte éclatée* and *Le Mirage de la paix*, and highlight the creation of the fragmented postcolonial female subject using *L'Interdite* and *Retour à la saison des pluies* as case studies. Examining the similarities found in the representation of the postcolonial woman in the two bodies of literature will show us how the use of the colonizer's language, as well as the influence of French culture and generic standards, have *created* a postcolonial female subject who is, as Françoise Lionnet states in the quotation referred to on the first page of this introduction, "quite adept at braiding all the traditions at [her] disposal, using the *fragments* that constitute it [her] in order to participate fully in a dynamic process of transformation" (1995: 5).[26]

NOTES

1. All references to *Mille Plateaux* will be taken from the English translation of Brian Massumi, *A Thousand Plateaus* (Minneapolis & London: University of Minnesota Press, 1987).

2. Here, too, I am calling these writers French because they write in French and have become part of the French literary canon. However, Duras spent much of her childhood in *Indochine*, and Sarraute is actually of Russian origin. Again, this proves the sometimes ambiguous, always problematic process of categorization based on national boundaries.

3. See, in particular, Vijay Mishra and Bob Hodge's essay, "What is Post(-)colonialism?" and Anne McClintock's "The Angel of Progress: Pitfalls of the Term 'Postcolonialism.'" Both in Williams and Chrisman, *Colonial Discourse and Post-colonial Theory: A Reader*. Valérie Orlando also discusses the use of this term in the particular context of women's identity formation in the Maghreb. See *Nomadic Voices of Exile*, 2–4.

4. See chapter 2 for more on the specific events surrounding decolonization throughout the former French empire.

5. This struggle can still be seen today. In Algeria, "The language which an Algerian chooses to speak is often tantamount to a political statement," according to Martin Stone (1997: 18), and Arabization is seen as a move toward further independence from the former colonizer. In contemporary Vietnam, the fight over how much of the West to accept has recently led to business investments from leading companies in the United States and Europe, but the weakening of resistance has taken some time due to the long history of conflict with both France and the United States.

6. Two interesting colloquia on Francophone literature and the question of nomenclature took place at both Yale University, Nov. 5–6, 1999, and at Columbia University, Apr. 7–8, 2000. In both instances, scholars agreed that the term "Francophone" presents conflicts and contradictions. Monique Manopoulos, in an unpublished paper given at the annual MLA convention on Dec. 28, 2000, suggested that our use of the term "postcolonialism" might give way to the use of the term "postfrancophonie." Farid Laroussi and Christopher Miller have also recently edited a volume for Yale French Studies, entitled *French and Francophone: The Challenge of Expanding Horizons*.

7. An excellent example of this is the case of Ho Chi Minh, the Viet Minh leader, who later became a Vietnamese and Communist hero. Ho Chi Minh received much of his education in France. For more on Ho Chi Minh's education and his life, see William Duiker's biography, *Ho Chi Minh*.

8. Witness, for example, the Algerian Front de Libération Nationale, which initially communicated in French among its members and in Algerian dialect with the people for whom they spoke.

9. Emphasis mine.

10. Although all of Saïd's work reflects his refusal of origin as authority, it is in the following works, in particular, that his theories of origin and authority appear the most clearly suited to this study: *Beginnings*, *Orientalism*, and *The World, the Text, and the Critic*.

11. See, in particular, chapter 1, "Introduction: Rhizome," in *A Thousand Plateaus*, 3–25.

12. All references will be to *Kafka: Toward a Minor Literature*, the English translation by Dana Polan.

13. Our current definition of what it means to "exoticize" something is generally pejorative in nature. Interestingly enough, according to Ashcroft, Griffiths, and Tiffin, "[t]he word exotic was first used in 1599 to mean 'alien, introduced from abroad, not indigenous.' By 1651 its meaning had been extended to include 'an exotic and foreign territory.'. . . During the nineteenth century, however, the exotic, the foreign increasingly gained . . . the connotations of a stimulating or exciting difference, something with which the domestic could be (safely) spiced" (Ashcroft et al. 1998: 94).

14. Lefèvre's initial nostalgic recollections of Vietnam in *Retour à la saison des pluies* are mixed with a sense of loss and a sense of distance that are not entirely negative. She is content to be in France and not in Vietnam. Her return to Vietnam is punctuated by her confrontations with reality, therefore directly putting into question the notion of nostalgic memories. The actual events of her return are narrated in such a way as to deny any exoticism.

15. Templer's observations on several French films dealing with Vietnam are particularly enlightening. He notes, specifically, Jean-Jacques Annaud's frustration with contemporary Vietnam when he was trying to film *The Lover*. Also, he mentions Tran Anh Hung's "Vietnamese" film, *The Scent of Green Papaya*, which was filmed entirely in studios in Paris (Templer 1999: 12–13). These examples are telling of a pervasive myth of Vietnam.

16. Pied-noir, literally "black foot," is the term used to refer to French nationals who were born and raised in North Africa, especially Algeria.

17. Although we will see Kateb's return to Algerian Arabic (in chapter two of this study) in his playwriting, it is true that his work was initially conceived in French.

18. Emphasis mine.

19. See Lazreg's section entitled "Education Fit for Colonized Girls" in *The Eloquence of Silence* (63–79).

20. This echoes the comments previously cited from Gail Kelly, who explained that wealthy city-dwellers often chose to send their children to France in order to obtain a "modern" education.

21. According to Martin Stone in *The Agony of Algeria*, approximately 90 percent of the one million pieds-noirs fled Algeria on the eve of independence (1997: 41).

22. "Beur" is the commonly used term referring to children of Maghrebian immigrants. They are, therefore, second-generation, and born in France.

23. The theme for the popular cultural television program on 18 April 1997 was "La Résistance algérienne." Pivot's selected bibliography included a work by Matoub Lounès, the assassinated Berber singer; Khalida Messaoudi, political and feminist activist; and Leïla Sebbar, a "beur" writer now living in Paris.

24. Some examples of these cinematic forays into colonial Indochina were mentioned in a previous footnote, and include Régis Wargnier's 1991 film, *Indochine*; Jean-Jacques Annaud's *The Lover* (1992); and Pierre Schoendoerffer's *Dien Bien Phu* (1992).

25. I take the term "nonuniversalist" from Mariniello and adopt her argument for a less restrictive and restricting form of feminism. See Mariniello, especially page 4.

26. Emphasis mine.

2

MAKING THE LINK

In *War and the Ivory Tower* David Schalk compares the wars waged by the French and the Americans in Algeria and Vietnam respectively. He notes that "[s]triking—one might want to use the word *painful*—similarities between the manner in which the Algerian and Vietnam wars were actually conducted once under way were pointed out long before the outcome of the Vietnam War was decided" (1991: 16). However, Schalk does not discuss the French war in Indochina, claiming that the French have chosen to bury it and its significance (1991: 174).[1] Although Schalk's statement may appear true for the vast majority of the French, historians have long pointed to the impact of this war and to the relationship fostered between the French and the Indochinese. In fact, as Panivong Norindr points out in his study, *Phantasmatic Indochina*, the French colonial era in Indochina has recently been at the forefront of media attention (1996: 132–33). Interestingly enough, Norindr goes on to note that the French media has dealt with Indochina in a highly nostalgic manner, de-emphasizing the colonial dominance of the French, and by extension, the war.

Perhaps part of the reason that the French war in Indochina has been perceived as less important than other wars of decolonization, in particular the one that took place in Algeria, is due to the relatively minimal support or interest it received at the time it was being fought. For example, Paul Clay Sorum indicates that the vast majority of the French metropolitan population during the early 1950s remained indifferent and relatively disinterested in the status of the French empire in Indochina (Sorum 1977: 8). As long as the empire was intact and presented no specific threat to metropolitan France, the population maintained a certain distance from it.

Remarkably, however, and in spite of the lack of a general draft, the number of French soldiers' casualties in Indochina between 1946 and 1954 is higher than in Algeria from 1954 to 1962 (Stora 1997: 40); yet, the war in Southeast Asia has consistently received much less attention. Figures indicate that French troops lost a total of 37,093 soldiers between 1945 and 1954 in Indochina, while in Algeria from 1954 to 1962, 35,500 French soldiers fighting were killed (Clayton 1994: 74, 175).[2] According to Benjamin Stora,

> L'Indochine reste une ombre, pas encore une tache dans la mémoire nationale française. Coincée entre les "années noires" de l'occupation-collaboration de 1940-1945 et les "événements" de mai 1968, la guerre d'Algérie demeure la référence dissimulée de la guerre. (1997: 40)
> [Indochina remains a shadow, not yet a stain in French national memory. Wedged between the "black years" of the occupation and collaboration from 1940 to 1945 and the "events" of May 1968, the Algerian war remains the hidden reference of war.]

Not only did the events that took place in France eclipse the war in Indochina, but due to extensive media coverage of subsequent American involvement in Vietnam, the earlier French-Indochinese colonial project, and nine-year battle to maintain it, faded more easily than memories of Algeria. The power of television began to surface during the Algerian Revolution and took on a pivotal role during the American war in Vietnam. The illusion of proximity that comes along with television footage gave way to an immediacy and familiarity that could not be attained with the French war in Indochina. "Ce 'décalage' dans la formation d'images est décisif: l'Indochine sera toujours une façade hors lieu, exotique, 'utopique,' hors guerre. Une façade historique passée, révolue. La guerre d'Indochine est lointaine et passionne peu les médias de l'époque" (Stora 1997: 14). [This "time lag" in the formation of images is decisive: Indochina will always be an unknown, exotic, "utopic" facade, far from war. A long-gone historical facade from the past. The war of Indochina is far off and does not excite the media of the era.]

Another important distinction that needs to be made between the Algerian and Indochinese wars lies in their rationalization. When the French soldiers began fighting in Southeast Asia, they were, in principle, waging war against the Japanese. In fact, posters designed to recruit soldiers for the French army stressed the continuation of the fight against totalitarianism

(Hémery 1990: 86–87). French troops believed, or were led to believe, that Japanese involvement in Southeast Asia was an extension of the same totalitarianism that had all too recently ravaged Europe (Stora 1997: 42). In spite of the military's efforts to convince all those involved, this line of thought was not uniformly accepted. The French Communist party, though excluded from political debates in Parliament after 1947, expressed strong opposition to France's empire and to the war in Indochina (Sorum 1977: 6). This ideological baggage may have allowed some French soldiers to justify their presence, but the Communist Party condemned the war as early as 1950 and labeled it a war of decolonization.[3]

In spite of these different perceptions of Algeria and Indochina, it is precisely the war in Indochina that served as a catalyst for nationalist movements in other colonial territories, especially Algeria. As Rob Mortimer states, "In a meaningful sense, the Indochinese and Algerian wars were part of a single historical process" (2003: 61). Ho Chi Minh, a Communist educated in both Japan and France, declared a new Republic of Vietnam in 1945, and thus destroyed any remaining unity within the Indochinese Union. Regardless of the distance between Algeria and Vietnam, Algerians were quite aware of the Vietnamese struggle for independence that was born out of the French war in Indochina. As French colonial subjects, they had been enlisted to fight, alongside other Africans, with the French army in Indochina. These Algerian soldiers participated in and witnessed firsthand the fighting between a colonial power and its subjects: "The inter-war years saw massive use of Maghreb troops for imperial purposes and policing; the Algerian *Tirailleurs* became the work-horse of the Empire" (Clayton 1994: 4). Additionally, many Algerian soldiers, captured by the Viet Minh, were subjected to anticolonial propaganda in prison camps. As Anthony Clayton explains, one of the most significant outcomes of the war in Indochina was this very process of indoctrination:

> Of greater long-term significance was the number of North Africans, particularly Algerians, who became ready converts to the cause of anti-colonial conflict expressed in these conditions. These were to return home with ideas on and experience in insurgency, to make an important contribution to the campaign to follow in Algeria. (1994: 75)

However, it would be erroneous to assume that all Algerians adopted an anticolonial stance as a result of inculcation at the hands of the Viet Minh. Mortimer has pointed out that collaboration between Vietnamese and Algerian revolutionaries can be traced back to Ho Chi Minh's Parisian newspaper, *Le Paria*. Messali Hadj, who would later lead the *Etoile Nord*

Africaine (ENA), the first truly nationalist party in Algeria, assisted Ho Chi Minh with this publication (Mortimer 2003: 61).

Along with these direct links, the Vietnamese also provided an inspirational case study. Their remarkable ability to overpower the French and defeat an imperial army left an indelible mark upon the future of wars of decolonization. The French historian Benjamin Stora, who has studied Algeria extensively, wrote in his 1997 study of Algeria and Vietnam, *Imaginaires de guerre: Algérie-Viêt-nam, en France et aux Etats-Unis*, that the Vietnamese victory at Dien Bien Phu in May 1954 was the first great military crisis of the "white man" in a very long time (1997: 13–14) and that it sealed the end of the French colonial empire (1997: 42). In other words, the European predominance in Africa and Asia came into question, thanks in great part to the demise of the French at Dien Bien Phu.

Decolonization was already riding a furious wave following World War II: India fell away from British rule in 1947, while Cambodia and Laos both declared independence in 1953, the year before Vietnamese victory at Dien Bien Phu. In Africa, colonized peoples gained confidence and imperial regimes began to lose power. Morocco and Tunisia were among the first to succeed in forcing the French out (both in 1956); eventually, Ghana and Nigeria would also break away from Britain (Ghana in 1957 and Nigeria in 1960); and the Belgian Congo became Zaire (today the Democratic Republic of Congo) in 1960. All of these countries achieved independence before Algeria; however, the breakdown of the British empire, due to its relatively nonviolent nature, influenced the Algerian struggle only minimally. The same can be said for the Cambodian and Laotian movements against the French. None of these successful examples of decolonization attracted the attention of the Algerians in the same way that Dien Bien Phu would. The dramatic capitulation of French forces at Dien Bien Phu made a significant impact upon contemporary and future Algerian nationalists. In *The Wretched of the Earth*,[4] Frantz Fanon, the Martinican psychiatrist who adopted Algeria as his country, writes:

> The great victory of the Vietnamese people at Dien Bien Phu is no longer, strictly speaking, a Vietnamese victory. Since July, 1954, the question which the colonized peoples have asked themselves has been, "What must be done to bring about another Dien Bien Phu? How can we manage it?" Not a single colonized individual could ever again doubt the possibility of a Dien Bien Phu. (1963: 70)

Fanon emphasizes the violent nature of the Algerian struggle and points out that violence is a necessary part of the Algerian fight for liberation. Thus, the bloodshed at Dien Bien Phu will predict the same in Algeria. Most importantly, the Viet Minh's liberation of their country proved once and for all that France and the Western colonial powers were not unconquerable adversaries.

Decolonization was also fueled in part by the advent of Marxist Communism, which recognized those oppressed by the capitalist West. In Europe, the Bolshevik Revolution and World War II both grabbed the attention of advocates for change in a dominant capitalist system. Colonial territories, such as Algeria and Vietnam, gained different degrees of support from Communism. Frantz Fanon, who took up residence in Algeria during the revolutionary war, writes extensively about the Algerian fight for independence, and makes reference to Communism as a possible means to the desired end. In Adolfo Gilly's[5] introduction to the 1965 English translation of Fanon's *A Dying Colonialism*,[6] he states that "[r]evolution is mankind's way of life today" and that "[c]apitalism is under siege, surrounded by a global tide of revolution" (1965: 1). In the mid-1960s when Gilly wrote this introduction, global revolution and attacks against capitalism, in general, did indeed describe the political climate of the day. In addition to the massive decolonization that was taking place and continued to occur throughout the world, American involvement in Vietnam was provoking strong reactions. Vietnam had by that time become a divided nation between those who fought for the nationalist, Communist cause and those who wanted to remain linked to a capitalist system inherited from the French and supported by the Americans. Gilly devotes two pages of his introduction to drawing a parallel between Fanon's revolutionary cry from Algeria and the American war in Vietnam. He comments most specifically on the American voices of resistance that were beginning to surface more and more forcefully:

> Resistance to the war in Vietnam, however weak it may seem in comparison with the apparent omnipotence of the imperialist apparatus, must be understood as a highly important symptom of what is gestating in the still unconscious depths of broad segments of the population. (1965: 15)

For Gilly, these voices of resistance linked the peoples involved, whether they were American, Vietnamese, or Algerian. He discusses revolutionary causes the world over and goes on to link "Santo Domingo, Vietnam, Bolivia, Algeria: they are expressions of a single revolution that embraces the world" (1965: 20). Highly Marxist in his rhetoric, Gilly illustrates the degree to which Communism was playing a great role in the movements of decolonization and revolution around the world.

When Fanon initially published this collection of essays in 1959, the Algerian war was still being waged, and France had not yet recognized the Algerian nation. By the time Gilly writes this introduction, however, Algeria is independent; and, in a reversal of influence, Algeria is now providing inspiration to Vietnam where a new struggle is taking place. Gilly comments that "the same masses who create it [the revolution], who live it, who inspire each other from across boundaries, give each other spirit and encouragement, and learn from their collective experiences" (1965: 1). The Vietnamese who had once inspired Algerians to fight against the French could now look to them, the Algerians, in their fight against the Americans.[7]

Echoes of this reciprocal influence appear scattered throughout literary works in French, especially those written contemporaneously to the events themselves. In 1960, five years before the Americans openly began bombing North Vietnam, the Algerian war for independence was escalating. It was at this time that the pied-noir, Jules Roy, returned to Algeria in order to give his account of the events. A longtime member of the Air Force until his resignation in 1953, Roy then became a writer (Dugas 1997: 989). During his military career he served in Indochina, to which he makes frequent reference in his narrative, *La Guerre d'Algérie*. Ostensibly a diatribe against war and its bloody consequences, Roy uses the forum of this book not only to relate his personal accounts of traveling throughout war-torn Algeria in 1960, but also to demonstrate the parallels he sees between the French military's current situation in Algeria and its previous, failed effort in Indochina.

Roy's journey through Algeria takes place in the ranks of the military where he discusses the war at length. The captain who serves as his main source of information and connection to the French troops in Algeria believes completely in the *Algérie française* cause, for as Roy notes, he believes he is defending the West, *just as* he believed he was defending it in Indochina against first the Japanese and secondly the Communists (1960: 135–36). It is this mentality that reflects perceptions of French soldiers in Algeria: a misguided notion that they were continuing the fight they had lost at Dien Bien Phu. Roy continues to condemn this belief by evoking the specter of Marxism that haunted most of the West following World War II. His conversation with the captain continues as follows:

> Pourquoi voulez-vous croire que vous vous battez ici contre le marxisme? L'Indochine ne vous a-t-elle pas obsédé? Personnellement, je pense que la rébellion algérienne est un refus du colonialisme et non un refus de l'Occident. Je suis même convaincu que si la France avait aboli ici tout vestige de

colonialisme depuis la fin de la dernière guerre mondiale, elle aurait pu faire
neuf millions de Français de neuf millions de Musulmans. Voilà ce qui nous
sépare. Vous craignez de voir l'Afrique du nord et l'Afrique tout court en
proie au marxisme et je crois que l'Afrique du nord, toute imprégnée de l'Oc-
cident, n'est nullement tentée de boire à la fontaine marxiste, sauf si nous l'y
forçons. (1960: 136)

[Why do you want to believe that you are fighting here against Marxism?
Didn't Indochina become your obsession? Personally, I think that the Algerian rebellion is a refusal of colonialism and not a refusal of the West. I am even
convinced that if France had abolished all vestiges of colonialism here after
the end of the Second World War, she could have made nine million French
out of nine million Muslims. That's what separates us. You are afraid of seeing
North Africa and all of Africa fall prey to Marxism and I think that North
Africa, completely impregnated with the West, is not at all tempted to drink
at the fountain of Marxism, unless we force it.]

It is interesting to note that Roy sees the French as pushing the Algerians
toward a Marxist solution. Thus, he is highlighting the fact that unlike the
Vietnamese (whose cause became rapidly linked with Communism), the
Algerian nationalist cause was not quickly and irrevocably tied to Marxist
doctrine. However, in Roy's view, if the French persist in their fight to
maintain power in Algeria, then the Algerians will look to the Vietnamese
for further inspiration, including political doctrine. Fanon's A Dying Colonialism, which we have already mentioned, illustrates the Algerian nationalists' repeated flirtation with socialism. Martin Stone affirms, "In 1956 the
FLN held a secret congress at Soummam in Kabylia, where it appointed a
central committee and the 34-member Conseil National de la Révolution
Algérienne (CNRA) and adopted an explicitly socialist political pro-
gramme" (1997: 38). Various emerging nations and Communist states later
supported the provisional Algerian government and the Algerians' rights
to self-determination in spite of the consistent French presence (Stone
1997: 39), which led nationalists to indeed be more and more inclined to
look to Communism as the political solution to create a successful revolution. Furthermore, Gilly's introduction highlights Communist ideology and
the way in which it links various nations and peoples.

At the same time, Roy warns the French not to envision Algeria as a way
to reevaluate the loss at Dien Bien Phu (Roy 1960: 146). Both the captain
and soldiers portrayed in La Guerre d'Algérie are fighting for an illusion of
French grandeur, which in Roy's view is erroneous, because this war is in
fact about people's desire to win self-determination. He emphasizes the
fickle nature of French military loyalty by reiterating that these same men

whom they now fight "nous les avons enrôlés dans notre armée, qu'ils s'y sont bien conduits et sont morts pour la France pendant quatre guerres: la première guerre mondiale, le Maroc, la deuxième guerre mondiale et l'Indochine" (1960: 112). [We enlisted them in our army, where they behaved well and died for France during four wars: the First World War, the Moroccan War, the Second World War, and Indochina.] Later, he says to the captain, "Vous les avez eus sous vos ordres, il y a peu de temps encore, en Indochine ou à Cassino" (1960: 179).[8] [You had them under your orders, only a short time ago, in Indochina or at Cassino.] Obviously, the French war in Southeast Asia is one of the many points of military connection between both Algerians and French. However, this common link has been buried during the fight in Algeria. To recognize the enemy as a former ally would annihilate the French belief in their cause.

Although historically both Algeria and Vietnam have benefited from reciprocal influence, in their respective national literatures, Algerian authors show a greater tendency to reference Vietnam. As we have already seen in the opening paragraphs to this chapter, Dien Bien Phu and its outcome left a great impact upon Algerian nationalists, and in the period following 1954, during the Algerian war, references frequently appear. For example, in 1965, when Mouloud Mammeri published *L'Opium et le bâton*, he saw fit to mention the significance of Vietnam.[9] The main character, Dr. Bachir Lazrak, reveals his frustration with the ongoing battles that the rebels are waging in Algeria. When the fighting began he was convinced that it wouldn't last, due to the inexperience of the Algerian forces and the expertise of the French. In his opinion, to fight against the French manifests a lack of judgment that is erroneously inspired by the Vietnamese and Dien Bien Phu:

> C'est les Viets qui leur ont tourné la tête avec leur guerre d'artisans, leurs officiers illettrés. On leur a dit que les paysans qui montaient en vagues hurlantes à l'assaut des puissants blockhaus d'une armée moderne étaient des paysans démunis et grossiers comme eux, que les mitrailleuses les fauchaient en vain parce que leur foi était la plus forte. Ce que les *nha qué*[10] immergés dans les rizières ont fait, ils rêvent de le recommencer dans les djebels.[11] Seulement, ils ne savent pas que la bombe embarquée à Marseille met des semaines pour atteindre Hanoï et une heure pour frapper Alger; ils oublient qu'à côté de l'Indochine il y a la Chine et ses immensités, ses hommes innombrables et derrière l'Algérie réelle les dunes vides du Sahara. (1992: 33)
>
> [It is the Viets who turned their heads with their war of artisans, their illiterate officers. They were told that peasants who went in roaring waves to attack the powerful blockhouses of a modern army were penniless and ignorant

like them, that the machine guns swept the ground in vain because their faith was stronger. What the *nha qué* immersed in the rice paddies did, they dream of doing again here in the *djebels*. Only, they don't realize that a bomb launched in Marseille takes weeks to reach Hanoi and one hour to hit Algiers; they forget that next to Indochina there is China and its vastness, its innumerable men, and behind Algeria the empty dunes of the Sahara.]

The doctor's statement illustrates what he believes to be the dangerous Vietnamese influence upon Algeria. He recognizes the way in which the struggles of the Vietnamese people affected the Algerian nationalist movement, but while acknowledging the Vietnamese inspiration, he also points out some of the major differences. These differences are the basis for his belief that the Algerians will fail. He alludes to the bitterness the nationalists felt during the war, due to the lack of foreign aid provided them. As he points out, Vietnam received backing from China and the Soviet Union, while Algeria struggled until nearly the end of its war without any support from the Communist Bloc. China finally provided some aid, but not until the war was nearly over. When the doctor speaks of the "empty dunes" of the Sahara being the only things behind Algeria, he is directly condemning all countries that refused to send help to Algeria. His tone is accusatory and bitter. The disillusionment to which he gives voice is the result of a long fight that has left him somewhat skeptical of the Algerian revolution. For him, as for many who experienced the war, the struggle was far too risky, and the thought of an Algerian nation independent of France was unfathomable.

Nonetheless, the doctor shows a certain familiarity with Vietnam. His choice of vocabulary in this excerpt shows the degree to which Vietnam had become less foreign and more familiar: he uses the Vietnamese term for peasant rather than the French "paysan." In addition, he does not gloss the term, assuming a certain degree of knowledge on the part of his reader. Although the meaning is readily discernible from the context, it is still a curious move on the author's part, one that leads us to believe the term appeared frequently enough in French to allow for its use here. Mammeri also utilizes geographically specific terms, such as "rizières" and "djebels," which represent stark contrasts: one is a low wetland; the other is a high mountain region. Once again the author employs a term, "djebel," that comes directly from another language, Arabic in this case. His utilization of the Vietnamese term (*nha qué*) and the Arabic term (*djebels*) within a paragraph which is otherwise exclusively French draws an implicit link between the "foreignness" of Vietnam and Algeria with regard to France. The

French words support and give context to both the Vietnamese and the Arabic words. Neither is rendered completely foreign, thanks to French. Here, the explicit message of the text, combined with the use of language, which can be read metaphorically, represents the revolutionary ties linking Vietnam and Algeria to Francophonie. While bitterly highlighting differences he still communicates how the Vietnamese victory inspired the Algerian fight.

Not only did Vietnam inspire historical events, which are then depicted in literary works such as Roy's *La Guerre d'Algérie* or Mammeri's *L'Opium et le bâton*, but Vietnam also had a direct literary influence upon one of the most well-known Algerian authors to date. In *L'homme aux sandales de caoutchouc*, celebrated Algerian author Kateb Yacine notes the historical importance of Vietnam to the process of decolonization in the world, placing particular emphasis upon Algerian reaction.[12] He echoes this in the following statement from his journalistic writing:

> Pour le peuple algérien, pour tous les peuples opprimés, Diên Biên Phu a éclaté comme un coup de foudre dans un ciel orageux. Un peuple colonisé venait de vaincre sur le champ de bataille la grande puissance coloniale réputée invincible. Pour tous les peuples qui subissaient encore l'esclavage et l'humiliation, Diên Biên Phu, c'était à la fois Octobre et Stalingrad: une révolution à l'échelle du monde et un appel irrésistible aux damnés de la Terre. (Kateb 1999b: 312)
>
> [For the Algerian people, for all oppressed peoples, Dien Bien Phu exploded like a bolt of lightening in a stormy sky. A colonized people had just vanquished the great colonial power, reputed to be invincible, on the field of battle. For all peoples still suffering slavery and humiliation, Dien Bien Phu was both October and Stalingrad: a revolution of global proportion and an irresistible call to the wretched of the Earth.]

It is this revolutionary call that Kateb uses as the premise for his 1970 play, *L'homme aux sandales de caoutchouc*. In it, he acknowledges the struggle of the Vietnamese people on both the particular level and the universal. He reminds the audience or reader of his play that the Vietnamese inflicted upon the French a defeat "*without precedent* in the history of the contemporary world" (Stora 1997: 23), a defeat that would not go unnoticed in Algeria.[13] Even before the battle of Dien Bien Phu in 1954, Kateb began thinking about Vietnam as a setting for his play. In 1949, while a journalist in Algiers, he sketched out the first scenes, which he further developed in the 1960s during his visit and stay in Vietnam (Kateb 1994a: 64). The final version would not be published until just after Ho Chi Minh's death.

It is significant that one of the most influential and well-respected writers of the Algerian war generation selects Vietnam as the setting for a play. This choice allows Kateb to reach beyond Algeria. His work prior to *L'homme* questions and criticizes myriad issues: colonial institutions, social injustice, poverty, government corruption, and hypocrisy. Most of his literary endeavors are set in Algeria, and as Bernard Aresu indicates, Algeria represents a "microcosm of a broader world view" (1993: 7). However, with this play he does not limit the setting to Algeria, his own nation; rather, he adopts another country, Vietnam, as the microcosmic land. As an Algerian Francophone writer, this alternative allows him to portray abuses of power in other nations beyond Algeria, while emphasizing the significance of Dien Bien Phu and the Vietnamese struggle to the world. This attempt to convey an international critique of injustice is demonstrated in the following ways: First, Kateb states an international political message and chooses a setting outside of Algeria to convey this message. Secondly, to enforce his message he employs thematic and linguistic satire, especially in order to render characters from various nations. At the same time, he draws a clear distinction between those personalities he ridicules and those he respects. Finally, he gets formal inspiration from Vietnamese popular theater.

As someone who believed and participated in socialist politics, Kateb's choice of Vietnam as the subject of an epic play allows him to discuss the politics of Communism in a forum outside of Algeria.[14] Although Kateb sympathized with the Vietnamese rebellion and admired Ho Chi Minh, he claimed that his play should not be reduced to mere propaganda. In an interview with Hichem Ben Yaïche in 1987, Kateb reproaches those who see his play only in these terms (1994b: 173–74). He stresses his belief in one existing world community that functions beyond the limits of politics.[15] Moreover, Kateb wishes to emphasize mutual identification and understanding among oppressed peoples, perhaps suggesting Communism as the solution, but nonetheless turning a critical eye to it at different moments throughout the play. Above all, he sees his play as a vehicle enabling the creation of ties that bind human beings to one another. It is Kateb's hope that oppressed peoples throughout the world will recognize themselves in this play and use this recognition to "se parler, se comprendre et agir ensemble" [speak to one another, understand each other and act together] (Kateb 1999b: 337).

L'homme aux sandales de caoutchouc reads as an ultimate call for political revolution, which according to Kateb is "une chose naturelle . . . le mouvement du monde. . . . Les révolutionnaires ne sont pas ceux qui veulent tout casser. Ce sont ceux qui veulent que le monde tourne comme il doit tourner" [a natural thing . . . the movement of the world. . . . Revolutionaries are not those who want to break everything. They are the ones who want the world to turn as it must turn] (Arnaud 1986: 565). It would seem that the way in which the world should turn, according to Kateb's vision, takes into account what Réda Bensmaia has called a "multiplicity of peoples with intersecting destinies" (1994: 225), a true unification of those who have experienced subordination.

As early as 1949, Kateb begins mentioning Vietnam in his journalistic work for *Alger-Républicain* (1999b: 50). He denounces colonial propaganda early in his career and exhorts people to resist and be aware of it (1999b: 68). *L'homme* is the first literary work in which Kateb crosses explicit geopolitical boundaries in order to target an international audience rather than a regional one.[16] His project is facilitated by the fact that the foundation on which he builds is Vietnam, a country whose political and cultural history has indeed played out on an international stage. Due to the foreign powers that maintained key interests in Vietnam's future, Kateb is able to include characters and scenes from the Soviet Union, Algeria, China, France, the United States, and Japan. All of these nations fit into the story of Vietnam, which allows Kateb to comment on each of them while he is recounting the history of Vietnam.

Divided into eight parts of varying length, the play follows a chronological progression, beginning in 40 AD and ending with the death of Ho Chi Minh in 1970. The design of this work is an enormous mural containing eight panels, which in turn constitute the history of Vietnam. Each panel can be seen individually or in relation to the preceding one. From the opening scenes of the play we are aware that unlike *Nedjma*, for example, this text does follow a specific chronological order; however, the time lapse within each panel is neither predictable nor proportional.[17]

Hundreds of years coexist within one small chapter, allowing history to be *re-presented* in an accelerated manner. For instance, within the first panel, consisting of thirty-four pages, Kateb goes from the Trung sisters (40 AD) to the Treaty of Versailles (1919). Trung Trac and her sister, Trung Nhi, vanquished the Chinese and became queens, only to commit suicide two years later as the Chinese crushed their empire. In the space of three pages, Kateb tells their story and mentions Thieu Thi Trinh, another revolutionary who suffered the same fate as the Trung sisters. Within the same three pages in which he tells the story of these famous nationalists, he also depicts a French missionary, who is laying the foundation for European invasion of Southeast Asia. Condensing all of these characters into such a small space allows for the play to become a massive, yet rapid, history lesson. Kateb's writing is thus rich and powerful due in part to its historical accuracy, the result of a massive amount of research (Arnaud 1986a: 588), and to the techniques he uses to communicate his message of international solidarity.[18]

One of Kateb's most effective literary techniques is his use of satire: "irony or caustic wit used to attack or expose folly, vice, or stupidity" ("Satire").[19] Since Kateb is creating a play that addresses political oppression and abuse of power on an international stage, he targets various figures with his satire. He also links events throughout French colonial history, thereby not limiting his satirical condemnation of corruption to French practices in Indochina or Algeria. He even includes colonial West Africa, as we will see shortly. The point of this historical overlapping is to draw his audience in so that he can show them to what degree corruption is prevalent throughout the world. His very didactic approach lends itself to overt satire. The satirical elements within this play come in two different forms: thematic and linguistic.

We see an example of the former in a poignantly hypocritical speech General Decoq utters. Decoq, a French general who is both incompetent and corrupt, has just forcibly rounded up troops from colonized Africa to aid the French forces in the First World War. In this passage Kateb highlights French colonial practices in West Africa, specifically to illustrate Decoq's dubious history.

> Vous vous êtes engagés en foule,/ Vous avez quitté sans hésitation/ Votre terre natale/ A laquelle vous êtes si attachés;/ Vous, tirailleurs, pour donner votre sang;/ Vous, ouvriers, pour donner vos bras./ Mes enfants, mes amis,/ Vous êtes les défenseurs du droit/ Et de la liberté. (1970: 32–33)
>
> [You have flocked to enlist,/ You have left without hesitation/ Your homeland/ To which you are so attached;/ You, soldiers, to give your blood;/ You, workers, to give your arms./ My children, my friends,/ You are defenders of the law/ And of freedom.]

On one level we have the obvious irony present in the speech due to the excessively hypocritical nature of the general's words. The general, *le coq* (the rooster), symbol of France, speaks to the colonial recruits as if they are the agents of their own destiny when they have actually been coerced into service to the French army. He is congratulating them for performing a duty that he has imposed upon them by way of his inhumane acts of aggression against their families. Kateb's ironic evocation of Decoq's violence against the recruits' families calls to mind the entire process of recruitment the French employed in French West Africa at the start of World War I. As Myron Echenberg notes, "France instituted universal male conscription in peace as well as in war from

1912 until 1960" (1991: 4). According to Joe Lunn, metropolitan France dictated only quotas to be met and left the methods relatively open to the colonial authorities in West Africa. They offered rewards, coerced chiefs, issued fines, and even imprisoned in order to recruit over 140,000 West Africans to serve in World War I (Lunn 1999: 1, 34, 38).

Furthermore, Kateb emphasizes the paternalistic overtones of the speech through Decoq's reference to these African soldiers as "mes enfants" [my children]. In the last two lines of his speech, the general's words are extremely ironic, highlighting the satire yet again: "Vous êtes les défenseurs du droit/ Et de la liberté." [You are defenders of the law/ And of freedom.] As we know, the soldiers are defending *European* rights and liberty, but the institutional framework that protects this freedom does not extend beyond the Mediterranean.[20]

In contrast to Decoq, a hypocrite and fictional character, Kateb introduces Henri Martin, an actual historical figure whose case was made famous in 1953 with the Gallimard publication of *L'Affaire Henri Martin*.[21] A French sailor whose initial good intentions serve as an ironic harbinger of things to come, Martin, a former Resistance fighter during World War II, joined the navy with the intention of freeing Southeast Asia from Japanese totalitarianism (Watts 2000). Kateb portrays Martin's intentions as follows: "J'ai combattu les Allemands/ Pour libérer le sol de France./ Je veux combattre les Japonais,/ Et libérer les colonies" (1970: 54). [I fought the Germans/ To free the soil of France./ I want to fight the Japanese/ And free the colonies.] The fighting he witnessed in Vietnam, however, outraged him, because he quickly learned that he was fighting a war of decolonization. The navy eventually transferred Martin back to France where he began publishing and distributing antiwar tracts to French soldiers. This ultimately led to his arrest and imprisonment. In the end, Martin was released from prison after serving only three of his five years (Watts 2000). Kateb retells this story and uses the Martin trial as another sign of the corruption of both France and "le Monde libre" [the free World] (1970: 78). In Kateb's play, Martin's response to the judge calls into question the fact that the "Free World" is not all-encompassing and shows that it is an exclusive club of fortunate Western nations. He reproaches the French and all those who would fight for a cause that is biased and hypocritical: "Celui qui aime la liberté,/ Ne l'aime pas seulement pour lui,/ Mais aussi pour les autres./ La défense nationale/ Doit se faire sur le sol de France,/ Et non pas contre un peuple/ Qui lutte pour être libre" (1970: 78). [He who loves freedom,/ Loves it not only for himself,/ But also for others./ National defense/ Must take place on France's soil,/ And not against a people/ Fighting for their freedom.]

Here, Kateb's treatment of Martin strikes us as markedly different from his treatment of Decoq. Through the satirical tone of Decoq's words and the decidedly ideological tone of Martin's, Kateb points out his own convictions. Martin reiterates the Communist Party's belief that France was fighting a colonial war in Indochina. Kateb emphasizes this opposition by satirizing only those characters whose beliefs do not coincide with his own. He is enjoining us to partake in his ideology, one that he clarifies in the following statement:

De Hitler à Johnson, le chemin parcouru montre bien toute l'ampleur de la débâcle impérialiste. Mais un autre Hitler, un autre Johnson, sont toujours possibles. Les guerres d'agressions, le pillage, la corruption, le racisme, le génocide universel, les intrigues innommables, les crimes quotidiens, les complots et les attentats, les charniers et les four à chaux [*sic*], le napalm, le dollar, la prostitution et l'obscurantisme, tels sont les attributs du prétendu Monde libre, habitué à prospérer aux dépens du fellah, du coolie et du prolétaire. Tels sont les maux qui nous menacent, et continueront à nous menacer, tant que les peuples ne sauront pas unir leurs forces vives, pour écraser l'impérialisme partout où il survit, chaque fois qu'il relève la tête. (1999b: 311)

[From Hitler to Johnson, the distance covered clearly shows the scope of the imperialist debacle. But another Hitler, another Johnson, are always possible. Wars of aggression, pillage, corruption, racism, universal genocide, unspeakable plots, daily crimes, conspiracies and attacks, open graves and lime kilns, napalm, the dollar, prostitution and obscurantism, these are the attributes of the supposed free World, accustomed to prospering at the expense of the fellah, the coolie and the proletarian. These are the evils that threaten us, and will continue to menace us, as long as the people do not know how to unite their living strength, in order to crush imperialism everywhere it survives, each time that it raises its head.]

Kateb wrote this statement in 1968 in an article linking struggles in Algeria and Vietnam. He draws a parallel between Hitler and Johnson, thereby equating the two leaders' imperialist projects and implicating Johnson, leader of the Free World, in war crimes equal to those committed by Hitler. This indictment of Johnson, combined with Kateb's list of the litany of crimes against humanity, bring to the fore his call for unified action by proletarians. This call to action is epitomized in Henri Martin's story. An international audience should find him sympathetic, thanks to his words, which are those of someone who believes in freedom.

Martin, like most of the characters in this play, comes directly from Vietnam's history. Kateb takes this opportunity to play upon the familiarity of their names. For example, Kateb's view of worldwide governmental corruption is echoed in the following instances: American President Richard Nixon becomes Niquesonne—which leads to a series of puns on his name. Colonel de l'Astre, a French commander, shows his disdain for Nixon by saying: "Viens, mon Niquesonne, / Viens que je te nique, / Et que je te sonne" (1970: 130). [Come, my Nique-sonne/ Come so I can screw you/ And so I can beat you.] U.S. President Lyndon Johnson is equally ridiculed when his name becomes Jaunesonne, or the "sonneur de jaunes" [beater of yellow people] (1970: 161).

It is not just the Americans who are satirized in this way, because Kateb also shows irreverence towards the names of Communist founding fathers Marx and Engels, along with their inheritors, Lenin and Stalin. In part IV of the play, Jaunesonne and Lancedalle, the two Americans in command in Vietnam, dress as astronauts and are transported into outer space. Symbolic of the imperialistic tendencies of the American government in the 1960s and of the desire to conquer more land, the scene parodies the first landing on the moon. Once again, this echoes Kateb's own political position: he was an outspoken critic of American imperialism, which led him to write an open letter to Richard Nixon in 1970 (1999b: 338–40). In setting the scene, Kateb notes two red planets, one of which is occupied by Mars (Marx becomes Mars, thus incorporating the name of the planet) and Engels; the other by Lunine (Lenin becomes Lunine, allowing for the inclusion of the moon, "lune") and Staline (1970: 162). The four men use a telephone to discuss the events that have been taking place before their eyes on planet Earth. At one moment, Lunine comments that he has to sleep while he walks because

> Suppose que la revolution/ Mondiale soit engagée/ Pendant que nous allons/ D'une planète à l'autre./ Où iraient les impérialistes,/ Sinon à la recherche/ D'un autre espace vital? (1970: 164)
>
> [Suppose that the world/ Revolution should begin/ While we are going/ From one planet to another./ Where would the imperialists go,/ If not in search/ Of another vital space?]

Immediately after he utters this last line, an American rocket lands on the moon and Jaunesonne and Lancedalle plant a flag in its surface. This gesture further indicates the grand scale of imperialism. To Kateb, this overwhelming desire to procure more land manifests the greed he associates with the so-called Free World. An all-consuming greed such as this cannot be contained even on a whole planet.

These character portrayals, name games, puns, and satirical dialogues all point to Kateb's irreverence for those who abuse their positions of power. He depicts internationally powerful figures in order to show specific examples of untrustworthy individuals. He does not rely on mere symbolism or subtle allusions; rather, his characters are very well known.

Other characters in *L'homme* are not necessarily famous political personalities. Take, for example, Face de Ramadhan. He is an Algerian man seduced by promises of money to join the French army in Indochina. He leaves his peasant's life behind and readily goes off to fight. Once in the ranks of the army, Face de Ramadhan is treated as a subordinate and asked to perform menial tasks. In short, he is a slave to the French officers. Through this character, Kateb shows us a vicious circle of injustice: the French mistreat Face de Ramadhan who, in turn, abuses the Vietnamese people with whom he comes into contact. The playwright attempts to explain how this violence erupts. He depicts Face de Ramadhan in a series of scenes where he observes French soldiers' lifestyles, where they reject him due to his difference (which is compounded by the fact that he is one of the colonized) and where he attempts to diminish this difference. In the end, his efforts to become someone else erupt into irrational violence. He drinks alcohol, begins to gamble, and eventually abuses a young Vietnamese boy who drives a bicycle taxi through the streets (1970: 101). Although the child gives him a ride, Face de Ramadhan refuses to pay him and treats him as an inferior, replicating the way he is treated by the French.

Face de Ramadhan makes every attempt to identify with the French, the dominant, imperialist power. This action represents the error in his ways. According to the philosophy professed by Kateb, Face de Ramadhan should be attempting to unite with his Vietnamese brothers. The international solidarity that can be created comes only through the unification of the oppressed. The dominant power will continue to see him as nothing more than the colonized, which means the French will never see him as an equal, regardless of the measures he takes to assimilate their way of life.

Of course, in choosing the name "Face de Ramadhan" for an ignoble Algerian character, the author wanted to create a certain reaction in the reader. Considering the satirical tone prevalent throughout the play, it is not surprising that he creates a name out of the holiest month in the Islamic year. However, even beyond the ridiculous nature of the name, it is interesting to note that this man is the *face* of Ramadan. In his name he embodies the exterior image of Ramadan as a pious and holy month. However, underneath this faciality is a complete black hole of subjectivity entirely different from what we expect to see. It is this subjectivity about which Deleuze and Guattari write in *A Thousand Plateaus* in the chapter entitled "Year Zero: Faciality." They point out that the identifying marker with which humans are predominantly obsessed is the face, although this external expression sometimes does not leave an accurate impression, nor does it give an individual any kind of identity. In fact, the face and its features deceive us into believing we know the subjectivity underneath. If we read the character of Face de Ramadhan in light of Deleuze and Guattari's theory, we can see him in effect as unidentifiable through his face. The face of Ramadan, the part that is presented to the world, is a holy, self-sacrificing image. The reality of this character, Face de Ramadhan, is that he is violent and disrespectful to both his religion and his fellow man. Moreover, Face de Ramadhan does not escape the trappings of faciality himself. Because he is unable to "escape the face, to dismantle the face and facializations" (1987: 171), he sees the Vietnamese people as infidels, as people to be despised. He is far too concerned with his exterior difference from the French, and by extension, the Vietnamese people's differences from him, to understand that the (sur)face is nothing more and nothing less than a societal construct, one that is very powerful. Deleuze and Guattari explain that this obsession with faciality is primarily a Western, especially Christian, phenomenon: "The face is not a universal. It is not even that of the white man; it is White Man himself. . . . The face is Christ. The face is the typical European" (1987: 176). Face de Ramadhan seems to have fallen victim to this Christian compulsion. In trying to be less Muslim he fixates on this exteriority, which will fail him, because he can never change his face; rather, he needs to overcome it. Furthermore, his name presents an irreconcilable situation in Islam. Muslims do not represent the human form in their art. This means that a face of Ramadan cannot exist. There is no external human form that can be rendered according to Islamic precepts. Thus, the faciality of this character is challenged on yet another level.

In an even more daring move, Kateb names Face de Ramadhan's Algerian friend Mohamed. However, this character reacts in a completely different manner, emphasizing the ties that bind Vietnamese and Algerian peoples:

Moi, les Viets,/ Je ne peux pas tirer sur eux, / C'est plus fort que moi./ Et quand je les vois/ Monter à l'assaut,/ Je suis fier, comme si c'étaient/ Des gens de mon village. (1970: 121)

   [Me, the Viets, / I can't shoot at them,/ It's beyond my control./ And when I see them/ Mounting an assault/ I am proud, as if they were/ People from my village.]

Mohamed is removed from the arguments of faciality because he realizes that the face is not a marker of individual identity—he says when he *sees* the Vietnamese soldiers it is as if they were from his village. He seems to be

echoing Deleuze and Guattari's statement that "[i]t is not the individuality
of the face that counts" (Deleuze and Guattari 1987: 175). In their explanation of racism, Deleuze and Guattari state the following: "From the viewpoint of racism, there is no exterior, there are no people on the outside.
There are only people who should be like us and whose crime it is not to
be" (1987: 178). We find an example of this theory of racism in Face de Ramadhan's thought processes. Mohamed, however, demonstrates its antithesis. Deleuze and Guattari's comment that "Its [racism's] cruelty is equaled
only by its incompetence and naïveté" (178) reflects the reader's perception
of Face de Ramadhan, while reinforcing the inherent goodness in Mohamed. Kateb could not have chosen a better mouthpiece than a character
named Mohamed, who is the Prophet, never represented with physical attributes. In his name alone, he opposes Face de Ramadhan. Mohamed's acceptance of an international bond with the Vietnamese ultimately pre-
scribes the message that Kateb wishes to express, a universal fraternity. The
contrast between the two characters, Face de Ramadhan and Mohamed,
highlights the didactic nature of the play. Kateb uses the first man to explain
the pitfalls of imperialist sympathies and the second to underscore the revolutionary hope to be discovered among the oppressed.

Throughout *L'homme* Kateb also deconstructs language by mixing English, Arabic, and Vietnamese with the dominant French. Colonel
Lancedalle's words are peppered with English words, such as "please"
(1970: 86, 87); General Harding, the English commander in Singapore, says
"fantastic" (1970: 117) at one point; the Algerian character, Face de Ramadhan, cries "Allah" (121) in a moment of fear. Even the Vietnamese language is briefly included among the myriad languages. In the following excerpt, Lancedalle is bragging about General Napalm's recent victory at the
battle of "Vien-Vien." General Giap and Uncle Ho, leaders of the Communist forces in Vietnam, are witness to this supposed victory, which in effect
represents only a small event. Here, he ties together both thematic and linguistic elements of satire in order to poke fun at the American troops who
think that this battle is significant. The scene takes place as follows:

Lancedalle:
Allo! Allo! Sensationnel!
Le général Napalm
Ecrase les troupes de Giap
A la bataille de Vien-Vien!
*Lumière sur l'oncle Ho et le général Giap. Ils parlent à distance au général
    Napalm.*

Général Giap:
Viens, Viens!
L'oncle Ho:
Viens, viens, poupoule !
Général Napalm:
Bien sûr, que je viens!
Général Giap:
Viens, viens, viens, viens, viens
A la bataille de trois fois rien! (1970: 124–25)
[Lancedalle:
Hello! Hello! Sensational!
General Napalm
Crushes Giap's troops
At the Battle of Vien-Vien!
*Light shines on Uncle Ho and General Giap. They speak at a distance from
    General Napalm.*
General Giap:
Come, Come!
Uncle Ho:
Come, come, little girl!
General Napalm:
Of course, I will come!
General Giap:
Come, come, come, come, come
To the battle of three times nothing!]

In line 5 Lancedalle gives the name of the battle in Vietnam, Vien-Vien. General Giap's and Uncle Ho's lines employ the second person singular form of the imperative for the verb *venir* (to come), which is written and presumably sounds like the name of the Vietnamese city. Although Vietnamese is a tonal language and therefore possesses a different sound system than French, this dialogue shows how the sounds of the Vietnamese language might be approximated in French. General Napalm repeats the verb in line 13, followed by General Giap's quintuple utterance of it in line 15. Kateb uses the absurdity of this dialogue to ridicule the American military and to show the arbitrary nature of language.

Linguistic experimentation is by no means exclusive to *L'homme*; in most of Kateb's work we see this process. Nevertheless, here he introduces new and perhaps more violent ways of expressing this arbitrariness. He forces us to reconsider the uniqueness of any given language, which by extension manifests Kateb's impertinence toward French. In an interview that Kateb granted to Jacques Alessandra, the interviewer notes his confrontation with the French language in this play: "Dans votre dernière pièce en français, *L'homme*, on a l'impression que vous prenez votre revanche sur la langue française; vous désarticulez, vous déchirez les mots et le langage." (Kateb 1994b: 78) [In your last play in French, *The Man*, we have the impression that you are exacting your revenge on the French language; you disarticulate, you tear apart both the words and the language.] It is through this breakdown, this disruption of words and language, along with the thematic satirical element present in this last dialogue, that we get a hint at Kateb's future literary endeavors.

Kateb designs *L'homme* to instruct the reader, or audience, to teach the lesson of Vietnamese history while sending a more universal message about the oppression of men and women. This didactic theatrical approach is reminiscent of Bertolt Brecht. In fact, all of Kateb's theatrical productions are similar to Brecht's in that he sees them as what the literary critic John Hodgson calls "weapons to bring about social change" (1972: 107) and tools with which to reach the people.[22] Influences upon Kateb are, however, not entirely European, nor solely accountable to Brecht. According to an interview that Kateb granted in 1958, his theater and the theater of North Africa differs from that of Brecht for two different reasons: "Ce que je refuse chez Brecht, c'est la façon qu'il a, lui qui est poète, de freiner continuellement la poésie au profit de l'enseignement d'une doctrine" [What I refuse in Brecht is the way he has, he who is a poet, of continually putting poetry in check in order to inculcate a doctrine] and "Le théâtre nord-africain se sent proche du théâtre de Brecht, mais il penche encore plus vers le théâtre chinois parce que celui-ci réalise une harmonie entre la tradition et la révolution" [North African theater feels close to Brecht's theater, but it leans even more toward Chinese theater because the latter realizes a harmony between tradition and revolution] (Kateb 1994b: 38, 39).

Equally instrumental in his didacticism is the Vietnamese popular theatrical genre, Chèo (Kateb 1994b: 160). Performed thousands of years ago in the northern provinces of Vietnam, specifically in the Red River Delta region, it is a popular musical theater that includes folk tales, traditional dances, history, and moral lessons (Ngoc 2000). As we have already seen, *L'homme* opens with the evocation of the Trung sisters, whose story is a prominent part of Vietnamese folklore. A popular and well-known story, the Trung sisters' exploits would undoubtedly figure prevalently in Chèo performances.

In Chèo, the performances inevitably end with the triumph of good over evil and the celebration of traditional village values. Kateb, in parallel fashion, concludes *L'homme* with the literal death of Ho Chi Minh, but the political death of Richard Nixon, thus depicting the triumph of his good (Ho Chi Minh) over his evil (Nixon). In the final scene of the play, the antiwar movement has taken hold in the United States and a secretary walks into Niquesonne's office and lights a memorial candle in order to signify the death of Niquesonne. Confused, Niquesonne asks why the secretary has placed this candle on his desk. The secretary responds, "Pour nous, vous êtes mort,/ Monsieur le président" (1970: 282). [For us, you are dead,/ Mr. President.] The chorus and Coryphée echo the secretary's words by calling Niquesonne a "cadavre politique" [political cadaver] (1970: 283). When Niquesonne insists that they have all made a mistake because it is actually Ho Chi Minh who has just died, the stage suddenly empties. The Vietnamese chorus arrives and begins to pay homage to Ho Chi Minh while facing his tomb: "Il marche dans nos rêves" (1970: 283). [He walks in our dreams.] Although it is clearly Ho Chi Minh who has died, Kateb illustrates the triumph of good over evil by indicating that Niquesonne's political power has waned and died, while Ho Chi Minh's has augmented even in his death.

In ancient times, farmers performed Chèo for fellow farmers, creating a truly popular theater. Any money they earned would be split among the actors who usually performed on a few straw mats serving as a stage (Ngoc 2000). Today, professional Chèo troops exist, especially in Hanoi, but amateur groups still make their way around the northern countryside performing for villagers. The actual production itself is always accompanied by music and basic props, much as it originally was. Stages, costumes, and backdrops have become much more modern, but the overall form has not been altered greatly due to its popularity (Ngoc 2000). Not only do actors play their roles, but they also narrate the story for the audience; thus, the action is both story and storytelling, allowing a didactic approach, which appeals to Kateb.

The didacticism is apparent in his choice of historical content and also in the above-cited conclusion to the play. Nevertheless, Kateb does employ the same direct communication with the audience that Chèo inspires. For example, the character of Mao speaks to the "public audience" in order to explain part of his philosophy (1970: 160). Later, a reporter also narrates directly to the audience in order to give information on Ho Chi Minh (1970: 217–18). In both cases, Kateb signals this change in format by literally altering the typography. Whereas most of the dialogue is written in verse (both rhymed and unrhymed), the passages where characters narrate directly to the audience are in paragraph form, as a prose passage would be. They are also informative passages that explain important background information either on characters or situations; thus they are highly didactic in content.

As we have seen, *L'homme* is infused with many elements of Chèo, a very particular and local form of theater. Kateb uses it to internationalize his own work, but then appears to become inspired by what he learns about it. While the subsequent changes in his career cannot be wholly attributed to his experience in Vietnam and with Chèo, it is noteworthy that *L'homme* signals a shift in Kateb's goals. With this play he begins a new phase in his literary career, which will lead him to an exclusively local theater.[23] It is as if he has utilized *L'homme* as a vehicle for disseminating his message of universal fraternity and resistance to the power structure; however, now he must go beyond that. Having written and performed *L'homme* in French, Kateb reconsiders his definition of the writer:[24] "La place de l'écrivain n'est ni près ni dans le pouvoir, mais près du public" (1994b: 33) [The place of the writer is neither close to nor within power, but near the people]; therefore, he begins to write in dialectical, specifically Algerian, Arabic.[25] *L'homme* provided him with the first glimpse of a didactic, yet popular theater, whose message is internationalized. He claims that: "C'était un pas en avant. . . . Ma pièce sur le Vietnam est une œuvre de théâtre déjà plus populaire, accessible à un plus grand nombre de gens que mes autres pièces. Le symbolisme est moins pesant, l'écriture est autre" (1994b: 79). [It was a step forward. . . . My play about Vietnam is a theatrical work which is already more popular, accessible to a greater number of people than my other plays. The symbolism is less weighty, the writing is different.] He is inspired to continue his evolution of theater. He decides to forego the *grand public* (general public) and focus on workers, students, and others who are directly involved and affected by the class struggle (Arnaud 1986: 587–88). To perform the plays, Kateb also forms his own acting troupe, *Action culturelle des travailleurs*, [Workers' Cultural Action], who travel with very modest means throughout Algeria.

The redefinition of Kateb's literary project and the change in direction of his career are the results of a desire to reshape theater, the genre he finds most appropriate to his cause:

> Le théâtre doit radicalement changer parce que l'homme d'aujourd'hui n'est plus celui d'hier. Il n'est plus l'homme d'un pays, d'un douar, d'une province, mais d'une planète. Il faut dire aussi que l'homme qui se fait honnêtement dans son pays est celui de tous les pays. (Arnaud 1986: 588)
>
> [Theater must change radically because today's man is no longer yesterday's. He is no longer the man of one country, one *douar*, one province, but of one planet. It must also be said that the man who acts justly in his country is a man of every country.]

If revolutionary literature acts as an educational tool to reach the people, then it must do so in a medium and language conducive to the people's interpretation.[26] Goals will ultimately govern choice of language. *L'homme* remains an international play that reaches out to a wide audience, but this audience is still Francophone. The internationalizing process Kateb undertakes with his choice of Vietnam as a microcosm, his thematic and linguistic satire directed at internationally powerful figures, and his adoption of certain Chèo standards leads him in the end to consider a kind of particularism. He decides to tailor his language and his message to the specific needs of his Algerian audience. Christiane Achour, in her article on Kateb Yacine, explains that theater is the only literary genre that aims to

> s'adresser plus directement au public, de ne pas se restreindre à un cénacle d'intellectuels, de sortir du champ étroit où l'institution confine les écrivains consacrés, d'autant plus étroit et pernicieux quand on est Algérien et qu'on écrit en français. (1986: 26)
>
> [address itself more directly to the public, to not restrict itself to an intellectual think tank, to get out of the narrow field, where the institution confines consecrated writers, a field even narrower and more pernicious when one is Algerian and writes in French.]

She recognizes Kateb's evolution as an Algerian playwright. He began writing in French, but ultimately in order to reach the Algerian public, Kateb turns to Algerian Arabic theater.[27]

L'homme aux sandales de caoutchouc is an excellent illustration not only of the historical parallels that can be drawn between Algeria and Vietnam, but also for the possibility of innovation that comes with the fusion of two distinct cultures. The theater born out of Kateb's encounter with Vietnam points to a new direction for him as a writer. The connection, which is possible for him because of the French language, is epitomized in his work. Without the linguistic connections, the product of a shared colonial history, it would be difficult to make any kind of initial link between Algeria and Vietnam. Thus, we can see that French played a pivotal role in Kateb's career and in his move back to Algerian Arabic. Using his experience as an example, we can see the importance of linking the two nations of Algeria and Vietnam with the French language. French facilitated communication, which would otherwise have made it an unlikely possibility that an author/journalist such as Kateb Yacine would have readily had access to Vietnamese culture. His play is therefore the result of political convictions as much as it is the product of the imposition of a colonial educational system in both Algeria and Vietnam.[28] Unwittingly, the French colonial pol-

icy contributed to the creation of an elite, politically conscious, Francophone class in both countries.[29] By extension, assimilationist French politics led to the creation of a Francophone literature.

In the introduction to his book, *The Vietnamese Novel in French*, Jack
Yeager discusses the ways in which various Francophone literatures are similar or different due to the place of French within each culture. He notes,
"French was an acquired, second, or other language, subsidiary in a cultural
sense to Arabic in the Maghreb[30] or Vietnamese or Cambodian in Indochina,
even though the written forms of these indigenous languages were not in
widespread use" (1987: 5). In Algeria and Vietnam, both Arabic and Vietnamese literature existed before the advent of a French-language tradition,
and Francophone works did not lead to the disappearance of indigenous-
language literature. The two coexisted in both countries and continue to do
so today.[31] Unlike the rest of the Francophone world, the Maghreb and Indochina had two (or more) written languages existing alongside one another
in a relationship of dominance and submission. In Francophone European
countries such as Belgium or Switzerland, for example, the linguistic relationship among several languages is not perceived as one of domination and
compliance. Rather, some speak and write in one language, while others do
so in another. Usually the language one writes is based solely upon the geographical background of that person, which means that no one language,
whether it be French, German, or any other, has a particular status assigned
to it. Obviously, Francophone European countries do not share the same experiences with the French language as countries such as Algeria and Vietnam. In addition, as Yeager indicates, these European countries share certain cultural and literary traditions, therefore rendering the literature much
less foreign (1987: 4). In Canada, similarly, the French-speaking regions of
Québec and New Brunswick utilize the language in order to identify themselves and differentiate from Anglophone Canada (Yeager 1987: 5). It is a
source of regional pride, and a conscious choice to promote their "Frenchness." Other Francophone countries, such as those in sub-Saharan Africa,
have dealt with French in yet another fashion. For many of them, French
was often the only written language available to those who wanted to write,
since the majority of African languages had no written form, or if they did,
few people were able to write it. Not only does this imply a forced choice to
write in French, but it also highlights the fact that many sub-Saharan
Africans who chose to write had little or no written tradition on which to
base their literature. For that reason much literary criticism surrounding the
Francophone texts produced in these various countries centers upon the oral
tradition and its incorporation of the French-language written tradition. Not

surprisingly, the same phenomenon occurred in the various island nations that came under French rule. In places such as Martinique and Haiti, Creole, the product of French combined with various African languages, as well as other European languages, eventually became the language of communication. Its written forms have, nevertheless, been slower to emerge.

In this chapter we have seen the historical, literary, and linguistic ties that bind Algeria and Vietnam. Two of the primary examples used to illustrate these links are Mouloud Mammeri and Kateb Yacine, who are both part of the first generation of Francophone writers. What about those who write after independence, whose generation did not experience the oppression of colonization firsthand? In the following chapters we will examine postcolonial women writers whose protagonists, all women, experience the French language, colonialism, and its implications in distinctive ways. Two describe bloody wars against all that is French (Yamina Mechakra and Ly Thu Ho); the other two experience French as both a curse and a blessing (Malika Mokeddem and Kim Lefèvre). Therefore, when we say that these authors *choose* to write in French, we must not overlook the fact that the choice may not be entirely free; however, we must also avoid interpreting *all* Francophone literature as maintaining the same sorts of relationships with the language and with France. As we will see, the linguistic experiences of each individual author dictate different encounters with the French language. Undoubtedly the educational system left imprints that carried over for many years in both Algeria and Vietnam, but writing in French in the 1980s, for example, implies a rationalizing process that would appear to be completely different from that which would have been used in the 1960s or 1970s (Gavronsky 1978: 846). One argument consistently put forth to explain the continued and growing publication of Algerian Francophone authors is that many Francophone authors see French as the only means of reaching a wide audience.[32] While it is true that French has a wider reading audience than Vietnamese, for example, assuming that an author writes in French exclusively for this reason is reductionist. Obviously the situation is much more complex than that, given that Francophone Vietnamese writers number very few. Vietnamese works are frequently translated into French, indicating that the French reading public is still interested in these works.

Today, authors from Algeria and Vietnam who write in French open themselves up for very different interpretations from their continental French counterparts. They are read in a different manner, because they are often classified in different departments. If the authors are women, the use of French inevitably poses the question of whether or not language serves as a tool of *women's liberation*.[33] This is especially problematic in Algeria, where French has become an instrument of women's opposition to government. My primary concern, however, is not with the concept of women's liberation; rather, my focus is on the literature itself and the way that it fits into the body of *all* literature written in French. These women demonstrate through their works how the postcolonial female subject has been created as a direct result of contact with the French. Each one presents a slightly different perspective upon what it means to be a woman writing in French in the postcolonial era; nevertheless, each manifests the ties that bind her, and therefore her writing, forever to France.

NOTES

1. In using the term "Indochina," I want only to situate the reader geographically. For an in-depth examination of the issue of naming "Indochina," see Panivong Norindr's book, *Phantasmatic Indochina*, in which he states the following: "If the name 'Indochina' was first coined as a geographical marker to describe the southeast Asian peninsula situated between India and China, in a relatively short period of time that coincided with the almost century-long French occupation of sovereign territories in the region, it was identified and confused with a political entity, the Union Indochinoise, which was created to bring together dissimilar nations and kingdoms under one centralized colonial administration" (1996: 2).

2. In Anthony Clayton's charting of the casualties in both Indochina and Algeria, he notes the different origins of the various soldiers who were killed or injured in the fighting. The statistics show that although they fought under the French army, many of those who were injured or killed were, in fact, not French.

3. An interesting case of a French soldier who opposed the war in Indochina and subsequently turned to Communism can be found in that of Henri Martin. For a look at his story, see Philip Watts's forthcoming article, "The Henri Martin Affair: A Forgotten *Cause Célèbre*."

4. Originally published in French as *Les Damnés de la terre* (Paris: François Maspero, 1961).

5. Gilly is an Argentine journalist who has published many works on revolution, especially in Cuba and Latin America. Felix Gutierrez translated his book, *Inside the Cuban Revolution*, into English in 1964.

6. Originally published in French as *L'An Cinq, de la Révolution Algérienne* (Paris: François Maspero, 1959).

7. Anthony Clayton notes that "[t]he FLN drew chiefly on the Viet Minh as a model for organization" (112).

8. Cassino is a city in Italy that was the scene of a pivotal battle during the Second World War. French and allied troops captured the city and were thus able to begin penetration toward Rome.

9. *L'Opium et le bâton* is a novel describing the Algerian revolution against the French.

10. This is the Vietnamese word for "people of the country" or peasants.

11. This the Arabic word for mountain, which, according to the *Petit Robert*, began to appear in the French lexicon as early as 1870.

12. In Arabic, Yacine is a common first name, while Kateb is a family name. The reversal of the author's name to Kateb Yacine is a result of French misunderstanding; therefore, throughout this study I will refer to him as Kateb, which is in fact his family name.

13. My emphasis.

14. For more information on the political nature of theater in Algeria, and specifically for Kateb Yacine, see chapter 5 of Kamal Salhi's book, *The Politics and Aesthetics of Kateb Yacine: From Francophone Literature to Popular Theatre in Algeria and Outside*.

15. For a corroborating view of my thoughts here, see Denise Louanchi, "Un essai de théâtre populaire: *L'homme aux sandales de caoutchouc*."

16. I agree with Bernard Aresu, who states that both *Le cercle des représailles* and "La Femme sauvage" were "already and essentially political theatre"; see Bernard Aresu, *Counterhegemonic Discourse from the Maghreb: The Poetics of Kateb's Fiction*, especially page x. What I am emphasizing here is both the explicit nature of Kateb's political message and the effort to internationalize his beliefs.

17. *Nedjma* is Kateb Yacine's most well-known work, published in 1956. This novel is revolutionary in its structure. The order in which the text is presented does not follow a clear-cut chronology. As a matter of fact, its complicated structure has inspired critics to attempt a deciphering method to facilitate reading the text.

18. Kateb even includes a bibliography at the end of the play.

19. *The American Heritage Dictionary*. 2nd College ed., s.v. "Satire."

20. Aimé Césaire similarly wrote in 1955 in *Discours sur le colonialisme* that the European does not abhor all crimes against humanity, but crimes against the *white man* (10-11).

21. The book also includes an essay by Jean-Paul Sartre.

22. For an explanation of the various uses of theater, see John Hodgson's book, *The Uses of Drama*. Among other playwrights, Hodgson discusses Brecht.

23. I use local instead of popular, because I believe that *L'homme* is already more or less popular. See Louanchi 203.

24. The editor of *Poète*, Gilles Carpentier, echoes this when he says: "En internationalisant son propos, en découvrant de nouvelles formes théâtrales, il peut enfin s'adresser directement aux siens et dans leur langue" (69). [By internationalizing his words, by discovering new theatrical forms, he can finally address himself directly to his own people and in their language.]

25. In her introduction to Kateb's *L'Œuvre en fragments*, Jacqueline Arnaud notes that Kateb continued to produce his first drafts in French, because that was

the most natural process for him. However, he ultimately converted his texts to dialectical Arabic (1986: 29).

26. Theater as a tool to reach the Algerian public is not a new idea. In Danièle Djamila Amrane-Minne's study of Algerian women who participated in the war, one of her interviewees, a former militant, discusses the importance of the theater as a tool in the revolution: "Le théâtre chez nous est un instrument. . . . Tu peux arriver à convaincre, à expliquer, tout en jouant, en donnant du plaisir aux autres" (1994: 22). [Theater is an instrument for us. . . . You can begin to convince, to explain, through playing a role, by giving others pleasure.] This didactic, political theater became a public manifestation of support for the FLN. Theatrical productions also enabled people to gather in a forum that could educate them about the goals of the nationalists and serve therefore as recruiting operations as well.

27. For French translations of some of Kateb's popular theater see Zebeida Chergui's collection of Kateb Yacine's theatrical works: *Boucherie de l'espérance*.

28. For more information on the colonial system of education in both Algeria and Vietnam, refer back to chapter one of the present study.

29. Ho Chi Minh was partially educated in France; the FLN communicated primarily in French. Both nationalist parties claimed to have been inspired by the French "philosophes" of the eighteenth century.

30. The Maghreb, Arabic word for both the west and the westernmost country in North Africa, Morocco, is alternatively spelled in English as Maghrib. In the French context, Maghreb is used normally to refer to the three Francophone countries of North Africa: Morocco, Algeria, and Tunisia.

31. Although literature in French still exists in Vietnam, it has become less prevalent over the years due to various factors. Now, the majority of those who speak French, for example, are of an older generation. Those who write do so for the most part in Vietnamese. In Algeria, on the contrary, the French-language tradition in literature has continued to grow.

32. See Jack Yeager's comments on Bui Xuan Bao in *The Vietnamese Novel in French* (1987: 50).

33. For more on this topic, refer back to chapter one of this study to read my discussion of feminism as it relates to this literature.

3

WAR

Historically, the wave of decolonization in the former French colonies began to spread following the Second World War. Since this study deals with the formation of the postcolonial Francophone female subject, it is imperative to discuss the wars and the role they play in forming her. In Miriam Cooke and Angela Woollacott's introduction to *Gendering War Talk,* they explain the importance of war in the production of gender meaning:

> A culturally produced activity that is as rigidly defined by sex differentiation and as committed to sexual exclusion as is war points to a crucial site where meanings about gender are being produced, reproduced, and circulated back into society. After biological reproduction, war is perhaps the arena where division of labor along gender lines has been the most obvious, and thus where sexual difference has seemed the most absolute and natural. (1993: ix)

If nationalist movements seek to include women or necessarily cannot forego women's participation in war, how do women's new wartime roles alter culturally produced gender meanings? And how is this specifically relevant in a postcolonial context? If, as Anne McClintock convincingly argues, controlling colonized women was an imperialist strategy of the West (McClintock 1995: 3–4), then what happens when these women rise up in nationalist struggle against the West?[1] How does all of this play out in patriarchal societies, where the question of power governs relationships between men and women? In both Algeria and Vietnam, war provided an arena in

which women could transgress boundaries, and were, paradoxically, also
further mired in the traditional divisions of patriarchal societies.

Nationalism by definition creates a homogenous community that defines
itself as a unified body and not as a heterogeneous group of individuals. In
order for the ideology of nationalism to work, a collectivity needs to take
precedence over individuality (Ashcroft et al. 1998: 150). Women, if they
actively participate in the war effort, thus become part of the national collective. They become citizens of the nation and not specifically *women* of
the nation. Although in a traditionally patriarchal society, men would be the
soldiers, in these specific instances, men accept and even encourage
women to partake in the struggle.

In this chapter I will focus upon the illusions and multiple realities of
women's roles in these two revolutions. Through an examination of the historical facts coupled with the representation of these roles, I will demonstrate how the effects of war helped create a postcolonial female subject,
who attempts to transcend the borders erected between past, present, tradition, modernity, colonialism, and postcolonialism.

While first the Vietnamese and then the Algerians struggled to free
themselves from the colonial grasp of the French, both nationalist groups
enlisted their women to fight alongside the men. Although these women
did not always participate in the same capacity or perform exactly the same
functions, history documents their active participation in the wars.[2] Their
depiction has been both mythologized and ignored; therefore, in order to
demystify and uncover some perceptions of women's involvement in the
two different revolutions, we will examine their portrayal in two novels: *La
Grotte éclatée* by Yamina Mechakra and *Le Mirage de la paix* by Ly Thu
Ho. Both authors create female characters who are defined and developed
by war, and to whom war serves as a way to affirm, deny, and most importantly, question prescribed identities within a given society. The war generation's questioning will leave a legacy for ensuing generations of women
to reconcile and/or resolve.

Folklore teaches us that Algeria claimed heroic women as early as the
eighth century A.D. It was then that the Berber queen known as *La Kahina*
fought against Arab invaders.[3] Marnia Lazreg points out in her study on Algerian women, *The Eloquence of Silence*, that *La Kahina* possesses a much
disputed identity which has served the purposes of many different groups.
Her real name is widely contested, as are her religion and her origins
(Lazreg 1994: 20–21). Lazreg also mentions several other legendary heroines in precolonial and colonial Algeria, proving that women throughout
history have played a role in armed struggles (1994: 21). Thus, women fight-

ing throughout the Algerian Revolution represent neither the first warriors nor the most famous to emerge.

One of the most well-known depictions of women's participation in the revolution can be found in Gillo Pontecorvo's 1967 screen version of Yacef Saadi's *La Bataille d'Alger*. Spanning the brutal years of 1956 and 1957, the film is based almost entirely upon Saadi's personal experiences. Filmed in black and white on location in Algeria, the movie also stars "actual FLN rebels,"[4] all of which gives one the sense of watching a documentary in spite of explicit indications to the contrary.[5] Controversial and originally banned in France, the film has become a highly regarded source of reference for the Battle of Algiers and is especially relevant to our discussion here of women's roles.[6]

Throughout the film women play a key role in the urban battle of Algiers. The FLN uses two different tactics, both dealing with dress.[7] First, the French soldiers who patrol the borders between the Algerian and French quarters of the city permit veiled women to come and go freely. Additionally, women who veil themselves achieve relative anonymity thanks to their traditional dress. In the film, the FLN uses these women as instruments to hide weapons destined for the hands of FLN assassins. When security becomes very tight following repeated assaults in the European quarter of the city, it is the Muslim women who pass through barricades much more easily than the men. The French soldiers avoid bodily searching these women because they don't want to offend the Algerians.

Following a period of violent ambushes of French law enforcement officials, the French police retaliate with a brutal attack on civilians in the Kasbah. Crying out for vengeance, the people protest; subsequently, the FLN promises retribution. An elaborate plan is devised in which three women will play key roles as agents of terrorism. This time, rather than use the Algerian dress as a cover, the women don European clothing, dye their hair, and apply makeup. The FLN is aware that the barriers between the Kasbah and the European quarter are open to Europeans; therefore, they use European prejudice to their advantage. Since the soldiers at the barricades judge mostly on appearance, the women stand a good chance of passing.[8] Each of the women carries a bag containing a bomb, which will be placed in a specific part of the European quarter of Algiers. According to the film, each of the three women we follow through this transformation is successful.

Women like the three in Pontecorvo's movie became known as the *porteuses de valises* (suitcase porters) and have obtained a mythical status in discussions of the Algerian war. While sources corroborate that women did

actively wage war in the urban setting of Algiers, and did participate in violent bombing attacks, according to Danièle Djamila Amrane-Minne, their
numbers were minimal. In the film *La Bataille d'Alger,* Pontecorvo examines the details of that specific battle; therefore, only a few representative
women are depicted. In reality, the female *fidayine*, or urban guerilla fighters, do not represent the majority of the female war effort in Algeria.[9] As a
former member of the FLN herself, Amrane-Minne has done personal interviews along with archival research in order to attest to the facts regarding female participation in the revolution. Depictions like the one seen in
La Bataille d'Alger, while important, tell only part of the story.

Amrane-Minne is quick to note that women were present in the revolutionary war from the very beginning of the movement for liberation, but
their roles were very often confined to those of caretakers, cooks, or re-
cruiters. Lazreg echoes this, stating: "It is clear that women's participation
in the war was instrumental to its success. Yet, with a few exceptions, the
nature of this participation fit in a 'traditional' pattern of gender roles,
where men held positions of responsibility and command, and women exe-
cuted orders" (1994: 124). Women also aided in forming political organizations that would become instrumental in the outcome of the war. Through
organizations such as the AFMA (Association des femmes musulmanes
d'Algérie) and the UFA (Union des femmes d'Algérie), Algerian women
promoted the war effort and gathered support for the work of political parties seeking independence from France. Amrane-Minne posits that the war
"marks the beginning of women making their presence felt" (1999: 62).

However, the level of women's activism remained on the sociocultural
level, never attaining the same prominence as that of men. Only 0.5 percent
of women participated in political positions within the FLN (Lazreg 1994:
125). Since 1962 women have achieved limited success within the political
framework of Algeria, but women's activist groups have managed to gain
voice. One of the most famous cases of a woman's participation in the government apparatus in Algeria is that of Khalida Messaoudi. Her situation
merits mention as an example of the perils awaiting women in politics in Algeria. Messaoudi is an outspoken proponent of women's rights and democratic government, a position that has led to the threatening of her life on
more than one occasion.[10] Political activism, even within the confines of the
recognized government, is both risky and rare. Women have been forced to
reconcile harsh laws, such as the Family Code of 1984, which takes nearly
all individual power away from them (Schemla 1998: xii), with an ever-
mounting engagement in politics. Winifred Woodhull explains that postrev-
olutionary Algeria was faced with the task of establishing a modern Social-

ist nation, which is what the leaders of the FLN had set out to do from the beginning of the revolution. In addition to creating this new entity, they were also attempting to resurrect the indigenous culture that French colonial power had annihilated through 130 years of occupation. According to Woodhull's analysis of David Gordon's work, women, as a group, "are the victims of this tension [created out of the confrontation between the modern Socialist state and the resurrection of the indigenous culture], and their present condition might be seen as its symbol" (1991: 113). In Algeria, as in other nations achieving independence immediately prior to or during the same time period, women's status became a relevant, even pivotal issue. In the Middle East, Elizabeth Warnock Fernea notes:

> In every national charter and constitution, proclaimed in triumph on the day of independence, one of the cited goals was the improvement of women's status. To achieve this end, and to improve and equalize the lives of all of the new citizens, laws were passed regulating what was seen as an inequity in the courts between men's rights and women's rights. Both men and women were to benefit equally from changes ranging from agrarian reform and industrialization to free public education and health care. Thus, much was promised. (1985: 1)

Fernea highlights specifically the governmental promises made to newly independent women in Middle Eastern countries. These promises, also uttered in Algeria, were never fulfilled, due, in part, to unchanging perceptions of women. In spite of women's activity in the war effort, women's roles in quotidian society did not ultimately transgress the boundaries of gender roles. Fernea points to governmental failure; however, Marnia Lazreg condemns an ill-fated revolutionary rhetoric and lack of concretely formed definitions of women's roles:

> Herein lies the apparent failure of the F.L.N. to transcend the sacrificial view of women, and replace it with a view that emphasizes control over one's life through action, as befits a woman revolutionary. Instead, women's involvement in the struggle for decolonization was presented as requiring some feminine qualities. Self-transformation through voluntary action for the national good was not brought up as an advantage for women in the movement. Rather, the abstract notion of "freedom," equated with entry in the war, was seen as the sum total of a presumed change in women's lives. (1994: 130)

In her view, women did not engage in the war out of a desire for social change; rather, they believed in an overriding notion of national freedom. Once independence was gained these women did not have the tools with which to transform their lives; thus, they returned to the same roles they had known prior to the revolution. The FLN and the revolutionary struggle had not actually rendered them capable of "self-transformation" or self-motivated action.

However, in an interview granted to Danièle Djamila Amrane-Minne, Fatima Benosmane, who was a militant member of the PPA (Parti du Peuple Algérien), reproaches her own generation for not passing the revolutionary torch to the younger one:

> Il y a, à mon avis, une faute que nous avons faite nous les militants: nous n'avons pas essayé d'expliquer aux jeunes ce qu'a été la guerre de libération. C'est une grosse lacune, nous n'avons pas donné aux jeunes ce qui leur aurait permis de juger à sa vraie valeur cette période. Nous ne leur avons rien donné pour sauvegarder nos acquis. . . . Nous avons lutté pour l'indépendance et, une fois l'indépendance gagnée, nous sommes partis[11] chacune de son côté. Chacune est rentrée tout doucement chez elle, se disant: laissons les autres se débrouiller. (1994: 24)
>
> [There is, in my opinion, a mistake that we have made, we the militants: we did not try to explain to the young people what the war of liberation was. It is a large gap, we did not give the young people that which would have enabled them to judge this period for its true worth. We gave them nothing to safeguard our accomplishments. We fought for independence and, once independence was won, we left, each of us going her own way. Each of us went quietly back home, saying: let the others figure it out.]

Benosmane's statement emphasizes the borders erected between the past and present. Interestingly, though, she blames the women themselves, not the men who hold political power. For Benosmane, the women failed themselves and the ensuing generation by not maintaining an activism following the war. Whether we point to Fernea's analysis, Lazreg's, or Benosmane's, the result is the same. Transgressing boundaries imposed by a phallocentric Algerian society and the French colonial ideology became an ongoing postcolonial struggle. Nevertheless, the revolutionary war forever changed the way Algerian women would see *themselves* and their roles in Algerian society. Regardless of social, political, or cultural transformations within Algeria itself, or the lack thereof, and regardless of the *reality* of women's participation in the war, ensuing generations of Algerian women have been forced to reconcile conflicting societal expectations that came out of the war.

One illustration of this forced reconciliation surfaces in Yamina Mechakra's 1973 novel, *La Grotte éclatée*. Too young to be a member of the war generation herself, Mechakra nonetheless chooses the Algerian War of Independence as the setting for her novel. First published in 1979 and republished in 1986, it remains a frequently cited text. We know little about the author herself, only that she was born in Meskiana, Algeria, in the 1950s and that she has studied both psychiatry and medicine.[12] Her body of work is limited to this narrative; one novella, entitled "L'éveil du mont," published in 1976 in *El Moudjahid culturel* (Caws et al. 1996: 169); and a novel, published in 1999 in the review *Algérie Littérature/Action*, entitled *Arris: roman*. For the 1979 publication of *La Grotte éclatée*, Kateb Yacine wrote the preface in which he discusses Mechakra's dedication of the book to her father, who was tortured and killed before her eyes. In the preface, Kateb writes: "Elle est née à la veille de l'insurrection. Quand elle entend parler de guerre, pour la première fois, elle croit à une tempête. En arabe populaire, 'guirra,' c'est à la fois un orage et la guerre de libération, un déchaînement de la nature" (1979: 7). [She was born on the eve of the insurrection. When she hears talk of war for the first time she thinks it is a storm. In popular Arabic, "guirra" means both a storm and the revolutionary war, an unleashing of nature.] *La Grotte éclatée* is a narrative that translates this storm/war in a dismal yet poignant way. Mechakra renders this storm called war tangible for the reader through the words and eyes of a female narrator who suffers through its tumultuous course.

Unlike Pontecorvo's film, Mechakra's novel is set in the *maquis* (underground), the primary battleground for most of the war. While decisive battles such as the Battle of Algiers were fought in an urban setting, the majority of Algerians battled in the countryside, the mountains, and the woods.

The narrator, a young Algerian woman, volunteers in the forces of the FLN as a nurse. We follow her story, which spans the years 1955 to 1962. Although we are tempted to read this as a chronological novel that has the style of a personal diary, Mechakra makes it difficult to define the genre. First, the text we read is marked by dates; however, the novel reads less as a journal and more as a series of stream-of-consciousness-like recollections. Sometimes the dates are very specific (4 juin 1962 on page 170); others are merely months and years (septembre 1958 on page 84), or seasons (automne 1960 on page 119). Some passages are not dated at all, and yet others repeat dates that have already been given. On several occasions Mechakra ignores her relatively linear chronology and jumps back in time by a month or forward by a year. Some of the most important events in the narrator's life, such as the birth of her son, do not coincide with specific dates, as one might expect. Rather, it seems that the dating process is somewhat arbitrary.

   This lack of a clear temporal structure functions in two different ways.
On the one hand, it makes it impossible for the reader to neatly categorize
this text as a historical novel. On the other, it makes us question the validity of the dates and their significance. In other words, Mechakra does not
recount all of the events in the exact order they happened, nor does she emphasize certain moments as more or less important than others. Rather than
following this straightforward narrative technique, she ventures in and out
of linear history and focuses on the way in which different moments im-
press ideas upon her. At times, the text consists of dialogue, flashbacks, and
poetic verse. It is a combination of various literary techniques and even
genres, juxtaposed to form one woman's story. Significantly, Mechakra's text
represents an obvious foray into fragmentation as a literary technique. She
presents us with fragments of dialogue and scenes that symbolize her role
as a nurse in the revolutionary army. She deals with literally fragmented
bodies, possesses a somewhat fragmentary memory, and loses her son in an
accident that will forever fragment her life.
   Throughout most of the text the narrator lives and works in a cave. Although actively participating in the war, she provides an example of the kind
of female activism we noted earlier: women remained primarily caretakers
throughout the war. She follows orders given to her by men who hold the
positions of power within the army, and she functions as a surrogate mother
figure for the wounded. She tries to heal the injured soldiers by whatever
means she can, although from the very beginning it is clear that her supplies
and expertise are lacking. Part of her job also consists in comforting the dying. Besides the narrator, there are two other characters who live in the cave
with her: Salah and Kouider. The former is a young boy whom she was able
to save from death by amputating his two legs. Kouider is the soldier who
stands guard over the cave's entrance. Along with her story, we learn fragments of Salah's and Kouider's.
   The most important part of Mechakra's literary project is a questioning
that forces us to confront borders between cultural traditions. In the opening pages of *La Grotte éclatée* the author writes the following:

Langage pétri dans les nattes tressées au feu de l'amour qui flambe depuis
des siècles au cœur de mes ancêtres et dans mon cœur vers lequel souvent je
tends mon visage gelé et mon regard humide pour pouvoir sourire. Langage
pétri dans les tapis, livres ouverts portant l'empreinte multicolore des
femmes de mon pays qui, dès l'aube se mettent à écrire le feu de leurs entrailles pour couvrir l'enfant le soir quand le ciel lui volera le soleil; dans les
khalkhals d'argent, auréoles glacées aux fines chevilles, dont la musique ras-

sure et réconforte celui qui dort près de l'âtre et déjà aime le pied de sa mère
et la terre qu'elle foule. (1986: 13)

[Language formed in the braids woven at the fire of love that has been
burning for centuries at the heart of my ancestors and in my heart to which I
often offer my frozen face and my moist eye to be able to smile. Language
formed in carpets, open books carrying the multicolored imprint of women of
my country, who at dawn begin to write the fire of their wombs to cover the
child in the evening when the sky will steal the sun; in the silver *khalkhals*,
chilled rings on their slender ankles, whose music reassures and comforts he
who sleeps near the hearth and already loves his mother's foot and the earth
that she treads.]

Two readings of this passage are possible. First, if we read the text in a
purely ethnographical sense, we find an ode to women's work. This dedication reveres expression through activity rather than through spoken or written language. *Langage* is repeated at the beginning of the two sentences
that form the entire paragraph. Both times it is a language that is *formed* in
something. In the first sentence, the language is formed in the woven mats
created out of love. The passionate quality of love is evoked through this
language and is emphasized with the vocabulary: *feu, amour, flambe, cœur*
(twice in the first sentence). The dry warmth and comfort of the fire are
placed in opposition to the narrator's cold and wet face. The practice of
forming this language is traditional (*ancêtres*) and therefore provides familiar solace. This language is not defined by words printed on a page; rather,
it is formed with the toil of hands creating a work of art, as is further elaborated in the second sentence. This traditional language is formed in carpets, which are *livres ouverts* (open books), in which dissimulation does not
take place – all the details are laid bare for everyone to see. These carpets
are books in the same sense that the text we are about to read is one. Here,
we read a specifically textual reference in the terms Mechakra uses: *langage, livres, écrire*. Mechakra seems to be setting up an opposition between
the Western predominance of language as a form of communication and
her own culture's refusal to bow to that imposition. However, her own work,
this book, is a text written in the French language. She is therefore juxtaposing two opposing traditions: language and handcrafts. For the author,
language—and, precisely, what is written with that language—serves to
warm and comfort: "écrire le feu de leurs entrailles pour couvrir l'enfant le
soir quand le ciel lui volera le soleil" [write the fire of their wombs to cover
the child in the evening when the sky will steal the sun]. Note that these
women do not *translate* the fire of their womb; rather, they *write* it directly
to protect and comfort the child. The mother is acting here as the child's

teacher and protector. In order to guide the child, she must teach him or her the language of her people. Paradoxically the text we read is in French, but tradition dictates that the language used here should be Arabic. The symbolic passing of the torch is caught up in the indigenous textuality (carpets) in opposition to the French textuality (books). The child speaks neither language yet, and it is the job of the mother to impart one of the two upon him or her.

Finally, Mechakra describes the music of the jewelry worn by women. This music is another form of comforting language that enables the child who sleeps next to the hearth (once again this idea of warmth and fire) to do so peacefully. The paragraph ends with the following phrase: "et déjà aime le pied de sa mère et la terre qu'elle foule" [and already loves his mother's foot and the earth that she treads]. It is the jewelry on the mother's foot, which will create the music of home, the language of comfort. But the earth that she treads is even more significant, because it is the land of Algeria. This language and all of the ways in which it is formed within this one paragraph laud Algeria and her traditions, especially those carried out by women. Language is a decidedly comforting element here, which seems to speak in sharp contrast to the powerfully violent account of war we are about to witness.

At the same time, a second, less ethnographically centered reading of Mechakra's opening text can give an interpretation that recalls the poststructuralism of the 1970s. Language is formed out of a braiding of threads that can be read as *codes* or *Voices* in the sense that Roland Barthes indicates in *S/Z*: "Chaque code est l'une des forces qui peuvent s'emparer du texte, l'une des Voix dont est tissé le texte" (1970: 28). [Each code is one of the forces that can take possession of the text, one of the Voices from which the text is woven.] Mechakra, like Barthes, emphasizes the polysemy present in language—these open books carry the *multicolored* imprint of her country's women. This idea of *multicoloring* indicates the plurality of language in much the same way that Barthes describes the "writable" text as one that does not have a unique plastic-coated system; rather, it manifests "la pluralité des entrées, l'ouverture des réseaux, l'infini des langages" [the plurality of the entries, the opening of networks, the infinity of languages] (11). The carpet that is created in the opening pages of *La Grotte éclatée* serves as a metaphor for the literary project that the author is about to undertake. She plans to create a form of literary language that will combine all of the women's voices heard here, but not in order to unify them and create one interpretation of their lives; rather, she wants to use this book to articulate their multiple opinions. She is in a sense acting as the interpreter of the text or the *tapis* (carpet or tapestry) of these women's voices. Thus, she echoes Barthes once again, who states: "Interpréter un texte, ce n'est pas lui donner un sens, c'est au contraire apprécier de quel pluriel il est fait" (1970: 11). [To interpret a text is not to give it a meaning, it is on the contrary to appreciate of what plurality it is made.] The woven layers present a plurality that creates a sharply modern text, complicating Mechakra's play on tradition in yet another manner. More than an anthropological study of women's work, this passage manifests a modern notion of writing within a traditional subject matter or context. In other words, the explicit theme masks an implicit message that completely contradicts it. This analysis seems ever more appropriate upon reading further into Mechakra's novel. Her narration is neither entirely logical, linear, nor univocal.[13] Thus, the opening passage on women's work acts as a harbinger for her modern text.

Mechakra's project is one of uniting traditions through techniques associated with the modern text in France. She ties together the language, women's work, modern textual interpretation, self-reflexivity, and the reality of war. As Karin Holter says: "*La Grotte éclatée* est en même temps concrètement ancrée dans une tradition culturelle donnée et universelle, en même temps ancienne et très moderne" (1989: 196). [*La Grotte éclatée* is concretely anchored in a given, universal cultural tradition, which is both ancient and very modern.] Throughout *La Grotte éclatée*, Mechakra pays tribute to various traditions. As we have seen, she uses an ostensibly "traditional" motif as the means by which to allow modernity to enter into the picture. However, neither her narrative strategy nor her narrator herself falls into the binary trap of tradition against modernity. She deftly weaves the reader's conceptions of these two opposites together, proving that they can and do work together. Mechakra questions these boundaries and what they mean for Algerians and especially Algerian women.

The narrator is constantly aware of the predicament into which women in her country have been placed due to the revolution. At various moments within the novel, she expresses a desire to connect everyday lives of Algerian women to the war. Even if these women are not participating in the way she is, she valorizes their thoughts and visions. The following passage presents one such example. In this excerpt the narrator contradicts officially sanctioned press releases with women's interpretations of current events:

Quelle serait, par exemple, l'opinion de ma sœur, pliée en deux par le poid [*sic*] d'une huitième grossesse, ayant mis à l'abri dans son corsage une lettre apportée par le facteur, le matin (ma sœur ne sait pas lire; il la lirait, lui, s'il rentre ce soir sain et sauf), les doigts roulant un couscous arrosé de larmes et l'oreille attentive à des voix algéroises, françaises, tunisoises, cairotes, des voix étrangères qui parlaient de l'Algérie, qui criaient leur colère, citaient des chiffres, disaient tout, absolument tout sauf ce qu'elle voyait, elle, ce qu'elle pensait, elle. (1986: 35)

[What would be, for example, the opinion of my sister, bent in two by the weight of an eighth pregnancy, having tucked away in her bosom a letter brought by the mailman that morning (my sister doesn't know how to read; he will read it, him, if he comes home this evening safe and sound), fingers rolling a couscous sprinkled with tears and the ear attentive to the voices from Algiers, from France, from Tunis, from Cairo, foreign voices that spoke of Algeria, that cried out their anger, that listed numbers, said everything, absolutely everything except what she saw, her, what she thought, her.]

More than an indictment of the manner in which information is diffused to the masses, this passage focuses on two important aspects of women's lives in the Algeria of the 1950s and early 1960s. First, the narrator describes a woman whom she calls her "sister," thereby implying a fraternity between the two and highlighting the rhetoric of the FLN (brothers and sisters in revolution). This woman carries out a daily routine completely alien to the nurse living in a cave. While the nurse, our protagonist, embodies one gender role that is born out of the revolution, this other woman's role is equally the product of war. She is responsible for the care of her home, presumably her children, and herself; however, she is completely uneducated and illiterate. In this passage, it appears that illiteracy among women is the norm, and this illiteracy leaves women powerless. This is depicted in the image of the letter the woman holds for her husband/son/brother/father to read to her. Not only is she illiterate, but she is also mute. Her voice is not expressed in spite of a plethora of languages surrounding her. None of it serves to interpret her thoughts, hopes, and worries. Rather, her opinion remains silently within her. The narrator seems to be reminding the reader of this forgotten woman. *La Grotte éclatée* attempts to acknowledge her voice and identify her, but not to place her in a fixed category. Literacy and its importance for the future of Algeria surface again in a conversation that occurs among Salah, the narrator, and Kouider:

[narrator to Salah] Tu sais écrire?

Non et j'en suis malheureux, j'ai toujours désiré avoir un cartable et prendre le chemin de l'école comme les autres. J'aimais beaucoup mes moutons et mes chèvres, mais. . .

Faut s'en foutre de l'école, brailla Kouider. L'écriture n'est qu'un piquet. L'apprendre c'est se retrouver une corde au cou. Les livres? Du maraboutisme intellectuel. Ils te disent tout de toi sauf ce que tu veux en connaître. J'en sais quelque chose.

Tais-toi, supplia Salah. Tu mens. L'écriture est belle. A cause d'elle je suis
malheureux. Ceux qui la savent ont un autre regard, une autre pensée que les
tiens, les miens. Ils sont heureux à cause d'elle. (1986: 46)

[Do you know how to write?

No, and I am unhappy about it, I have always wanted to have a school
satchel and to follow the road to school like the others. I liked my sheep and
goats a lot, but. . .

Have to not give a damn about school, shouted Kouider. Writing is nothing
but a stake. Learning it means finding yourself with a cord around your neck.
Books? Intellectual sorcery. They tell you everything except what you want to
know. I know something about it.

Be quiet, begged Salah. You're lying. Writing is beautiful. Because of it I am
unhappy. Those who know how to write have another gaze, other thoughts
than you and me. They are happy because of it.]

Kouider adamantly renounces literacy, seeing it as a colonial tool of domination, but the narrator, in a follow-up to the above-cited passage, highlights alternate forms of communication, such as music. She tells Salah:
"Tu t'y tailleras une flûte, tu y souffleras ta musique; c'est une écriture qui
parle. Elle a la force de plusieurs écritures. . . . [T]u transformeras nos regards et nos pensées, les regards et les pensées de tout un peuple" (1986:
46). [You will carve yourself a flute, you will blow your music into it; that's
a writing that speaks. It has the strength of multiple writings. . . . You will
transform our gazes and our thoughts, the gazes and thoughts of an entire
people.] Again, as in the opening dedicatory passage, the narrator emphasizes music and links musical and linguistic communication. She explicitly
tells Salah that music is the equivalent of the written word. Unlike Kouider
the narrator does not condemn the written word, but she readily finds an
alternative that comes from familiar traditions for Salah. As a former
sheepherder he has practice with the flute, and the narrator wants him to
realize that it can carry a message, transform and inspire a people in the
same way that a book can.

Only pages later she highlights the powerful literary influences in her
own life. She mentions both Pierre de Ronsard and André Gide. Although
Ronsard appears only briefly in the text, she echoes his poetry by stating:
"Je ruminais le nom de Ronsard qui effleura jadis mon âme d'enfant close
et l'entrouvrit comme une rose" (1986: 48). [I ruminated over the name of
Ronsard which long ago touched my closed childhood soul and opened it
up like a rose.] Ronsard's poems, the beauty of his verses, bring her solace
and enable her to feel happiness in an otherwise dark childhood. To this literary reference she will add that of Gide and *Les Nourritures terrestres*.

Initially she reflects back upon this book in the context of her current situation in the cave. Her memory is triggered and she suddenly recalls her first encounter with it, and the punishment that ensued. As a fourteen-year-old girl in an orphanage, her reading is strictly monitored by nuns. When she comes upon Gide's novel, she is intrigued, indeed she is moved by his words, to the point that she transcribes her feelings into her diary. Called before the mother superior and three other nuns (including the one who actually owned the copy of *Les Nourritures terrestres*), young Marie[14] is questioned about what she has understood from the book: "J'ai compris que j'ai faim. . . . Je veux les nourritures terrestres. . . . Je les porte en moi et je ne les connais pas" (1986: 49). [I understood that I am hungry. I want earthly nourishment. I carry it within me and I am not aware of it.] This is her condemning confession, which leads to her expulsion from the orphanage and her internment in a correctional facility. When Marie is a child in a convent, worldly, physical desires, such as those extolled by Gide, remain repressed. The inspiration and creative force that she gleaned from reading Gide is linked with sin and danger, specifically sexual freedom. In the eyes of the nuns she has committed a criminal offense in reading and enjoying something so sexually explicit. The narrator condemns the cold, unfeeling reaction of the nuns, who could not understand what Gide represented for her: "Régies par des lois abominables elles voulaient gérer ma personnalité profonde et tuer toute créativité authentique" (50). [Governed by abominable laws they wanted to control my innermost personality and kill all authentic creativity.]

Her innermost personality is linked to creativity and thus explains why she encourages Salah to explore his creative impulses and not to become frustrated because he cannot read. Additionally, the narrator's true identity comes to the forefront through Ronsard and Gide, two French, male authors. Ronsard's poetry of the Renaissance exudes beauty, often in the name of love. Gide's novels explore sexuality, morality, and identity in general, all of which link very closely to the narrator's idea of not belonging to one specific group. Gide, like the narrator, confronts boundaries and questions them explicitly in his writing. The narrator's bond with the written French language appears therefore to be very strong. Through her invocation of two of France's literary giants, Mechakra is confirming the power of words. This valorization of the French language and literary tradition serves to deemphasize national, as well as sexual, identity. Male, French authors and their messages are not distant from her message as a female, Francophone author. In addition to this clear literary connection, Mechakra is also demonstrating how the narrator in *La Grotte éclatée* constructs her *self* around various ideas gleaned from different sources. Even though she is an

Algerian fighting for a nationalist cause against the French, this does not immediately imply a total disconnection from French language or literature.

At the same time that words and written literature become extremely important in the self-definition of the narrator, she never denies a second
bond with other forms of literacy, such as music, gestures, and handicrafts.
We see this in the opening passage and in her discussion with Salah. These
examples, tied with the mention of French literature, link together a multitude of means to communicate, thereby paralleling Mechakra's literary
project with *La Grotte éclatée*.

Her project, rendered poetic in the opening lines of the text, is to bring
life to a metaphorically dead Algeria. The first page of her text begins: "Je
m'en allais vers ARRIS, les yeux fixés sur mes doigts qui, à l'horizon se tres-
saient avec d'autres doigts pour ramasser les nuages du ciel et les presser
sur une terre brisée d'oubli" (1986: 14). [I headed out toward ARRIS, my
eyes fixated on my fingers, which in the horizion wove together with other
fingers to gather the clouds from the sky and press them onto an earth broken with neglect.] The narrator's departure toward ARRIS is undertaken in
an optimistic frame of mind. She is heading out toward ARRIS and looking
toward the sky for help in repairing a broken earth. Note the lexical re-
minders of traditional work, in particular the use of the verb *se tresser*. Immediately we are reminded of the braiding and weaving that she describes
in her opening dedication. The handicrafts, symbolic of Algerian tradition,
are invoked from the very beginning of the book. Here, the narrator's fingers are intertwined with other fingers in much the same way that the individual braids of a mat are woven together, or like a text is woven with its various Voices. This weaving is a collective effort, which will produce one
richly interwoven fabric in the end. Since the earth is broken from neglect,
because colonialism has destroyed its beauty, the narrator chooses to participate in the war and thus hope for an independent Algeria. Ultimately,
and as a result of the bloodshed brought about by war, she envisions her
country anew: "Des hommes s'étaient mis à effacer de leur sang toute la
honte qui pesait sur l'histoire de mon pays pour recommencer une histoire,
plus juste, plus digne, plus humaine" (1986: 29). [Men had begun erasing
with their blood all of the shame that weighed on the history of my country
in order to start a new history that is more just, more dignified, more human.] This idea of restarting history, of a clean slate, as she accentuates it
here, implies the combination of values, and significantly, the disappearance of preconceived, strictly divisive borders between people.

Throughout *La Grotte éclatée* the narrator makes explicit references to
the uselessness of categorized identity. She questions the way we interpret

ourselves according to specific barriers. "J'avais compris qu'il était grand
temps de vivre, qu'un nom n'avait point d'importance" (1986: 29). [I had
understood that it was high time to live, that a name had no importance.]
As an illegitimate child who is abandoned to the orphanage, she begins to
recognize that one's identity is formed through one's experiences rather
than one's lineage. Until her enlistment in the FLN, the narrator's existence
as an orphan and ward of the state is governed by childhood service agencies. Authorities in these various agencies shuffle her around from home to
home, leading to various parental figures attempting to construct an identity for her. "Chez les uns on m'appelait Marie ou Judith, chez les autres
Fatma" (1986: 33). [Some called me Marie or Judith, others Fatma.] None
of these attempts succeed; if anything, all of the competing forces create a
subject who defies categorization. Religious divisions, as implied in the
naming choices above, are manifestly ignored by the young girl: "Pour moi,
le ciel comprenait trois grands mondes où je n'avais pas de frontière: celui
de Moïse, celui de Jésus et celui de Sidna Mohammed" (1986: 33). [For me,
the sky included three big worlds where I didn't have any borders: that of
Moses, that of Jesus and that of Mohammed.] She sees herself as a person
who can easily transgress boundaries created by and for others. "J'étais
heureuse de n'appartenir à aucune communauté. Je m'inventais des
hommes et un pays aussi libres que moi" (1986: 34). [I was happy not belonging to any community. I invented men and countries for myself that
were as free as I was.] The narrator expresses two very important concepts
relating to identity in these two sentences. One is the idea of not belonging
to a *community*, which is normally conceived of upon lines of identity (sexual, racial, religious, and national). The other idea that she brings forth here
is the one which we shall explore in greater detail in chapter 4—that is, the
idea of a freely multiple identity constantly in a state of becoming.[15]

The narrator's belief in not belonging to a community serves as a catalyst to her participation in the war for independence. In her childhood
wanderings from one community to another, she witnesses the violent cohabitation of Algeria's population. As Benjamin Stora illustrates in *Algérie:
Formation d'une nation*, it is the exclusivity of the *pied-noir* community,
the direct result of French colonizing practices, which leads to identification among Muslim Algerians. In other words, he sees the formation of the
nationalist movement as the product of a *phénomène d'exclusion* (phenomenon of exclusion) (1998: 16). One of the most effective methods of
colonization used by the French in Algeria was to exclude Algerians by
populating their soil with French citizens.[16] By 1962, there were a million
Europeans in Algeria (1998: 23), most of whom had been given land by the

French government. This land was, obviously, taken from the Algerian people. Thus, the end result was a group of landowning Europeans who saw themselves as belonging to an exclusive community within Algeria. In reference to this phenomenon, Stora states the following: "Le refoulement foncier et le déracinement culturel de la population 'indigène' hors des territoires les plus riches, construisent un système de dépossession de l'identité" (1998: 23). [The taking away of land and the cultural uprooting of the indigenous population out of the richest territories construct a system of identity dispossession.] The indigenous people are stripped of their possessions, excluded from land ownership, and relegated to an inferior status by a European minority. Politically, thus, power has been reappropriated by the colonist elite, allowing them to form an identity of "other-ness" in relation to the native Algerians. Mechakra's narrator stands as an example of someone who has internalized these politics of colonization and now is dispossessed of identity. She waits for someone to name her, but this name will mean nothing to her, only to the person who is trying to categorize her, based upon demarcation lines established by and as a result of European colonialism.

Confirming Stora's thoughts on the creation of nationalism and the dispossession of identity, Benedict Anderson examines the concept and delves into its origins in his book *Imagined Communities*. Anderson explores the historical processes that created the belief in belonging to one larger community, the nation. In his introduction, he states that "all communities larger than primordial villages of face-to-face contact (and perhaps even these) are *imagined*" (1991: 6).[17] Consequently, if we place Mechakra's narrator within this context, we begin to understand her predicament more clearly. She describes her identity as it has been conceived through colonialism for her. She has no agency in the creation of her identity; rather, she has passively been forced to observe borders that communities have erected between each other, thereby creating an ever-deepening bond among those dwelling within certain boundaries. While the narrator believes that she is fortunate not to belong to any one definable community, she also knows that every individual community will try or has already tried to form her according to its own customs. The communities to which she makes explicit reference are those centered on religion. The narrator, through her irreverent attitude toward Judaism, Christianity, and Islam, takes a stand against organized religious communities that define themselves in opposition to other religions.

In order to escape all bonds of community, she invents a country for herself. In doing this, she symbolizes Algeria's fight for its own unique identity;

she metaphorically creates a nation. Once again, Anderson's study shows that this is perhaps the same process whereby contemporary nations were created – they were invented as a result of historical exclusions. In reality, Algeria as a united community did not exist; rather, it was divided into groups according to race and religion. Nationalism was born out of this very divisiveness, allowing for people to see unity where they previously saw only differences. The nationalists who fought to gain independence from France did not fight for the Algeria of the 1950s or 1960s. They envisioned a future nation in which they all had a stake. This *imagining* allowed for the formation of the FLN.

In *La Grotte éclatée*, the narrator explains that her childhood identity could not be defined through the traditional, bureaucratic means propagated and enforced by colonialism: "Je me promenais sans fiche d'état civil, sans nom, sans prénom. Je vivais clandestinement sur terre. J'étais une hors-la-loi" (1986: 34). [I walked around without a birth certificate, without a family name, without a first name. I lived clandestinely on earth. I was an outlaw.] Existing outside the norms of society she resisted colonial domination, even if this was not her conscious intention as a child. Her current role in the novel, as a militant for the Algerian Nationalist cause, is the logical outcome of her rebellious childhood.

The question of identity is also exploited through the recurring use of "Arris" as the name of both a place and a person. In order to distinguish one from the other, "ARRIS" in all capital letters signifies the village, whereas "Arris," written with just the first letter capitalized, represents either the narrator's son or her lover, the father of her son. The first notation of AR-RIS appears in the first line of the narrative following the opening dedication ("Je m'en allais vers ARRIS"). The word is followed by a marker indicating the footnote, which says "ARRIS: petite ville de l'Aurès" [ARRIS: small city in the Aures mountains] (1986: 14). Two pages later the narrator mentions "Arris" for the first time. The name is once again marked by a numbered footnote, which explains the following: "Arris: nom d'un maquisard" [Arris, name of a *maquisard*] (1986: 16). Since we are expressly given two definitions in the form of footnotes, it would seem to illustrate the narrator's desire to keep the two distinctly separate from each other. Nevertheless, the way in which both typographies are used within the text leads one to believe otherwise. Note the following passage:

Il nous fallait remonter jusqu'à ARRIS, où une réunion devait avoir lieu.

J'étais infirmière du groupe. Je devais survivre à tous les obstacles: la vie, la santé, le sort de cette liberté que nous défendions, dépendaient de la volonté de ceux qui avaient pris les armes et je me surprenais en train de penser comme Arris.

"O Arris, si tu savais, si tu savais. . ."

ARRIS ce soir-là avait froid et peur.

Elle tremblait, faibles lueurs entre un ciel sombre et une montagne de neige. (1986: 19).

[We had to go back up to ARRIS, where a meeting was supposed to take place.

I was the nurse of the group. I had to survive all the obstacles: life, health, the fate of this liberty that we were defending, depended on the will of those who had taken up arms and I surprised myself thinking like Arris.

"O Arris, if you knew, if you knew. . ."

ARRIS that evening was cold and afraid.

She trembled, weak glimmers of light between the dark sky and a mountain of snow.]

In this excerpt from the text we witness the vacillation between the two different terms. The narrator's group is climbing up a mountain to the city of ARRIS, which is personified as a woman in the last few lines. This personification immediately follows the narrator's comment that she has begun to think like her lover, who is a soldier strongly committed to the cause of a free Algeria. Juxtaposing Arris, the brave, with ARRIS, the fearful, signals the narrator's own state of mind. While the city and the man are inextricably linked to each other because of their names, the narrator herself becomes intertwined in this duality. The fluid nature of identity is highlighted and embodied in this particular passage.

In addition, this passage is the opening of a new chapter, which follows the one in which Arris is introduced to us for the first and last time. He helps the narrator as she is forced to drink the blood of a jackal in order to stay alive. The gruesome scene garners little sympathy from other rebels in the camp, with the exception of Arris. As he encourages her to drink the blood in spite of herself, he says: "Au bout de notre chemin, il y a des frères qui nous attendent. Il nous faut la force d'arriver jusqu'à eux; et puis là-haut sur nos monts, nous serons nombreux à aimer la liberté, nombreux aussi à la défendre" (1986: 17). [At the end of our route, there are brothers who are waiting for us. We must have the strength to get to them: and then up there on our mountaintops we will be many to love liberty, many also to defend it.] When the narrator claims in the formerly quoted passage that she is thinking like Arris, it is this moment that she is referencing. Arris's patriotism is fortifying in both moments, and in the end helps her to reach the village of ARRIS.

This superposing of connotation and denotation in the usage of the two terms extends to a further degree later in the novel when the narrator gives birth to a son, whom she names Arris, after the boy's deceased father. Following an explosion in the cave (the most obvious source for the novel's title, *La Grotte éclatée*), Arris, the infant son, is forever maimed. At this point, the family that the narrator has created for herself explodes. Not only is her biological son impaired, but her *brothers* in the war effort also perish. The war has destroyed this *imagined* family/community, the one to which Arris, the father of her child, alludes when he describes the "frères" waiting for them in the village of ARRIS. This complete scattering of the *imagined* family unit leads to serious psychological trauma for the narrator. Here, she writes a poem to her child:

Sur le chemin d'ARRIS, je rencontrerai le regard indifférent de quelques rares voyageurs.
Le soleil se noyait de chaleur.
Je retrouvai un instant Constantine.
J'arrêtai mon regard sur les yeux de mon fils.
Arris, mon fils, tu étais ma révolte.
A toi, aujourd'hui, mon enfant,
Je dis ton père mort, sur ses lèvres mon amour.
Je dis ma maison tuée là-bas au pied d'un arbre qui blasphème à la face du ciel.
Je dis mes amis écrasés d'oubli, mais vivants encore dans la mémoire du vieux chacal; il vient chaque soir déchirer la nuit de lents sanglots.
Je dis ma foi demain, clouée sur ma poitrine.
Je dis ARRIS mon pays et ses moissons
ARRIS mes ancêtres et mon honneur
ARRIS mon amour et ma demeure. (1986: 172)
[On the route to ARRIS, I will meet the indifferent gaze of several rare travelers.
The sun drowned with heat.
I discovered Constantine for a moment.
I held my gaze upon the eyes of my son.
Arris, my son, you were my revolt.
To you, today, my child,
I tell your dead father, on his lips my love.
I tell my house killed over there at the foot of a tree that blasphemes in front of the sky.
I tell my friends crushed with neglect, but still alive in the memory of the old jackal; he comes every evening to tear through the night with his long sobs.
I tell my faith tomorrow, nailed to my chest.

I tell ARRIS my country and its harvests
ARRIS my ancestors and my honor
ARRIS my love and my home.]

Arris/ARRIS can once again be read as pertaining to either the person or the place, in spite of the typographical indications. Arris, the name of her child, is specifically mentioned only once, and exemplifies the narrator's revolt. He symbolizes her revolt against colonialism, against societal norms (she has this baby out of wedlock with a man she barely knows), and in addition, he is the product of two revolutionaries. Beyond all of these possible meanings, we can also see that Arris could be read as the place name, because it is in that village that she fights in the revolutionary struggle. The first line of the poem, along with the final three lines, all utilize the ARRIS which should pertain to the village. ARRIS's path in the first line is also the path that Arris, the father of her son, took when he left to fight and eventually die. It is also the path of Arris, her son, because he was born and killed in the same cave. This path leads to that cave. Since ARRIS is the location of the cave, and it is within the cave that she gave birth to Arris, the metaphor of the harvests (*moissons*) that take place in this village links AR-RIS/Arris in yet another way. She goes on to invoke ARRIS in the name of her ancestors and her honor. A child carries within him all of the ancestry that has created him in the same way that a land/village/country does. The narrator's honor is also tied up in ARRIS, the place, Arris, her son, and Arris, her lover. Finally, the last line ties together both meanings of the word—it is her love and her home.

The overlapping of meanings, along with the utilization of the exact same name for two different characters and one place, indicates in a definitive way Mechakra's desire to undermine our normal process of identification. In other words, by blurring the lines of identification between people and places, she makes us question the meaning of naming yet again.

As we mentioned earlier, the fragmentary techniques employed by Mechakra serve to metaphorically depict the war and its impact upon both the narrator and her family. The dismembering of fellow soldiers, as portrayed in scenes of amputation, further expands upon this notion of fragmenting the individual. Through these various examples, the author enables us to refute divisions and oppositions that tend to categorize individuals in the "Self versus Other" dichotomy. She destroys barriers and shows how the *imagined* communities created by colonialism—communities that thrived upon exclusionary practices—cannot survive the Algerian war for independence. Individual identity is eventually exploded by way of the scenes of amputation, leaving only the *imagined* community of a future Algerian nation. This community binds together those who believe in a nation that does not yet exist, disempowers colonial divisions among classes and races, and devalues the importance of each individual's identity. The main character's struggles against division throughout the text demonstrate how she perceives individual identity. It is not the product of one global, all-encompassing category; she is a fragmented individual. However, while she does not neatly fit into the categories created by colonial divisiveness (remember her criticism of the barriers erected among the Muslims, Christians, and Jews in Algeria), she does manage to identify with the Algerian revolution. In it, she does not discover an intact, preconceived notion of who she *is*; rather, she confronts the fragmentary nature of existence. The narrator shows the failure of many concepts of identity, because those she has witnessed try to define the individual as a whole, an impossibility for a postcolonial woman in Algeria. She reinforces what Iris Marion Young explains: "The self is a product of social processes, not their origin" (1990: 45). The woman about whom we read in *La Grotte éclatée* does not have a unique origin; rather, she is the product of linguistic, historical, and practical interaction (1990: 45).

In Vietnam, as in Algeria, folkloric tradition allows that the history of women warriors harks back to 40 AD when the Trung sisters defeated Chinese invaders. Not only did the two women force the Chinese to retreat, but they subsequently took over ruling power in Vietnam. Their revolutionary roles led directly to their political involvement in the country. When the Chinese returned two years later, however, the Trung sisters were unable to vanquish them again and instead of suffering humiliating defeat, chose to commit suicide by throwing themselves into a river (Karnow 1983: 100). Revered as heroines for the Vietnamese nation, they continue to be honored with celebrations throughout contemporary Vietnam. Although the rituals have become much less elaborate over the years,[18] the temple erected in their memory still stands and serves as the center of festivities for what has now become not only "Two Trung Sisters' Day," but also a day to celebrate Vietnamese women throughout the nation.[19] During the war against the Americans, the names of the sisters were invoked to inspire women and call for their support. This is seen in newspaper editorials, especially in the North (Chiem T. Keim 1967: 49), and in the actions of President Diem's sister-in-law, Madame Nhu, in the South. Madame Nhu used the Trung sisters as a means of self-promotion: "[She] erected a statue in Saigon in 1962 to commemorate their patriotism—and also to promote herself as their reincarnation" (Karnow 1983: 100). Madame Nhu went on to organize her own group of female soldiers, even helping to train them (Karnow 1983: 243, 266–67).

The Trung sisters are just one example of evidence from popular Vietnamese legends that would indicate that women have not always been conceived of as substandard to men. In Vietnamese society, the feudal system and philosophical foundation that came with the successful invasion of the Chinese impacted every aspect of the society, making it difficult to surmise what the true situation of Vietnamese women was prior to Chinese domination. Nonetheless, it is irrefutable that when the Chinese brought Confucianism to Vietnam, they made a significant impact upon women's lives (Eisen 1984: 12). With the subsequent one-thousand-year rule of the Chinese, Confucianism and its doctrines became an integral part of Vietnamese society, forever changing the perception of women who, at least from this point on, became subservient to men. Confucius himself equated women with servants, banishing both to an inferior status and claiming that, "[w]omen and servants are most difficult to deal with" (*Analects* 17:25).[20] Women could therefore carry out all domestic chores, including physically demanding work for which they often became quite literally beasts of burden. When the French invaded Vietnam in the nineteenth century, they saw to it that the patriarchal and feudal systems derived from Confucianism were kept in place in the rural villages—this served as an excellent foundation on which to build their new colonial regime (Eisen 1984: 23). The French governed directly in the cities, but from afar in the villages where they employed the feudal lords to collect taxes and enforce laws. As for women, their status fell even lower under French rule, because they became "slaves of slaves" so to speak (Taylor 1999: 21). In other words, while the women were once slaves of men in their society, now the men were slaves to a higher colonial power, therefore pushing women even further down on the social scale. In speaking of subaltern women's situations, which resulted from colonialism, Gayatri Spivak echoes: "[B]oth as object of colonialist historiography and as subject of insurgency, the ideological construction of gender keeps the male dominant. If, in the context of colonial production, the subaltern has no history and cannot speak, the subaltern as female is even more deeply in shadow" (1994: 82–83).

In order to come out of this double shadow, women took notice of the nationalist movement's need for their help. As nationalists slowly gained voice in the twentieth century, first in the northern parts of Vietnam, they began to include women among their ranks, realizing that they needed to gather as much support as possible in their fight against the French. Some Vietnamese women, in addition to striving to break the yoke of colonial oppression, saw revolution as an instrument by which to achieve their own liberation.[21] They joined the Communist Party and fought alongside the

Northern Vietnamese soldiers in various capacities. As early as 1930, the Indochinese Communist Party made the following statement: "The revolutionary potential of women constitutes one of the main forces of the revolution. Without the participation of masses of women in the revolution, the revolution will never succeed" (Eisen 1984: 94).

During the war with the French from 1945 to 1954, Vietnamese women played roles in the resistance and maintained some high-profile positions in the armed forces. According to Arlene Eisen, over 1 million women actively participated in the war against the French (1984: 29). However, Eisen notes that we must define the meaning of "active" so we are not misled. In other words, while the most notorious women to come out of the fighting in Vietnam were soldiers, in reality only a very small number participated in this capacity (1984: 99). Photos circulating in the West, especially during the subsequent American war in Vietnam, often showed Communist female soldiers carrying guns, taking prisoners, or working in the rice paddies while holding a weapon. Nonetheless, these pictures, veritable representations of women's involvement, show only one meaning of the term "active" and only one side of the fighting that took place throughout Vietnam. During the American war in Vietnam, the Vietnam Women's Union instituted a policy known as the *Three Responsibilities*: "It consisted of 1) responsibility in production; 2) responsibility in caring for the family; and 3) responsibility in serving the state and being ready to fight against the aggressors" (Soucy 2000: 124).

As in the case of the Algerian women we have already discussed, Vietnamese women did indeed play a key role in the struggle for independence, but much of their work was "women's work." Vietnamese writer Duong Van Mai Elliott, author of *The Sacred Willow*, an autobiographical study of her own family's history, discusses her sister's involvement with the Viet Minh. Her sister followed her husband into the nationalist movement and joined the Viet Minh. Although her husband became a cadre, her responsibilities did not grow in the same way. Out of the group of five cadres' wives in her community, only one of them actively participated in military operations. "Revolution was primarily seen as a man's work, and women tended to do things like sewing flags and writing slogans on banners" (1999: 162). Elliott acknowledges that some greater involvement did exist for women, but it was on the sociocultural level:

A higher level of participation would be working in the Women's Association to encourage women to support the resistance, but "supporting" usually meant standing behind husbands and sons, taking care of their families so the men could focus their attention and energy on the fight against the French, or serving as porters to carry weapons and supplies for the army. (1999: 162–63)

This is confirmed in Eisen's work on Vietnamese women; she notes that they were in charge of "spreading the [nationalist and eventually Communist] movement like a drop of oil" (1984: 100). Their job was to convey the message of the party to other women who would then perform the same duties in order to gather essential support. Eventually this would allow for the political motivations and intentions of the nationalists to reach everyone in Vietnam. Similarly, in South Vietnam in 1955, President-to-be Diem had women from Saigon travel to the villages in order to encourage people in the rural areas to vote for him.

Women helped to win the decisive battle at Dien Bien Phu in 1954 by transporting weapons and supplies. They also sacrificed their lives and on many occasions their children's lives in order to help the nationalist forces gain ground. In Christine Pictet's photographic narrative of Vietnamese women, *Femmes du Vietnam: Visages d'hier et de demain*, she highlights one woman's testimony:

Elle insiste sur l'importance de leur rôle tout au long de la guerre et surtout décrit l'ampleur de leurs sacrifices: pour laisser la voie libre aux résistants, leurs bébés sur le dos, elles détournaient l'attention de l'ennemi s'exposant à son feu. (1996: 23)

[She insists on the importance of their role all throughout the war and especially describes the extent of their sacrifices: to leave the path free for the rebels, their babies on their backs, they diverted the enemy's attention, exposing themselves to their fire.]

Those who fought alongside the Communists continued their struggle against the American forces that came to Vietnam following the French defeat at Dien Bien Phu. In spite of their important contributions to the Communist Party and the armed struggles in Vietnam, women did not suddenly become major political leaders in Vietnam following the reunification. In reality, the Vietnamese government that came to power following the American war did not make much effort to recognize women's roles. In Robert Templer's book, *Shadows and Wind*, he examines contemporary Vietnam and discusses how the Vietnamese have constructed their memory of Vietnam. He notes that the first gesture of recognition given to Vietnamese women was the title of "Heroic Mother." In 1994, this award was "given to those whose children had died in the conflicts that blighted Vietnam from 1945 to 1989. . . . Several hundred women,

dressed in formal black velvet *ao dais,* attended a ceremony at the Presi-
dential Palace in Hanoi where they were serenaded by a rock band and
greeted by past luminaries such as General Giap and Pham Van Dong"
(1999: 30). The official recognition of these women was intended to
"heighten patriotism," according to Templer, but served to remind many
Vietnamese that heroism had been reserved almost exclusively for men.
The contradictory position of women in Vietnam proves difficult to analyze because of the constant shifting between traditional values and modern concessions. For example, Dr. Duong Quynh Hoa, an active member
of the Communist Party and Women's Union, served as vice minister of
health and became a deputy to the National Assembly in Ho Chi Minh
City after the reunification of Vietnam. However, she removed herself
from politics in 1976 to run a pediatric center (Pictet 2000: 23). In a 2000
report for National Public Radio, journalist Daniel Zwerdling traveled to
Vietnam and examined the current state of women's affairs. One of the
people whom he interviewed was the author Duong Van Mai Elliott, who
confirmed that:

> in some ways Vietnam's rules for women have always been somewhat contra-
> dictory, as they are in many countries. For roughly 2,000 years, women's daily
> behavior in Vietnam has been defined by the Chinese philosophy called Con-
> fucianism, and it still is. Mai grew up learning that women have to live ac-
> cording to what they call the three submissions and the four virtues, which ba-
> sically dictate that women must always obey the men in their lives and
> sacrifice everything for them. ("Vietnam" 2000)

At the same time, as we have seen, women throughout Vietnamese history
and into the modern era have played important roles in shaping their country. Zwerdling notes that "women have been playing a growing role in public life. A woman serves as vice president; they're getting jobs as professors
and managers" ("Vietnam" 2000). Does all of this suggest that women have
achieved liberation?

Mary Ann Tétreault explains that women's liberation in Vietnam was indeed a goal of the Indochinese Communist Party, but it was listed in tenth
place out of ten objectives, implying its relative lack of importance (1994:
38). According to Tétreault and other feminists, the reality is that Vietnamese women have "fail[ed] to maintain solidarity with one another"
(1994: 53). While this is undoubtedly true in part, women's liberation has
also proven to be a very nebulous concept, especially in a country such as
Vietnam. Gender roles have always been contradictory, as Elliott indicated
above. Furthermore, Neil Jamieson points out in *Understanding Vietnam*

that Vietnamese society, prior to colonial domination and war with the West, possessed an ambiguous definition of women's roles:

> The role of women was a source of tension in society. There was often a grating disjuncture between ideological ideals and sociological reality. Vietnamese myth, legend, and history are filled with stories of strong, intelligent, and decisive women. In all but the uppermost strata of society, men and women often worked side by side. Women performed many arduous physical tasks, ran small businesses, and were skilled artisans. . . . Yet ideologically women were subordinate to men in the nature of things. . . . They were supposed to be submissive, supportive, compliant toward their husbands. Husbands were supposed to teach and control their wives as they did their younger brothers and their children. (1993: 18)

Thus, while a lack of solidarity may explain some women's disappearance from the active political arena, a certain degree of inherited ambivalence further hampers complete equality. In addition, Vietnam was until very recently split along political lines, leaving many scars among those who participated in or witnessed the fratricidal war. Those who did not believe in the Communist cause fled to the South, flooding cities, especially Saigon (present-day Ho Chi Minh City), to well beyond its saturation point. Bitterness abounded between northern refugees and southern residents. In addition to the drama of overpopulation, political strife and corruption divided allegiances and created an even murkier political situation. Women and men in southern Vietnam struggled with questions of alliance.[22] Henceforth, the legacy bequeathed to ensuing generations of Vietnamese women is one of reconciliation among the reality of women's participation in the wars, interpretations of their roles, the internal division propagated upon their country, and the subsequent reunification under Communism.

If scholars and history itself have proven that women did indeed actively participate in the war effort, then it would seem that the fiction dealing with the periods of war in Vietnam would indicate likewise. Contemporary novels coming out of Vietnam illustrate the myriad roles played by those who supported the Communists. For example, Duong Thu Huong's poignant depiction of the end of the "American War," *Novel Without a Name*, traces the war's destructive path through the narrative of a young man who encounters female "comrades" along the way. Originally written in Vietnamese, this novel was a bestseller in Vietnam before being recently translated into En-glish. Each female character in the novel demonstrates her importance to the war effort in a different way, leaving us convinced that the war against the Americans could never have been won without the help and support of women. Among Duong's female characters are mothers who recite slogans as they watch their young sons go off to war, then deprive themselves and their youngest children of food so that they can send it off to the soldiers at the front.[23] She also portrays a middle-aged, unbearably ugly woman who lives a solitary existence in the middle of the forest. Her sole occupation is to provide food and shelter to any soldiers passing through the area in need. Finally, the most glamorous woman is a young liaison agent who guides male soldiers to their meeting place. Each character embodies a different, yet equally important, role. It is interesting to note that the author herself is a former member of the Communist Youth Brigade, in which she participated for seven years. An active member of the Communist Party until 1989, Duong is one of the few women to have participated in the war and written about it.[24] Her characters have therefore a firsthand knowledge of the war and of the Communist doctrine encouraging them to fight.

However, in *Francophone* Vietnamese fiction, as one would expect, there are few novels exhibiting Communist sympathies.[25] In sharp contrast to Duong's novel is Ly Thu Ho's *Le Mirage de la paix* (1986). Deceased in 1989, she is from a different generation than Duong and her experience as a bourgeois Vietnamese from the South brings another perspective to the searing realities of war. In Ly's southern Vietnam setting women do *not* actively participate in the American war; rather, they are depicted as passive observers to the fighting. The women in this novel strive for a recomposition of the family unit and desire to re-create the community that was destroyed in Vietnam as a result of war. In other words, Ly's text provides us with a follow-up to Yamina Mechakra's description of the Algerian war in *La Grotte éclatée*. While Mechakra shows war's destruction of communities, Ly attempts to illustrate a reconstructive approach to postwar fragmentation. What I propose to explore here is not what could be viewed as a *returning* to tradition, especially since the women in this novel have never truly *left* their traditional way of life. What is more interesting to examine is what Gayatri Spivak hails as the "reconceiving [of] customary law so that tradition can become a vehicle of change" (Spivak interview with Landry and Maclean 1996: 308). Spivak notes that tradition does not necessarily have to equate with regression or lack of progress. Customs may remain intact while a society advances into the modern world. In order to fully grasp the importance of Vietnamese women's struggles, we need to first realize that the past does not always stand as a barrier to the future. This, I would argue, is exemplified in this text, which appears at first to relegate women to a more traditional status. In addition, Ly's work does not participate in the Communist restructuring of women's roles (as in Duong Thu Huong's novel); nevertheless, it is in reality not a regressive historical project. Rather, the author is allowing for the creation of another space within which women lay claim to each of the roles they have encountered. They struggle in a society faced with a sudden confrontation between new values and Socialist dogma. They endeavor to recreate a community that now exists only in their imagination, a community that is nothing more than a *mirage*. These women are *reclaiming* traditions in an effort to utilize them as elements to construct a new identity for themselves, one that incorporates long-established ideals with recently altered roles. The female characters in the novel serve as examples of this strategy. Some succeed, while others do not. However, they all demonstrate, as Françoise Lionnet points out, that "[a]ll of us inhabit an interdependent late 20th century world, which is at once marked by borrowing and lending across porous cultural boundaries" (1995: 15).

Ly Thu Ho was born in South Vietnam and received a French education in Saigon. She later moved to France where she made her home until her death in 1989. Jack Yeager indicates in *The Vietnamese Novel in French* that she depicts many of her own experiences throughout her works (1987: 104). She draws heavily upon the twentieth-century history of Vietnam and sets her novels within specific periods of that history. *Le Mirage de la paix* represents the final text in her trilogy of novels. Her first text, *Printemps inachevé*, was published in 1962, and although it is a fictional work, it is very concretely based upon the historical events that took place in Vietnam between 1935 and 1955. Her follow-up to this novel, *Au milieu du carrefour*, was published in 1969, and deals with the Vietnam of the mid-1960s. Finally, seventeen years later, in *Le Mirage de la paix*, she tries to bring together ideas and characters from her two preceding novels in order to demonstrate the way in which history, war, suffering, and intercultural encounters have affected lives of Vietnamese people and changed their perceptions of their individual place within the world. This third installment in the series begins in 1970 and deals primarily with the reunification process of North and South Vietnam that began to take place formally in 1975.

The novel centers on the family of Tran-Huu-Phuoc, who is a wealthy landowner in southern Vietnam. Sympathetic to the southern forces, his family undergoes the transformations common to the bourgeoisie that came under Communist rule after 1975. The Agrarian Reform movement instigated by the ruling Communists created major upheaval in the system of land ownership throughout all of Vietnam; however, those living in the North had undergone the transformation several years earlier. Therefore, after reunification, property redistribution took place primarily in the South. Wealthy landowners had their assets sectioned off and began to work their

own land for the first time. The newly established Socialist government expected every Vietnamese citizen to consider her- or himself the equal of all
others and to therefore do the same kind of work. No exceptions were to be
made for those who didn't know how to work the fields. Tran-Huu-Phuoc's
family, bourgeois landowners, provide an example of this land redistribution
process. He and his family, for the first time, begin to work sections of the
land that have been allotted to them. In addition, along with the other members of their village, they must attend reeducation classes where they learn
Communist doctrine and hear party slogans repeated continually. In sum,
this family has lost all of its privileges.

Much like a play, the first page of the novel contains a list of all the characters. They are divided into the following categories: "La famille de M.
Tran-Huu-Phuoc"; "Le personnel du domaine"; "Les militaires sous les ordres de Huu-Loc" (Huu-Loc is Huu-Phuoc's son); and "Les amis de la
famille" (1986: 7–8). Out of thirty-four characters listed on these two pages,
ten of them are women. None of those women fall under the rubric "Les
militaires." All of the characters are described in terms of their relationships
to the others within each given section. Professions are listed where appropriate, although it is significant to note that none of the women possess professional titles in spite of the fact that at least two of them work. The majority of these female characters play very small roles in the novel.

In Huu-Phuoc's family, there are three women: Mme Them (his oldest
daughter), Ngoc-Suong (his youngest daughter), and Bâ-Sau (his first
cousin and housekeeper). Mme Them is an unsympathetic social climber,
living now with her husband and children in Saigon. She seldom appears in
the novel and when she does, she embodies "modern" bourgeois values, including city living and avarice. Ly does not appear to be explicitly condemning these qualities, but she does paint this ambitious social climber in
a negative light, especially in contrast to Ngoc-Suong, who epitomizes modest behavior.

As the novel begins, Ngoc-Suong is a young girl who is completing her
years at the boarding school in Dalat, Le Couvent des Oiseaux. She is in
love with the son of her father's overseer. Initially both fathers oppose the
love, because it straddles class boundaries, but eventually they overcome
their objections and the two marry. Ngoc-Suong spends much of the novel
either pining away for her love or worrying about his safety, as he is a soldier in the South Vietnamese army. Her role is highly traditional throughout the novel, exemplified in her longing to be married and have children.
Ngoc-Suong acts as a model Vietnamese woman who follows Confucianism's teachings of filial piety and virtue. According to the teachings of Con-

fucius in *The Great Learning*, "Wealth makes a house shining and virtue makes a person shining" (Wing 1963: 90). The wealthy older sister illustrates only the first part of this adage, because she is not virtuous, just rich. Ngoc-Suong, however, has a wealth, thanks to her father's prosperous land, and she remains virtuous throughout the entire story. She represents the ideal Confucian principle of comportment.

Bâ-Sau serves the function of caretaker, cook, housekeeper, and confidante to the Huu-Phuoc family. In short, her purpose in the novel seems to be to replace Huu-Phuoc's dead wife. As the oldest member of the family, she instructs the younger women on how to cook, provides advice in matters of the heart, and primarily serves as a figure that the younger women in the family should strive to emulate. Bâ-Sau has her own son, who deals clandestinely with black market merchandise, supplying both the northern and southern forces with food and medical supplies. His "immoral"[26] behavior saddens his mother, who suffers through disappointment at her son's behavior and then remorse at his death.

Two other female characters who play significant roles include Manh and Thu-Thuy. Manh is a highly respected worker but her character traits show that she has loose morals and defies traditional social conventions. She is neither married nor intending to be so; Ly portrays her as something of a free spirit who has frequent romantic encounters with men, but always remains unattached to them. As the Communists take over the South, Manh is the only person who seems to benefit both on a personal and on a larger social scale. For example, she describes her improved physical appearance along with the disappearance of a social ladder that was impossible for her to climb. Under Communist rule she is essentially the equal of even the wealthiest women in the village. Through the eyes of Manh we witness the dismantling of the class system. While acknowledging some of the advantages of the new system through her portrayal of Manh, the author still never shows great sympathy to the Communist cause; she continues to dedicate most of the novel to the trials and tribulations of the displaced bourgeoisie.

Thu-Thuy is a refugee from the North who initially takes a position as business manager at Huu-Phuoc's estate, but she quickly becomes part of the family. She meets and almost instantly falls in love with Huu-Loc, Huu-Phuoc's son. They eventually marry and have children, thereby completing Thu-Thuy's adoption into the family. Much of the plot revolves around her story, focusing on the sad plight of refugees, her renewed hope in her future thanks to the marriage and her children, and finally, the devastating effects of war. When we are privy to Thu-Thuy's thoughts they deal primarily with worries similar to those of Ngoc-Suong. She is concerned for her husband's safety above all else. Consequently, when he dies toward the end of the novel, Thu-Thuy abandons hope and despairs to the point of near death. Realizing she must rediscover a will to live for her children's sake she slowly recovers to become the narrative voice throughout the remainder of the text. She recounts the events following Communist takeover of southern Vietnam while sitting at her husband's tomb.

With the exception of two central female figures (Ngoc-Suong and Thu-Thuy), the remaining women play either secondary or completely irrelevant roles to the plot. Nevertheless, the female characters in this novel provide us with a telling portrait of Ly's perceptions of war and its effects on gender roles. None of the women we meet are soldiers nor do they participate actively in the war effort. When the men discuss politics the women are either preparing the meals, playing with the children, or otherwise occupied at some purely domestic duty. They serve very traditional, if somewhat unimaginative, female roles: prostitute, young virgin, loving housekeeper, faithful wife, loyal daughter, and devoted mother. Ly depicts women who exist in a universe that is completely contrary to the Socialist way of life. They are not workers, whereas under the Socialist government that was instated during the reunification, everyone was assigned a specific job, even women. The middle and upper classes were to become equal with the peasants, and women and men were to be equally responsible for working and earning money.

Allegedly, the government officials believed that liberating women meant putting them to work, which would enable them to provide their own financial support to the family unit. Women were to become economically independent and therefore completely equal to men. In Mai Thu Vân's study of Vietnamese women following the reunification, she conducts interviews with women from various geographical regions (both North and South, urban and rural) who have different political beliefs. The women generally agree, however, that the situation of women did not greatly improve following the war. In other words, the Socialist system of government did not nullify years of traditional inequality between the sexes. While women did begin to work, their jobs remained mostly confined to that of physical labor. Men gained office positions or managerial work, along with other less physically demanding positions (1983: 203). The government has nevertheless maintained that Vietnamese women, unlike those in Algeria, for example, were not "renvoyées à la cuisine une fois la libération nationale achevée" [sent back to the kitchen once national liberation was achieved] (Mai Thu Vân 1983: 136). This alone is seen as constituting liberation. Not all women see it that way: "Lorsque vous voyez ces femmes en tenue de maçon sur les chantiers, passant des paniers de terre de l'une à l'autre, sous un soleil de plomb, appelez-vous cela la libération de la femme?" (Mai Thu Vân 1983: 190). [When you see these women in the clothes of a bricklayer on at construction sites, passing baskets of dirt from one to the other, in the blazing sun, do you call that women's liberation?]

Ly echoes this critical point of view through her traditional female characters. What is traditional has become new and even subversive. Women's roles have been redefined—the state wishes all people to work, and no division of labor will supposedly be based upon sex. Rather than embodying this idea, the women in Ly's novel choose to reconstruct traditional gender roles, those that were in place for the Vietnamese bourgeoisie prior to the war. Our first inclination is to read the two main female characters, Ngoc-Suong and Thu-Thuy, as traditional, therefore *nonliberated* women. What we realize, however, is that these two women are actually revolutionary in their resistance to modern Socialist reform. Not only do they not participate as soldiers in the fight, but they also do not condone the Socialist means toward achieving *female liberation*. Obviously, political allegiance plays a large role in this text, and it is undoubtedly very clear that Ly's perspective is influenced by her status as a southern bourgeois woman. However, her point of view is significant because it aids in destroying the myth that all Vietnamese women were soldiers, therefore *liberated* thanks to the war. We must constantly remind ourselves of the divisions between North and South, Socialism and capitalism, and political allegiances. Both parts of Vietnam experienced the war, but in different ways. As we have already seen, in *Le Mirage de la paix* it is only Manh, the least traditional woman of the group, who reaps any benefits from the new economic and political systems. Manh stands to gain the most because she is a "worker" and therefore part of a previously underprivileged class. Although Ly speaks very little of women warriors and avoids discussing women's issues in depth, she does allude to both.

Only twice in the text do we have any mention of women's active participation in the war. Ironically, the first character to even broach the subject of women's involvement and subsequent liberation is Kieu-Lien, the prostitute: "[La guerre] . . . a permis à nombre de femmes vietnamiennes d'avoir l'occasion de servir leur pays, de lutter pour son indépendance et même de mourir sous l'étendard du pays" (1986: 175). [War permitted a number of Vietnamese women to have the opportunity to serve their country, to fight for its independence, and even to die for the country's flag.] The glorious exploits of women fighters seem to somehow become diminished in the mouth of the prostitute who admits that she is not willing to do what these women have done because sacrificing oneself for a "noble cause" is in the end a futile act: "Je trouve absurde le fait de se sacrifier pendant que d'autres exploitent vos cadavres" (1986: 175). [I find it absurd to sacrifice oneself while others exploit your cadavers.] Kieu-Lien also mentions that she has no faith in the peace talks or negotiations. She claims that her sole mission with regard to the war is to convince soldiers to desert. Remarkably, although it is a very short episode in the book, of all the women in the novel, Kieu-Lien is the only one who discusses her political beliefs. Rather than speaking directly of women's *liberation*, she focuses on the participation and death of women in the war. Interestingly enough, she never describes the women who are fighting. Is she referring to women who are actually fighting in the North for the Communist cause, or is she making allusion to women who are participating in some capacity in the South? Since the author gives us no examples of women soldiers in the South, it is hard to pinpoint Kieu-Lien's reference. We have no idea in what capacity the women about whom she speaks are participating. Her emphasis on the absurd nature of dying for an ideal seems to predict the attitude of many following the fall of Saigon. During the war they felt they belonged to a community and their actions had a purpose. Following the war, this solidarity was destroyed as a result of geographical divisions and economic discrepancies, among many other societal woes: "Pendant la guerre, la vie avait un sens, elle était précieuse. . . . Il y avait un élan commun pour combattre l'ennemi commun" (Mai Thu Vân 1983: 120). [During the war, life had meaning, it was precious. . . . There was a common impulse to fight the common enemy.]

Kieu-Lien's antiwar statement, while far from an outright political manifesto, nevertheless sends a subversive message about Communism. The fight for independence is a virtuous cause, and it is thanks to Communist doctrine that nationalists achieved their goal of a unified, independent nation; however, Kieu-Lien does not see the Socialism born out of this as providing anything more than an elusive ideal of women's liberation. Through Kieu-Lien's irreverence for this idea of women's liberation, we gain some insight into the perspective women such as Ly, living in the South, may have had. The only freedom that she sees coming out of the women's war effort is the freedom to die. As we saw with *La Grotte éclatée* and the Algerian war, the nation as symbol calls to mind the *imagined communities* of Benedict Anderson. War collectively unites a group during the struggle—they can envision a future as a community, but when the war is over, to what community do these women soldiers belong? Kieu-Lien's cynical, skeptical view forewarns the lack of women's involvement in contemporary Vietnamese politics. She seems to understand that the idealized project of attaching a change in women's status to national liberation requires much more than participation in a war for independence.

The second and only remaining mention of women warriors comes from le Vénérable Buu-Tam, who is a Buddhist monk. He recites the story of Nguyen-Thai-Hoc, a member of the nationalist party who led a protest against the French administration in 1930. French officials publicly guillotined him along with other members of his party. Buu-Tam mentions Nguyen-Thai-Hoc's female companion, Cô-Giang, and describes her as an "[a]rdente patriote et membre actif du parti, chargée de dangereuses missions de liaison, très connue de la police française" [ardent patriot and active member of the party, charged with dangerous liaison missions, well-known by the French police] (1986: 259). Then, he goes on to say that "elle ne survécut pas à Nguyen-Thai-Hoc à qui elle avait juré un éternel amour. Le lendemain de l'exécution de son bien-aimé, elle retourna au village de ce dernier et en habit de deuil, elle se tira une balle de pistolet en plein cœur" (1986: 259). [She didn't surive Nguyen-Thai-Hoc, to whom she had sworn an eternal love. The day after the execution of her beloved, she returned to his village and in mourning clothes, she shot herself once in the heart.] If we examine these lines carefully, we notice a similar subversion to that noted in Kieu-Lien's political discussion of women's roles in the war. Here, Buu-Tam is describing a female warrior, a great patriot, who carried out dangerous missions against the French. However, she is relegated to the role of grieving widow, overcome with the loss of her loved one; thus, she tragically commits suicide—a desperate act distancing her even further from her role as a warrior. I am not questioning the validity of the story here, nor am I suggesting that Buu-Tam not tell it; rather, I think it quite telling that the words Ly chooses to put in the mouths of both Kieu-Lien and Buu-Tam actively work to undermine a belief in the predominance of female soldiers. Buu-Tam mentions, quickly following his explanation of Cô-Giang's death, that her sister was also "une grande patriote . . . [qui] avait trouvé une mort aussi tragique et héroïque" [a great patriot who also found a tragic and heroic death] (1986: 259). This time he gives no details about the woman's militant activities, nor does he explain how she died. His only qualifier is that her death was "also tragic and heroic." This "also" obviously refers back to Cô-Giang, whose suicide we are apparently supposed to interpret as tragic (this would seem evident) and heroic. How is Cô-Giang's death heroic? She commits suicide out of grief over the loss of her lover (or so we are led to believe) not out of political motivation, nor in order to obtain concessions from the French government. Her suicide, based on the information given by Buu-Tam, does not come close to emulating the heroism of the legendary Trung sisters. Furthermore, her death appears to be a climactic moment in a romantic tragedy, not at all politically motivated. The story is all the more problematic because it refutes the notion of political heroism that Buu-Tam otherwise describes in relation to Nguyen-Thai-Hoc and his followers.

The question that remains then is why does *Le Mirage* seem to downplay the female soldier's role in the wars in Vietnam? Why does the author paint this traditional portrait of Vietnamese women? The vast majority of characters in *Le Mirage* revere traditional values in spite of the social transformations taking place within their country. It is not surprising, then, that the notion of a strong, intact family unit remains of primary importance throughout the novel. Again, if we return to Confucius and his teachings we see that he believed in utilizing traditional values "as a remedy for the social and political disorder of his times" (Honderich 1995: 151), and he believed the regulation of the family was a prerequisite for the ordering of the state and everything that followed (Wing 1963: 90–91). Confucius claimed in his teachings that the family was pivotal in all matters relating to the country: "There is no one who cannot teach his own family and yet can teach others" (Wing 1963: 91). In order for all things to run smoothly, one's own household must be in order and harmony: "When the individual families have become humane, then the whole country will be aroused toward humanity" (Wing 1963: 91). When the Communist government descends upon Huu-Phuoc's plantation and orders that the land be divided up, the family suffers greatly, but by keeping their *community* intact, they are maintaining strength.

The transformations that the female characters undergo throughout the course of *Le Mirage* focus almost exclusively upon their standards of living; underneath the obvious changes brought about by the Communist takeover, there is also a *reclaiming* of tradition. While this works on the one hand to contradict the Socialist rhetoric of work, at the same time it foretells the appeal to tradition that Alexander Soucy highlights in his 2000 article, "Vietnamese Warriors, Vietnamese Mothers: State Imperatives in the Portrayal of Women." Soucy convincingly argues that feminism in Vietnam has become a "Trojan horse" of nationalism (2000: 123). For example, the contemporary Vietnamese government has constructed a museum dedicated to Vietnamese women and to their contributions to the nation. The museum is, however, organized in such a way as to promote both women's contributions to the revolution and economy of Vietnam, as well as a postwar return to traditional gender roles. Soucy notes: "Women are represented in a way that encourages an increase in labour output, and it is done in such a way that implicates a particular vision of a gender order, (and not necessarily an emanicipatory one)" (2000: 124). With nationalism as the primary focus of the museum, it is not surprising to read the following:

> In the Vietnamese Women's Museum women are shown as workers, but the most eye-catching display shows a woman in a kitchen preparing food for her family. The occupations that women are represented as engaged in are mostly in the unskilled labour sector: labour that has little or no social prestige and small financial reward. Only minor displays are dedicated to the exceptional professionals. For instance, there is a small display that shows female doctors, but the display relates to gynecology and obstetrics, somehow locating even the exceptions back in an area that is traditionally women's domain. (Soucy 2000: 125)

Le Mirage echoes this with Thu-Thuy, for example. Although she initially travels to the plantation in search of work, relatively little narrative space is devoted to her job. For all of the women in the novel, in spite of their abilities and potential, professional development takes a back seat to family. It is familial values, traditional social norms, which allow for these two women to survive and maintain some kind of hope. In the closing lines of the novel, Thu-Thuy, kneeling at her husband's tomb, swears that she will always remain faithful to him and to his memory. She also promises to stay in South Vietnam in spite of the difficulties she is bound to endure. It is her faith in familial, therefore traditional, values that gives her the strength to remain (1986: 308–9). Though this appears to be a somewhat melodramatic ending to the story, once again it illustrates the importance of traditional values and of the reconstruction of the familial community.

However, we must keep in mind that the novel does not refuse a change in values altogether. Take, for example, Manh, Huu-Phuoc's employee. In the final pages of the text, she reveals to both Ngoc-Suong and Thu-Thuy, the models of tradition, that two men have expressed interest in making them their concubines. Manh states the following:

> Je n'ignore pas qu'on vous a inculqué les principes moraux très rigoureux qui régissent la conduite des mères et des épouses; c'est pourquoi, dans le but d'écarter de votre chemin ces oiseaux de proie gênants, et sans demander votre avis, j'ai pris sur moi l'initiative de faire courir la rumeur que vous êtes atteinte d'une certaine maladie de femme et que vous êtes en train de vous faire soigner pour de longues années en perspective. Que voulez-vous? *Autre temps, autres mœurs. Tous les moyens sont bons pourvu que l'on arrive à ses fins.* . . . J'ai inventé cette fable pour mettre à l'abri votre vertu et votre honneur à toutes deux.[27] (1986: 307–8)

[I am aware that you have been taught very rigorous moral principles that regulate the conduct of women and spouses; that's why, in the interest of brushing aside these annoying birds of prey from your path, and without asking your opinion, I took it upon myself to start a rumor that you are infected with a certain women's illness and that you are undergoing treatment for many years to come. What do you want? *A new time, new morals. All means are good provided that one arrives at her ends.* . . . I invented this fable to protect both of you, your virtue and your honor.]

It is Manh, the socially unconventional, former peasant, who employs whatever means necessary to preserve the ideal of honor for Ngoc-Suong and Thu-Thuy. The antiquated notion of fidelity to one's dead or missing spouse does not fit with current conditions in Vietnam; thus, Manh invents a case of venereal disease that is anything but virtuous. The sheer impropriety of such a daring claim receives its justification in Manh's statement: "Autre temps, autres mœurs." If, as Manh indicates, all means are good if one arrives at one's desired ends, then we can read Ly's message of women's survival as a combination of traditional values and modern circumstances. Upon closer examination, however, we realize that Manh's actions are necessary only because they enable the two women to remain within the family unit. In other words, the reconstruction and maintenance of the family as a community dominates all other sentiment and action. The *Mirage* that is peace following war is actually nothing more than a period of reconstruction and reunification, not only in a purely political context, but also in the psychological realm. If we read the novel as a lesson (and I would argue that it is didactic in nature) on surviving war, then we need to disregard the borders erected between past and present, old and new. In the end, we see the melding of tradition and modernity, which leads to the very dissolution of these binary categories. It is only through the modern maintenance of some traditions that certain communities can survive war.

In both Yamina Mechakra's and Ly Thu Ho's narratives, the fundamental element of transformation is war. It brings conflicting interpretation of women's roles, as well as the perceptions of these roles. The reality of the participation of women in both Algeria and Vietnam seems to be effaced in two different ways in these two works. Mechakra depicts a woman who is engaged firsthand in the armed struggle in Algeria (although as we have seen, she functions less as a warrior and more as a caretaker); while Ly chooses to distance her characters from female soldiers in Vietnam. Neither author aims to render an account of the situation that is purely historically referential; both focus either explicitly or implicitly on the more important legacy of revolutionary war rhetoric surrounding women. Were they indeed warriors who were completely liberated thanks to Socialism? Has the role of women changed within these societies? And, most significantly, *should* it change? Without discussing contemporary Algeria or contemporary Vietnam in their books, these authors still bring to the forefront the ambiguous responses to these questions. Transformations caused by the wars do not provide clear-cut answers, but their repercussions are profoundly felt today. While colonialism itself created a divide, its demise led to the further fragmentation and destruction of categories formed by Europeans and adopted by the former colonized peoples.

La Grotte éclatée shows the complete breakdown and literal destruction of the community, and Le Mirage de la paix attempts to reconstruct the postwar community through more traditional gender roles. The two works, therefore, can be in dialogue with each other regarding the final outcome of war. Ultimately, the female characters have undergone splits that leave them trying to negotiate the wars: fragmentation becomes both the result (in La Grotte éclatée) and the solution (in Le Mirage de la paix).

NOTES

1. See Anne McClintock's book, *Imperial Leather*. This argument is one of her three primary themes.

2. For detailed studies on the roles of women in the Algerian war, see Danièle Djamila Amrane-Minne, *Les Femmes algériennes dans la guerre*; *Des Femmes dans la guerre d'Algérie*; and "Women and Politics in Algeria from the War of Independence to Our Day." For the participation of Vietnamese women in the war with France, see Arlene Eisen, *Women and Revolution in Viet Nam*; Sandra C. Taylor, *Vietnamese Women at War*; and Christine Pelzer White, "Vietnam: War, Socialism, and the Politics of Gender Relations."

3. *La kahina* means "the sorceress."

4. This is quoted from the jacket of the video and the opening credits of the film. FLN stands for the National Liberation Front, which was the primary political group behind the Algerian Nationalist movement.

5. There is a notice prefacing the film, which states that this is neither a documentary nor a product of newsreel.

6. So controversial was the film that General Jacques Massu, who led French forces in Algiers, wrote a book entitled *La Vraie Bataille d'Alger* in direct response to both it and Saadi's claims.

7. For a discussion on the use of the veil and/or Western dress in the fight against the French, see Frantz Fanon, "Algeria Unveiled" in *A Dying Colonialism*, and Winifred Woodhull, "Unveiling Algeria."

8. In Massu's book, he refutes the idea that Algerian women's appearances had any effect upon the French soldiers. He states: "L'utilisation de la grâce féminine à des œuvres de mort n'a pas dupé les paras" (1971: 191). [The use of feminine grace for death operations did not dupe the soldiers.]

9. According to Amrane-Minne, the term literally means one who decides to give one's own life.

10. See Khalida Messaoudi, *Unbowed: An Algerian Woman Confronts Islamic Fundamentalism. Interviews with Elisabeth Schemla.*

11. Although this could just be a typographical error, the missing feminine marker "e" on the verb is striking here in a discussion about female fighters. Note that in the very first sentence of the quote, Benosmane also states: "nous les militants" indicating a masculine element, rather than exclusively feminine "militantes." One would expect her to use the feminine forms given that she speaks about the women's job of passing along the revolutionary message to the next generation.

12. In the *Dictionnaire des œuvres algériennes en langue française* (Paris: L'Harmattan, 1990) edited by Christiane Achour, Mechakra's birth year is listed as 1949 (166).

13. According to Barthes, in *S/Z*, "Le texte classique . . . suit un ordre logico-temporel. Il s'agit d'un système multivalent mais incomplètement réversible. Ce qui bloque la réversibilité, voilà ce qui limite le pluriel du texte classique. Ces blocages ont des noms: c'est d'une part la vérité et d'autre part l'empirie; ce précisément contre quoi—ou entre quoi—s'établit le texte moderne" (37). [The classical text . . . follows a logico-temporal order. It is concerned with a multivalent but completely reversible system. What blocks the reversibility is what limits the plurality of the classical text. These blockages have names: on the one hand truth and on the other empiricism; exactly what the modern text establishes itself against or between.]

14. In the next section we will examine the multiple names imposed upon the narrator. Here, the nuns have christened her Marie; nevertheless, we should not assume that is her "real" name.

15. I take the idea of becoming from Deleuze and Guattari in *A Thousand Plateaus*.

16. For more information on the colonizing process in Algeria, see Stora, *Algérie, Formation d'une nation*; and David Prochaska, *Making Algeria French: Colonialism in Bône, 1870–1920*.

17. Emphasis mine.

18. See Mai Thu Vân, *Viêtnam: un peuple, des voix.*

19. In a 1960 North Vietnamese newspaper editorial, August 3 is referred to as "Two Trung Sisters' Day" as well as "International Women's Day." See Chiem T. Keim, *Women in Vietnam.*

20. The quote from the *Analects* is taken from the translation by Wing-Tsit Chan, *A Source Book in Chinese Philosophy* (1963: 47). Wing-Tsit Chan notes on the same page that "From Confucius down, Confucianists have always considered women inferior."

21. Minh Khai, a founder of the Women's Union, is quoted as having said, "Revolution is our way of liberation" (Eisen 1984: 7), and Ho Chi Minh said: "If women are not free, half of the nation is not free" (White 1989: 175).

22. For an excellent view of the political upheaval in Vietnam throughout the first seventy-five years of the twentieth century, see Wendy Wilder Larsen and Tran Thi Nga's moving collection of poetry, entitled *Shallow Graves: Two Women and Vietnam*; or Duong Van Mai Elliott's autobiographical *The Sacred Willow*.

23. "A plow in one hand, a rifle in the other, we will be worthy of our loved ones at the front" (Duong 1995: 30).

24. Duong Thu Huong's novels have all been banned in Vietnam although she was a best-selling author there before the government's censorship of her work. She was expelled from the Vietnamese Communist Party for allegedly revealing state secrets in her novels. She was imprisoned without trial for seven months in 1991 and currently resides in Hanoi.

25. When the Communists came to power in the North, sympathizers with the French regime fled to the South. Catholics and those educated in the French system (primarily the bourgeoisie) also had no choice but to move southward. Therefore, we can safely assume that the majority of Francophone writers would not have been writing novels glorifying Communism or describing war from the Northern point of view.

26. This judgment belongs to Bâ-Sau, who sees her son's behavior as immoral. Once again, the teachings of Confucius come to mind, especially as regards filial piety. Out of respect for his mother, Bâ-Sau's son should not be doing things that would dishonor her or the family, especially since his motivation is financial gain.

27. Emphasis mine.

4

POSTWAR FRAGMENTATION

Fragmentation, as we have seen in the closing to chapter 3, represents an important technique, which serves to represent the upheaval brought about by war to women's lives in both Algeria and Vietnam. On one hand, it resembles the fragmentation that is prevalent throughout twentieth-century metropolitan French prose.[1] However, according to Françoise Lionnet, the technique is used among female Francophone writers in a different manner. In her study on postcolonial women writers, *Postcolonial Representations: Women, Literature, Identity*, Lionnet indicates that the fragmentation is not necessarily "a fatal breakdown and dispersion," an *undoing* of one specific element; rather, it emphasizes "dispersed images that reflect the contingencies of multiculturalism, whose social relations are constantly in a state of negotiation" (1995: 173). In Lionnet's understanding, these women are negotiating an existence that takes into account the multiplicity present in the contemporary postcolonial world; therefore, the technique of fragmentation will be used not to reduce, but to multiply. A multicultural postcolonial subject must extend beyond borders of nation, language, and race, therefore remaining in a constant state of negotiation.

In Lionnet's study, she goes on to explain that the postcolonial women authors she studies redefine "traditional conceptions of history and culture, literature and identity. They create new paradigms that represent, through innovative and self-reflexive literary techniques, both linguistic and geographic exile, displacements from the margins to a metropolitan center, and intercultural exchanges" (1995: 7). In both Malika Mokeddem's text, *L'Interdite*, and Kim Lefèvre's *Retour à la saison des pluies*, the authors are in fact depicting fragmented subjects who attempt to go beyond this creation of new paradigms.

In order to explain and develop my readings of these works I am borrowing Lionnet's use of the term *transculturation*, a concept that she in turn has borrowed from the Cuban poet Nancy Morejón. The term is used in the following manner: "to describe a process of cultural intercourse and exchange, a circulation of practices which creates a constant interweaving of symbolic forms and empirical activities among the different interacting cultures" (Lionnet 1995: 11). Lionnet notes that the spatial connotations of the prefix "trans" are significant in indicating the movement that is taking place between and among cultures (1995: 13). She stresses that *all* cultures are involved in a transcultural process, and that the interaction is in no way unidirectional. In order to express herself in French, the Francophone author, if she follows binary oppositions, is forced to divide herself between one cultural heritage (in this case, Algerian or Vietnamese) and that which is intrinsic to the language in which she writes (here, French). Rather than placing these women and their works in an oppositional framework such as this, I will examine the way in which they work to reject the idea of difference as a defining notion.[2] Within their struggles to reject difference, however, these women are not always successful.[3] What we shall see through our examination of these works is the constant battle being waged between the ideal of multiculturalism and the pitfall of binary oppositions. In other words, these authors symbolize through their writing the cultural and historical splits between Algeria and France, as well as those between Vietnam and France. In their attempts to go beyond the "broken" relationships created out of colonialism, the wars for independence, and the current political climate in which they live, we witness their fight to overcome the ideological trap of duality. This entire complex predicament is filtered down into the literature.

Born in the western part of the Algerian desert in 1949, Malika Mokeddem is the daughter of illiterate nomads who slowly became sedentary, settling in Kenadsa. She is the oldest of either ten or thirteen siblings (figures vary depending upon where you look) and was the only girl in a class of forty-five at her high school in Béchar. Not unlike some of her heroines, she refused to marry an Algerian man whom her parents chose for her. Instead, she went on to study medicine in Oran and later continued her studies in nephrology in Montpellier.[4] Eventually, she did get married, but to a Frenchman in France. Thanks to the popularity of her novels in France, she spends much of her time now writing, although she still works occasionally as a doctor in a nephrology clinic in Montpellier. Since her immigration to France she has returned to visit Algeria only seldom. Her body of work includes the following novels: *Les Hommes qui marchent*, which was printed in 1990 and republished in 1997; *Le Siècle des sauterelles* (1992); *L'Interdite* (1993); *Des Rêves et des assassins* (1995); *La Nuit de la lézarde* (1998); *N'zid* (2001); and *La Transe des insoumis* (2003). At the moment her books can be found in the *Livre de poche* series and published by Grasset. In addition, translations of *L'Interdite* are available in many languages, including English. There is also talk of turning *L'Interdite* into a screenplay.

In 1993 violence was at a peak in Algeria. In May of that same year Islamists killed the young, celebrated author Tahar Djaout. Following his murder, killings of artists, journalists, musicians, and writers became commonplace in the headlines coming daily from Algiers. Much of the intellectual community was either forced to leave or tragically, silenced forever by bullets.[5] Published in 1993, *L'Interdite* reverberates with the violence of contemporary Algeria. In its dedication, Mokeddem evokes Tahar Djaout and in so doing, she acknowledges the peril of writing in Algeria.[6] This sets the tone for her novel.

Amidst this backdrop of violence and repression, she places two narrators, Sultana and Vincent. Sultana is an Algerian-born woman who has chosen to live and practice medicine in France. Vincent is a Frenchman who has recently undergone a kidney transplant. Here, we catch a glimpse of what will be Mokeddem's narrative strategy throughout the novel. By using two distinct narrators, she plays into a duality on several levels. On one level we have the obvious duplicity inherent in choosing both a female and a male narrator; on yet another we recognize the juxtaposition of a Muslim name with that of a Christian. Both "Sultana" and "Vincent" are names whose etymologies imply power and strength. "Sultana" comes from the Arabic word meaning power and implies royalty. "Vincent" comes from Latin and means "to conquer." It is interesting to note the seemingly innocuous choice of names that is in fact symbolic once we have read *L'Interdite*. Although Vincent's name reminds us of France's conquering, colonizing past, Sultana is portrayed as a powerful woman, for whom Vincent is a somewhat weak adversary. Mokeddem has reversed the traditional colonizer/colonized along with male/female roles the reader expects to find. Here, it is the formerly colonized woman who is the stronger character of the two. In this reversal, Vincent, representative of the former conqueror, is dominated by Sultana. Throughout *L'Interdite*, and thanks to the two narrators, Mokeddem questions the dominant/submissive myth between men and women.

In addition to the textual representation of duality, the two narrators are experiencing personal confrontations with fragmentary natures. Sultana is a product of both her Algerian childhood and her French adulthood, while Vincent has involuntarily become a part of two opposing cultures. Mokeddem herself is embodied in Sultana's character, because as she states: "I am from both coasts, a woman flayed alive" (Marcus 1998: vii). It is colonialism that has flayed her, created such a violent image in her mind. Even as the child of the postcolonial generation, Mokeddem suffers through the remnants of colonialism, which is arguably more difficult than colonial domination itself. She acknowledges the difficulty of such a situation through her depiction of Sultana. Even before delving into the complexities of the novel, we can see that the surface elements of plot and narrative indicate that the author aims to emphasize a duality, which illustrates fragmentation that ultimately characterizes the historical relationship between France and Algeria.

The text begins with Sultana disembarking from a plane in the small airport of Tammar, Algeria. We learn that she has come to Algeria rather unexpectedly. While still in France she was feeling nostalgic for a former lover in Algeria. When she finally decided to telephone him, she was greeted on the other end by the news that he was, in fact, dead. The shock of this death coupled with her longing to see him again set in motion plans to return to Algeria for the first time in many years. For Sultana it is a bittersweet return home, one punctuated by time, sentiment, and a deep sense of loss.

Within the opening paragraphs of the novel, she describes the contradictions she feels within herself and the effects they have on her: "Je n'aurais jamais cru pouvoir revenir dans cette région. Et pourtant, je n'en suis jamais vraiment partie. J'ai seulement incorporé le désert et l'inconsolable dans mon corps déplacé. Ils m'ont scindée" (1993: 11). [I would have never believed it possible to return to this place. And yet I've never really left it. All I have done is incorporate the desert and the inconsolable into my displaced body. They have split me in two] (Marcus 1998: 3). When she physically left Algeria, she could not envision actually returning in the future, but as she herself notes, her experiences in Algeria stayed with her to the point that she never truly felt that she had left the country behind her. As she returns to the village where she grew up, she describes her body as "déplacé"; in other words, it exists in a sort of void. While in France she carries with her the distinct characteristics of the desert and the feeling of inconsolability that stems from such a harsh climate. What is the desert if not a void of nature, where nothing can grow except the most resilient of plants, where human life is, at best, difficult to sustain. The final sentence in this paragraph is one of the keys to Sultana's personality. She is "scindée"—in other words, cut or sectioned off. She is "flayed alive" much as Mokeddem herself claims to be in the previously cited interview. Sultana is fragmented, but not in the positive way that a theory such as Lionnet's advocates. She is split between two binary opposites, yet trying to negotiate them into a multi- or trans-cultural alternative. On the one hand, Sultana seems to be describing an existence that is multiple, not easily defined in binary terms. On the other hand, however, Sultana claims to possess two completely different versions of herself:

> Je m'enroule avec prudence sur mes Sultana dissidentes, différentes. L'une n'est qu'émotions, sensualité hypertrophiée. Elle a la volupté douloureuse, et des salves de sanglots lézardent son rire. Tragédienne ayant tant usé du chagrin, qu'il se déchire aux premiers assauts du désir. Désir inassouvi. Envie impuissante. Si je lui laissais libre cours, elle m'anéantirait. Pour l'heure, elle s'adonne à son occupation favorite: l'ambiguïté. Elle joue au balancier entre peine et plaisir. L'autre Sultana n'est que volonté. Une volonté démoniaque. Un curieux mélange de folie et de raison, avec un zeste de dérision et le fer de la provocation en permanence dressé. Une furie qui exploite tout, sournoisement ou avec ostentation, à commencer par les faiblesses de l'autre. Elle ne me réjouit, parfois, que pour me terrifier davantage. Raide de vigilance, elle scrute froidement le paysage et, de son aiguillon, me tient en respect. (1993: 14–15)
>
> [I carefully envelop myself in my dissident and different Sultanas. One is nothing but emotions, exaggerated sensuality. Her voluptuousness is painful, and bursts of sobs split her laughter. A tragedienne having so worn out her sorrow that it tears at the first assaults of desire. Unsated desire. Impotent longing. If I let her run free she would annihilate me. For now, she devotes herself to her favorite pastime: ambiguity. She swings the pendulum between pain and pleasure. The other Sultana is sheer will. Demoniacal will. A curious mix of insanity and reason, with an outer layer of contempt and the sword of provocation permanently raised. A fury that exploits all, cunningly or ostentatiously, starting with the weaknesses of the other. Sometimes she delights me, only then to terrify me all the more. Vigilant and rigid, she coldly scrutinizes the landscape and with her goad keeps me at a respectful distance.] (Marcus 1998: 6)

In the first sentence of the above-cited paragraph, she seems to be highlighting the multiplicity she feels within herself. Throughout the remainder of the quotation, nonetheless, she depicts diametric opposites. These two personalities are forced to coexist, much as Algeria and France have been forced to do the same. In the first Sultana we have emotion, exaggerated sensuality, painful pleasure, and sobbing that intermingles with her laughter. Furthermore, even within this first personality contradictions exist, which indicate a deeper level of fragmentation. Her personality does not consist of only two opposing voices, but rather a multitude of them. This initial division that she describes characterizes the "hysterical" woman who is incapable of controlling the pendulum that sways between pain and pleasure. On the other hand, this Sultana works side by side with a second one who is described as nothing more than pure will. "Un curieux mélange de folie et de raison" [a curious mix of insanity and reason] that defies conventionality because of its possession of so much fury and volatility. Our Sultana would appear then to possess myriad personalities that are disjointed. In order to understand the significance of these two personalities and the fracturing that takes place within each of them, we must put them into a historical context.

Without oversimplifying Mokeddem's strategy, it would seem that within this simple description of one woman's inner battles, we have a metaphor for the complex historical situation about which the author speaks. Her main character embodies the split inherent in many postcolonial societies and serves as an allegory for national identity.[7] Like Sultana's two personalities, the former colonizer, France, and the former colonized, Algeria, possess completely different cultural practices, mores, and norms. One would assume that because the two are diametrically opposed, they could not therefore coexist. Yet they are forced to do so. Sultana is representative of both the positive and the negative outcome of this coexistence. On the surface, she is divided between two places (France and Algeria, or Personality One and Two), never feeling that she fully belongs to one or the other. At the same time, she has internalized contradictions in order to maintain unity. Furthermore, her situation as an Algerian *woman* renders the analysis more poignant. As a product of the French educational system and an immigrant, she has adopted French ideas of feminism. At the same time, she is intimately tied to the vision of independent Algeria by her gender alone. Deniz Kandiyoti elucidates this fact when he speaks of women's stake in nationalism:

> On the one hand, nationalist movements invite women to participate more fully in collective life by interpellating them as "national" actors. . . . On the other hand, they reaffirm the boundaries of culturally acceptable feminine conduct and exert pressure on women to articulate their gender interests within the terms of reference set by nationalist discourse. Feminism is not autonomous, but bound to the signifying network of the national context which produces it. (1994: 380)

It is the national context about which Kandiyoti speaks that creates the impasse for Sultana. Her definition of feminism is decidedly Western, therefore making it impossible for her to come to terms with the way in which the concept has been interpreted in Algeria since independence.[8] In Winifred Woodhull's terms, Sultana is part of a social order in Algeria that "depends on [her] exclusion as [an] *agent* who produces social meanings that contest tradition, or more dangerously still, attests the 'betweenness' of Algeria" (1991: 116). Therefore, as Fatima Mernissi illustrates convincingly, Muslim societies must exclude women in order to maintain the power structure they have created.[9] In the specific case of Sultana, Algerian men in power must exclude her; otherwise, the order they have established will fall into disarray.

During a conversation with Salah, a friend of Yacine's, Sultana realizes that this is the status quo for feminine behavior in Algerian society. Salah criticizes her for what he deems to be her unnecessary excesses. She responds to his criticism in the following manner:

> Une femme d'excès? Le sentiment du néant serait-il un excès? Je suis plutôt dans l'entre-deux, sur une ligne de fracture, dans toutes les ruptures. Entre la modestie et le dédain qui lamine mes rébellions. Entre la tension du refus et la dispersion que procurent les libertés. Entre l'aliénation de l'angoisse et l'évasion par le rêve et l'imagination. Dans un entre-deux qui cherche ses jonctions entre le Sud et le Nord, ses repères dans deux cultures. (1993: 47)
>
> [A woman of excess? Is the feeling of nothingness an excess? I'm more in between the two, on a fractured line between the two, in the midst of all ruptures. Between modesty and disdain that erodes my rebellions. Between the tension resulting from refusal and dispersion resulting from liberties. Between the alienation caused by anguish and escape through dreams and the imagination. In an in-between place searching for its connections between the south and the north, its markers in two cultures.] (Marcus 1998: 36)

Although this identity provides a disturbing portrait of a chaotic existence, it compounds upon the initial idea of fragmentation. Her existence seems to be a precarious one, teetering on a tiny line that barely supports her. She describes her predominant sentiment as one of "nothingness." It is within the framework of this void that she has etched out an identity for herself. Given that we have already seen Sultana describing herself in pluralistic terms, this evocation of a completely fractured self does not shock us. However, Mokeddem does not simply repeat the same formula we have previously examined. In order to emphasize the point of fragmentation, within this small excerpt there are but two complete sentences. The force of this message lies in the bulk of its explanation being done through fragments, incomplete sentences. Stylistically we are drawn to each of the first three

"definitions" of the "entre-deux" because they each begin with the preposi-
tion "entre." This repetition emphasizes the problematic situation, which
when juxtaposed with the fragmented sentence structure only strengthens
our grasp of the "betweenness" in which Sultana lives.

Indeed, this state of being between two places and never really in one or
the other creates the "néant," the void, where she operates. To borrow from
Deleuze and Guattari, she is always in *a state of becoming* (1987: 232–309).
We cannot understand Sultana in terms of filiation or a progressive/regressive
linear interpretation. She is not proceeding from the fixed point of one identity to the finality of another. Rather, we need to see Sultana as part of "a line
of becoming [that] has neither beginning nor end, departure nor arrival, origin nor destination" (1987: 293). Sultana's body is an incarnation of this
process of becoming because of her encounters with the French. She is constantly crossing imaginary borders in search of an identity that does not exist
because "a becoming is neither one nor two, nor the relation of the two; it is
the in-between, the border or line of flight or descent running perpendicular
to both" (1987: 293). There is no final resolution that will cause her to stop
becoming and *become* definitively one or the other personality. The self that
she may build is not of a singular voice, but intrinsically plural.

> [Maintaining this plurality] . . . does not signify an abstract principle of toler-
> ance but rather the labor and practice that keep the spaces open where these
> discourses can clash with one another and exchange and transform their
> rules. . . . To keep these spaces open, to keep these confrontations open,
> means to struggle so that just those social and historical realities that have not
> fit within the framework of classical reason and discourse can speak. (Rella
> 1994: 54)

The social and historical reality of Sultana's situation is that she is a plural
subject who does not fit into the classical categorization of *French* or
Algerian. She is both and neither. As she says later in the same conversation
with Salah: "cet entre-deux mijote dans ma tête en permanence" (1993: 47)
[the place in between permanently simmers in my head] (Marcus 1998: 36).
It is impossible and irrelevant to force her into a preconceived paradigm,
because her identity cannot be defined so easily, not even through revolution as we know or understand it. For national revolution, as we have already seen in chapter 3, merely replaces one identity with another. In the
case of Sultana, belonging to the Algerian nation does not immediately create a sense of unity within herself. She still possesses an element of French
identity within her. The most important act that she can carry out is

accepting the plurality, multiplicity of herself and her situation. She struggles with this act throughout the novel, because others want to place her within an old paradigm, pitting what is perceived to be *French* against what is perceived to be *Algerian*.

In addition to her inability to "identify" with one fixed postcolonial subjectivity, Sultana also undergoes a "becoming" in the sense that she is not conceived by her peers as an Algerian woman. Not only can she not overcome the imaginary borders that prevent her from *being French* or *being Algerian*, but she is also faced with a gender conflict. Mokeddem mentions the women's movement in the village of Aïn Nekhla and shows us how Sultana does not fit into it. Despite the fact that Sultana receives their support and encouragement, she does not wish to be like these women. In a conversation between Sultana and Salah, he reprimands her for not acting like an Algerian *woman*:

> Je te demande seulement de te comporter comme une femme intelligente et responsable. Les femmes, ici, sont toutes des résistantes. Elles savent qu'elles ne peuvent s'attaquer, de front, à une société injuste et monstrueuse dans sa quasi-totalité. Alors elles ont pris les maquis du savoir, du travail et de l'autonomie financière. Elles persévèrent dans l'ombre d'hommes qui stagnent et désespèrent. Elles ne donnent pas dans la provocation inutile et dangereuse comme toi. Elles feintent et se cachent pour ne pas être broyées, mais continuent d'avancer. (1993: 131)
>
> [I'm only asking you to behave like a responsible and intelligent woman. The women here are all in the resistance. They know that they can't attack head-on an almost totally unjust and monstrous society. So they have taken to the underground of knowledge, of work, and of financial autonomy. They're persevering in the shadow of men who stagnate and despair. They don't lapse into useless and dangerous provocation, like you. They pretend and hide, not just to avoid being crushed, but to continue advancing.] (Marcus 1998: 111)

Salah's discourse describes the silent, almost stoic resistance of women who hope to gain gradual advancement through education and financial autonomy without expecting immediate ramifications. He calls them the "true" Algerian women. Sultana responds that she is not a "true" Algerian woman because she is not "whole" like they are: "Elles sont entières" (1993: 131) [They're whole] (Marcus 1998: 111). Here, once again invoking Deleuze and Guattari, I would question this very notion of wholeness because of the impossibility of an entire, complete postcolonial female subject anywhere that encounters between two cultures have taken place. However, while the reality may be that *whole* subjects do not exist,

Sultana sees these other Algerian women as different from her due to specific circumstances. She feels that because of her differences she can never belong to a category. In a world where interpretation comes through questions of identity and difference, Sultana suffers. Unlike her "true" Algerian counterparts, she does not have the luxury of believing she belongs to only one place, of assuming she is "whole." She is all too aware that she is "multiple et écartelée, depuis l'enfance. . . . Maintenant en France, je ne suis ni algérienne, ni même maghrébine. Je suis une Arabe. Autant dire, rien" (1993: 131). [I've been many-faceted and torn apart since childhood. . . . In France now, I'm neither Algerian nor even North African. I'm an Arab. That's as much as to say nothing] (Marcus 1998: 111–12). The all-important act of naming is questioned here, as it will be throughout Sultana's discussions of her *self*.[10] Within the boundaries of France, Sultana is assigned the identity of the *Arab*. According to the *Petit Robert* (1993), the adjective *Arabe* designates an "Originaire de la péninsule arabique; des peuples sémitiques d'Arabie *et par extension* des populations arabophones du Proche-Orient et du nord de l'Afrique" [Native of the Arabian peninsula; Semitic peoples from Arabia *and by extension* Arabophone populations of the Middle East and North Africa]. The current usage (*usage courant*) in the *Robert* is noted as a "Personne originaire du Maghreb" [Native of North Africa]. An Arab signifies in the first definition three different and distinct groups of people, who may or may not share a religion, a culture, or even a language.[11] In the current usage, we see that one employs it to mean anyone from the Maghrib. Subsequently, we see why Sultana states that being called an Arab means nothing—it reduces multiple groups of people to one monolithic term. The reduction isolates her from the French, but remains meaningless as a descriptor of her.

As for the conflict she faces regarding gender, this comes to Sultana in the form of her inability and unwillingness to adopt the plight of all Algerian women as her own. She is not part of a uniform group known as "women" or "Algerian women" or even "women of Aïn Nekhla" any more than she is part of a monolithic Arab culture. She traverses all of these borders, along with those of France and Algeria. In the above statement that she makes, we witness the power of nomenclature and the desire people have to create an identity *for* her, but this is only an external process, thus it does not work. Internally she cannot appropriate any of these terms; they do not define her because she is pluralized. The initial and continued "betweenness" of her existence creates a fragmentation to which no unique name can be attached.

The climax of the novel comes near the end, as the village begins to divide into two camps: those who side with the mayor, who is a supporter of the Islamist party, and those who support Sultana and her work at the hospital. It is the women of the village who make the biggest impact, because they finally speak up and act out against the mayor, who is trying to force Sultana to leave. Among the villagers, one woman speaks to Sultana, saying "Nous les femmes, on a besoin de toi. . . . C'est une ancienne du maquis qui te parle. Une femme qui ne comprend pas par quelle perversion l'indépendance du pays nous a déchues de nos dignités et de nos droits alors que nous avons combattu pour elle" (1993: 166). [We women need you. . . . I'm a former resistance fighter speaking to you. A woman who doesn't understand by what perversion our country's independence deprived us of our dignity and our rights, when we fought for it] (Marcus 1998: 141). We are reminded here of chapter 3 in this study in which we examined the roles played by women in the revolutionary war. Through Danièle Djamila Amrane-Minne's studies on women's participation in the revolution, we observed that women's roles in the war were instrumental, but that following this period of high activity, many women disappeared from the political sphere. The prestige associated with women who fought in the *maquis*, but who are now involved in a much more resigned and silent fight, presents a contentious moment. This woman's self-description portrays the contemporary situation of a generation of women in Algeria. Her involvement in the war for independence immediately gives her a certain amount of credibility; however, it is important to note Sultana's reaction to both this woman and the invitation to join the group: "Non, non, je ne serai pas votre présidente. . . . La rébellion contre les injustices est une chose, le vrai désir de liberté en est une autre qui exige un pas beaucoup plus grand, parfois quelques ruptures" (1993: 170–71). [No, no, I won't be your president. . . . Rebellion against injustice is one thing, the true desire for liberty is another, which demands a much larger step, sometimes some changes] (Marcus 1998: 145). Here, we witness the deep division that exists between Sultana and the women of the village. According to Mokeddem's narrator, *true desire for freedom* is something that requires a much greater effort than rebellion against known or at least perceived injustices. In other words, Sultana is in effect reminding this woman that she cannot rely on historical events to shape her present and definitely not her future. This linear interpretation of cause and effect (participation in the war leads to political power) has been proven not to work; therefore, Algerian women must search for another solution. According to Sultana, some *ruptures* are inevitable in order to reach a place in which true liberty exists. In the end, too, Sultana's separation from the women of the village, and her desire for such a distancing, indicate the inaccuracy of seeing *The Algerian Woman* as a collective identity. Instead, we are forced to see *women*, a group constituting different individuals with more than one ideology. This distinction is important to our overall understanding of the novel, and our search for an answer to the difficulties facing contemporary Algerian women, whether they live in Algeria or France, because, as Spivak notes, "the solution [does not] lie in the positivist inclusion of a monolithic collectivity of 'women' in the list of the oppressed whose unfractured subjectivity allows them to speak for themselves against an equally monolithic 'same system'" (1994: 73).

Postcolonial maneuverings have made it impossible for people like Sultana to neatly fit into one group or the other. Western interpretations of feminism do not apply to her because her entire history, from her childhood to the present, has made her an isolated woman. She does not belong with these women any more than she belongs with the French who define her as an Arab. The villagers are asking her to conform to their ways, to not receive male guests in her home, to behave, as Salah would say "as a true Algerian," but she refuses to give up any of her individual freedom. She is in a sense accusing them in her final reply. For Sultana, true freedom is more than rebellion against oppressive forces; it is individuality, which does not really exist without certain "ruptures." The women want her to be their president, their spokeswoman, because of her unique past, of her Western education. Here, they are buying into a neocolonial attitude that assumes a Western-educated woman can help *her people*. Not only does Mokeddem reject this assumption, but she also demonstrates how these Algerian women, through their assignation of a French identity to Sultana, are placing her in a predefined category just as the French attempt to do when they call her an Arab. In the final lines of the novel Sultana comes to the realization that she cannot stay in Algeria and that her return to Montpellier will be definitive. Her final words express her complex situation once again: "Dis aux femmes que même loin, je suis avec elles" (1993: 181). [Tell the women that even from afar, I am with them] (Marcus 1998: 154). While she empathizes with the women and believes in their quest, she feels that she is incapable of helping them because she does not belong *to* Algeria.

In Sultana's view, she has never truly been a part of this village. Throughout the novel we are privy to moments of flashback, where she gives us a glimpse of her past. From the very beginning when she arrives in Tammar and takes the cab to Aïn Nekhla, her encounter with the driver indicates that her past must be colored in some way. She recalls painful childhood memories: name-calling (once more emphasizing the role of nomenclature in defining or attempting to define a person), others making fun of her. Therefore, she is hesitant to reveal her name to both the cab driver and to the others in the village. The power of naming is made explicit here, since her identity will be defined by her past. Eventually, they discover who they *think* she is, who history dictates she should be; thus, their distrust for her grows considerably. In other words, the discovery of her name, therefore her categorized identity, triggers a powerful reaction from the villagers. As a stranger she is an object of curiosity, but as a named entity she becomes a threat.

The story of Sultana's parents created quite a stir in Aïn Nekhla when she was still a child. They were from different Algerian tribes and married out of love. The man who is now the mayor of the village, a fervent Islamist, intended at one point to marry Sultana's mother. When she chose another man over him, he began to spread rumors of her infidelity. In her most revealing flashback, Sultana describes the day her father finally gave in and believed the rumors. He flew into a furious rage, pushed her mother down, and killed her. Then, out of remorse and regret he fled the village, never to be seen again. Sultana was left alone with her dead mother and an infant sister, who survived only a short time after the mother's death. Relatives should have taken her in, but they eventually abandoned her because of their fear that she came from a cursed family. The turning point in her story is the entrance of a French doctor and his wife onto the scene. They befriend her, encourage her education, and introduce her, for the first time, to Western ways of life. Unfortunately for Sultana this interaction with the benevolent French couple does not make her any more acceptable to the villagers. Her name still conjures up memories of trouble, pain, and misfortune. The power of her filial identity is overwhelming and extraordinarily condemning. The villagers will of course continue to shun her because of her familial background, but now they may add a new damning trait to the list: her crossing of the border between colonizer and colonized. Through her newly found friendship and quasi adoption, she is rejected even more violently. "Je suis devenue la putain du roumi. . . . Paul et Jeanne Challes ont eu les pires problèmes à cause de moi" (1993: 155). [I became the roumi's whore. . . . Paul and Jeanne Challes had the worst problems because of me] (Marcus 1998: 133). Her banishment from the village society is compounded upon by attacks upon her benefactors as well.

Within this revelation through flashback we grow to understand Sultana's complexity even more. From the time Sultana was very young, the people in the village singled her out as cursed and different. The alienation that she experienced came first from her family history and second from her association with a French couple. It seems almost inevitable that she would show an affinity for the West, because two representatives from that part of the world were the first to show her compassion and acceptance. The Challes become both her salvation and her damnation. By accepting and encouraging her, they open new doors for her future; in fact, without their tutelage one wonders if Sultana would have survived the tragic death of her family. Although she does indeed physically survive, psychologically she is marred forever. Once again this situation epitomizes the ambiguity of the postcolonial situation. The Challes are creating a woman who will be accepted in neither France nor Algeria. No matter how much she begins to feel akin to the French couple, she is in fact an Algerian girl. Slowly her alienation progresses to the point that she feels she can no longer stay in her own country, which is why she flees and pursues an education in France. A victim of the ideological trap of duality, she still feels a tie to the village, the Algerian people, and especially the women. This bond is intrinsic and impossible to annihilate, which leads her to initially consider remaining in Algeria:

> L'actualité du pays et le sort des femmes, ici, me replongent sans cesse dans mes drames passés, m'enchaînent à toutes celles qu'on tyrannise. Les persécutions et les humiliations qu'elles endurent m'atteignent, ravivent mes plaies. L'éloignement n'atténue rien. La douleur est le plus fort lien entre les humains. Plus fort que toutes les rancœurs. (1993: 155–56)
>
> [The country's current events and the fate of women here constantly plunge me back into my past dramas, link me to all those women who are tyrannized. The persecutions and the humiliations endured by them reach me and reopen my wounds. Distance attenuates nothing. Pain is the strongest bond between humans. Stonger than all resentments.] (Marcus 1998: 133)

In addition to this tie she feels to people in Algeria, she is still searching for that reconciliation with her past. She feels she has not yet achieved it; therefore, she wonders if a definitive return to Algeria would enable her to do so. As we know, however, in the final pages of the novel she realizes that she can do nothing useful or productive in Algeria. The situation in the village has spun out of her control. Instead of joining with the women in the village, she leaves for Montpellier. During this entire period of indecision (should she stay in Algeria or return to France), appropriation (she knows she should *feel* Algerian, because she is, after all, defined as such due to her birth there), and finally acceptance (she will never *belong* within the walls of either place), we witness the distinctively destructive nature of the borders of nationality.

Sultana is the *product* of the violent cohabitation with colonialism. This internal violence is depicted poignantly in Sultana's physical descriptions of her suffering. A physical malady as a result of sentimental or emotional events is not a new concept. Take, for example, Claire de Duras's 1823 narrative, entitled *Ourika*. The young Senegalese woman who has lived her entire life in France under the care of a metropolitan family suffers extreme anxiety once she realizes she is different from her French counterparts. Eventually she retires in a self-imposed exile to a convent. In the opening to the text, a doctor attends to the now dying nun and describes her in the following manner: "Sa maigreur était excessive, ses yeux brillants et fort grands, ses dents, d'une blancheur éblouissante éclairaient seuls sa physionomie; l'âme vivait encore, mais le corps était détruit, et elle portait toutes les marques d'un long et violent chagrin" (Duras 1994: 4). [She was excessively thin. The sole things that gave light to her face were her extraordinarily large and luminous eyes and her dazzlingly white teeth. Her mind still lived, but her body was destroyed. She showed every sign of having suffered from prolonged and acute melancholia] (Fowles 1994: 4). Ourika herself explains that her current poor state of health is the result of her life as an outsider: both she and her doctor explain her disease in a very nebulous way—she has suffered from profound sorrow which has led to the destruction of her body. Her symptoms manifest themselves only in her physical appearance and appear to be directly linked to tuberculosis. This physical description of Ourika calls to mind Susan Sontag's study, *Illness as Metaphor*, and especially her discussion of the role of tuberculosis in the conveyance of romantic notions. Sontag explains: "TB was a disease in the service of a romantic view of the world" (1978: 69). This disease was particularly well suited to serve as a metaphor for the melancholia associated with Romanticism.

This extremely romantic notion of suffering is put into question in Sultana's rendition of her own displacement between Algeria and France. Using a medical lexicon, she explains the effect each country has had on her life. She says the following:

J'ai fait un infarctus de mon Algérie. Il y a si longtemps. Maintenant mon cœur frappe de nouveau son galop sans algie. Mais une séquelle de nécrose reste: sceau de l'abandon à la source du sang à jamais scellé. J'ai fait une hémiplégie de ma France. Peu à peu, mon hémicorps a retrouvé ses automatismes, récupéré ses sensations. Cependant, une zone de mon cerveau me demeure muette, comme déshabitée: une absence me guette aux confins de mes peurs, au seuil de mes solitudes. (1993: 82)

[I had a heart attack over my Algeria. Such a long time ago. Now my heart is again pounding without pain. But an aftereffect of necrosis remains: the

bucket of abandonment at the never-sealed source of blood. I'm half para-
lyzed over my France. Little by little, half of my body has again found its au-
tomatic functioning, recuperated its sensations. Yet a zone of my brain remains mute to me, as if not lived in: an absence lies in wait for me at the
borders of my fears, at the threshold of my loneliness.] (Marcus 1998: 67)

The division and coexistence, contradictory terms, are described as chronic
and pathological. This literal translation of pathology pushes the nineteenth-
century sentimentality shown in *Ourika* to an extreme, thereby creating a
new, more concrete effect for the reader. Rather than dealing in purely sentimental terms, the narrator utilizes medical vocabulary that paints a vivid
picture of pathology. Hers are physical reactions to emotional circumstances.
In an innovative way, the familiar nineteenth-century sentimentality is re-
worked here to create a more violent response. For example, Sultana talks
of her heart, but here, the heart is recovering from a heart attack and is
learning to work with its deadened parts alongside it.[12] In other words, the
injured part of the organ has sealed itself up and closed itself off from the
rest. This is the description she gives of "her Algeria" and the effect it has
had upon her. Rather than speak of the clichéd "broken heart," Mokeddem
employs the medical equivalent. It does not appear as an outside symptom;
rather, it is an internalized injury. When speaking of France in the same
passage, she wants to discuss the feeling of absence; therefore, she once
again turns to medical terminology. She speaks of an absence, one that is
the result of a loss of blood flow to the brain. This lack of something leaves her
feeling at a loss, fearful and alone. France has created a deaf, silent zone within
her brain. Thus, as we can see, Mokeddem's description of self-alienation is
made all the more powerful by the terms the narrator employs. The use of
strong, unusual metaphors impacts the reader to an even greater degree than
a simple narrative strategy of recounting events. As a literary device it acts as
a rewriting of nineteenth-century sentimental discourse. Mokeddem is,
in part, rewriting Romanticism and reconsidering metaphorical
illnesses.

In addition to this one example of her confrontation and subsequent
rewriting of romantic literary norms, she also questions erotic discourse associated with Orientalist literature. If we accept Edward Saïd's notion of
Orientalism as a "Western style for dominating, restructuring, and having
authority over the Orient," (1979: 3) then to rewrite Orientalism is to refute
this Western domination, to restructure in order to reinscribe authority in
the Orient. Mokeddem's project unleashes an Oriental authority with a female voice. Sultana becomes the antithesis to Gustave Flaubert's Salomé.

According to Saïd, in the Oriental woman, and in this specific instance, the Oriental prostitute, Flaubert found "an occasion and an opportunity for [his] . . . musings; he is entranced by her self-sufficiency, by her emotional carelessness, and also by what, lying next to him, she allows him to think.[13] [She is] [l]ess a woman than a display of impressive but verbally inexpressive femininity" (1979: 187). Flaubert will go on to translate this "verbally inexpressive femininity," observed in the form of a prostitute, into his novels and short stories. One such example is the Salomé who appears in *Hérodias*. With great care the author describes Salomé's erotic dance:

> Elle dansa comme les prêtresses des Indes, comme les Nubiennes des cataractes, comme les bacchantes de Lydie. Elle se renversait de tous les côtés, pareille à une fleur que la tempête agite. Les brillants de ses oreilles sautaient, l'étoffe de son dos chatoyait; de ses bras, de ses pieds, de ses vêtements jaillissaient d'invisibles étincelles qui enflammaient les hommes. . . . Sans fléchir ses genoux en écartant les jambes, elle se courba si bien que son menton frôlait le plancher; et les nomades habitués à l'abstinence, les soldats de Rome experts en débauches, les avares publicains, les vieux prêtres aigris par les disputes, tous, dilatant leurs narines, palpitaient de convoitise. (1966: 148)
>
> [She danced like the Indian priestesses, like the Nubians of the cataracts, like the bacchanals of Lydia. She tilted from all sides, similar to a flower that the tempest stirs. The diamonds on her ears leapt, the fabric on her back shimmered; from her arms, her feet, her clothing flew invisible sparks that set men ablaze. Without bending her knees while spreading her legs, she bowed down so well that her forehead brushed the floor; and the nomads, used to abstinence, the Roman soldiers, experts in debauchery, the stingy tax-collectors, the old priests embittered by disputes, all, dilating their nostrils, quivered with desire.]

As she nears completion of her dance, the king, who has been lecherously partaking in the spectacle, summons her to him. Since the promise had been to grant Salomé whatever she might wish, the king asks her desire. At first, Flaubert writes that she didn't speak; she and the king just looked at each other; then, finally, she spoke as a child would (1966: 149). Her voice is initially absent, yet when it does produce an enunciation it is diminished to possessing a childlike quality. Thus, the Oriental, or Orientalized, Woman serves a sexually explicit purpose, and if she remains within a sexual frame she maintains power. As soon as she steps outside of that role, however, she possesses no authority whatsoever.

Mokeddem's response to this erotic, yet silent, scene in Flaubert can be construed through her own male narrator, Vincent. In order to justify his role in the novel, she has recourse to medical vocabulary once again—this time relying on a surgical procedure: the transplant. The operation links him to Algeria in a very contrived way, because the transplanted kidney once belonged to an Algerian woman. In the second chapter of the book, he decides to travel to Algeria in order to reconnect with this unknown woman who allowed him to live through her death. He is searching for a link to appease his curiosity. In a sense, he is the grateful gift recipient looking for the donor. In another sense, and although Vincent is a male character, he is a unique receptacle of a fragmented postcolonial Algerian woman. In other words, the concept of fragmentation is visualized corporally through Vincent. In the following excerpt, he rhetorically asks if he has accepted the woman's kidney, or if the kidney has accepted him:

> J'ai accepté le rein. Ou peut-être est-ce lui qui a fini par m'intégrer et par digérer, filtrer et pisser mes tourments? Sans crise de rejet, sans raté. Assimilation et pacification mutuelle. . . . Mais cette tolérance ne pouvait empêcher l'idée qu'avec cet organe, la chirurgie avait incrusté en moi deux germes d'étrangeté, d'altérité: l'autre sexe et une autre "race." Et l'enracinement dans mes pensées du sentiment de ce double métissage de ma chair me poussait irrésistiblement vers les femmes et vers cette autre culture, jusqu'alors superbement ignorée. La fréquentation de Belleville et Barbès m'a guéri de deux autres tares: la résignation et la solitude. La résignation à la solitude. (1993: 30)
>
> [I accepted the kidney. Or is it maybe the kidney that ended up integrating me into it and digesting, filtering, and pissing out all my tormented feelings? Without rejecting the organ, without failure. A mutual assimilation and truce. . . . But this tolerance couldn't keep me from thinking that with this organ, surgery had implanted in me two seeds of strangeness, of difference: the other sex and another "race." And the feeling of this double *métissage* of my flesh became deeply rooted in my thoughts and pushed me uncontrollably toward women and toward this other culture, which until then I had haughtily disregarded. My frequent visits to Belleville and Barbès cured me of two other defects: resignation and loneliness. Being resigned to be alone.] (1998: Marcus 21)

The vocabulary in this excerpt is loaded with connotations of the relationship between France and Algeria, and between women and men. Vincent speaks of integration, rejection, assimilation and pacification. In all of these terms we can see the vocabulary of colonization and French governmental policy.[14] Algerians were *integrated* into French colonial schools; however, the French also *rejected* them. The colonists lived apart from the *indigènes*, creating a segregated society. *Assimilation* was official government policy and *pacification* turned into the key word surrounding Algerian uprisings against the French during the war for independence.[15] All of these terms have become irrevocably linked with

French presence in Algeria, and their mere invocation by Vincent calls to mind colonial discourses.

Moreover, we can also see a commentary on the erotic perception that the colonizer (generally a French male) has of an Algerian woman. Vincent fantasizes about the donor: "J'enlace son absence, j'étreins le vide de sa présence. Un rein, presque rien, un défaut, une faute à rien, nous unit par-delà la vie et la mort" (1993: 31). [I embrace her absence, I squeeze the emptiness of her presence. A kidney, almost nothing, a flaw, a simple twist of fate, unites us beyond life and death] (Marcus 1998: 22). He embraces her even in her absence; for she, the silent *Oriental Woman*, retains value to him only in a physical and even sexual sense. Her lack of voice is allegorically indicated by her death and therefore Vincent's inability to ever hear her in any capacity. Furthermore, the additional sexual connotation of *rein* (kidney, but also "loins") in French links itself easily to an erotic interpretation of Vincent's words. He is focusing upon her as an object, or so it would seem upon our first reading.

Just like the lustful king in *Hérodias*, Vincent becomes a voyeur akin to the colonial consumer present in Malek Alloula's *The Colonial Harem*.[16] As Barbara Harlow indicates in her introduction to this collection of pictorial representations of Algerian women: "The postcards . . . no longer represent Algeria and the Algerian woman but rather the Frenchman's phantasm of the Oriental female" (1986: xiv). Alloula shows us how the French metropolitan public of the late nineteenth and early twentieth centuries would have seen the Algerian woman. His project is to turn the gaze of the European around upon himself by returning a voice to each of these postcards. Used to communicate with metropolitan France, these postcards succeeded in perpetuating various imagined ideals regarding Algeria. For our purposes, I will call attention only to the specifically erotic images of women in Alloula's collection. He demonstrates how the French photographer created fantastic and fantasmatic situations in order to suggest a confirmation of stereotypical Oriental eroticism. Whether imitating a harem scene or displaying a veiled woman's breasts, the photographer seeks to appease the voyeuristic appetite of his viewers. Significantly, too, in most instances, the model, subject of the photographer's lens, remains anonymous. Void of any identity, other than that of *L'Algérienne*, she, like Salomé, is silenced or trivialized. She may be a femme fatale, but her only power comes through a silent sexuality. This image, replete with erotic overtones and void of identity, seems to coincide with Vincent's dreams and thoughts in *L'Interdite*.

Because he is fascinated by the thought that an Algerian woman resides within him, he desperately searches for a woman with whom he might speak. Given the cultural constraints, he has difficulty encountering any women at all, except for Sultana. Under the pretext of needing a physical, he goes to the hospital where she works. Sultana performs a routine medical examination and informs him that his body is still reacting well to the transplant. Nothing remarkable occurs during their meeting. All the same, Vincent awakens slowly the following morning while having a sexual fantasy involving an imaginary Algerian woman. In his mind she is the organ donor. At the same time, he realizes that he has been reanimated sexually for the first time since his surgery. Is it a coincidence that this happens after his first real encounter with Sultana? She has ignited his fantasies and allowed him to feel sexually aroused once again.

With all of these examples Mokeddem seems to be telling us that Vincent is a stereotypical Frenchman straight out of Flaubert or Alloula. He is the Western subject who is objectifying the *Other*. However, Sultana's own sexual hallucinations involving the deceased Yacine appear in the chapter immediately following Vincent's awakening (1993: 87). One sexual episode is followed by another, indicating that the author has placed the two in parallel, thereby forcing us to recognize the importance of sexuality to both characters. Therefore, through a closer reading of both passages, we can conclude that Sultana is not being victimized by Vincent's sexual desires, because she possesses and struggles with these same desires. Before she fantasizes about Yacine, she likens Vincent to him, giving a purely physical description—objectifying him (1993: 86–87). When she has intimate contact with Vincent later in the novel she once again mistakes him for Yacine, showing Vincent's complete lack of identity and subjectivity in Sultana's mind. He is depersonified to the point that he becomes a token male symbol for Sultana's female desires. Sultana's actions therefore depict a complete reversal of the Algerian woman's image portrayed in Alloula's postcards because she, as the woman, is no longer symbolic of male fantasy and colonial desire. It becomes apparent that the author is forcing us to confront and refute the stereotype of the Algerian and Muslim woman. Rather than engaging in the facile project of pointing out the well-known misguided conception of the Algerian woman that the West has grown accustomed to seeing over the past three hundred years, Mokeddem uses Vincent's and Sultana's sexuality as an instrument to guide us toward a new understanding of the postcolonial Algerian woman. By automatically assuming that the Western man is exploiting the Oriental woman (as Alloula does), we, no matter who *we* are, are taking power and thus, voice, away from the woman. If we accept this position we are in effect attempting to re-present the subaltern woman as a voiceless victim.

Instead of being in the "shadow" of subaltern studies (Spivak 1994: 83), Sultana is actually reinforced as the agent of her own sexuality and therefore is more than the object of Vincent's desire. Whereas the women photographed in Alloula's book epitomize the *objectification* of femininity, Sultana *subjectifies* it. The very presence of her sexuality refutes a simple reading of her as a victim, or as Amal Amireh puts it, "of a monolithic Islam and tribal Arab culture [in which women] . . . are permanently locked out of history and allowed to be only objects—of study, of pity, and of liberation" (1997: 186). Not unlike Vincent, she has dreams and fantasies that are fueled by sexual desire. Sultana's role in *L'Interdite* effectively works to eradicate falsely preconceived notions of Algerian women through a rewriting of romantic and eroticized discourse that deconstructs Orientalism. The end result is an Algerian woman whose authority and power cannot be undermined by Western constructs of her, nor by unjust interpretations of her role within the Algerian society.

While Vincent is the most significant male character in the novel because of the important revelations he produces with regard to the heroine, he is not the only one. As we have already discussed, the pretext for Sultana's visit to Algeria is the death of her former friend and lover, Yacine. Once she arrives in Aïn Nekhla she meets one of his very close friends, Salah. Her relationship with Salah is ambiguous, especially because of his wary nature. As the novel progresses, however, it becomes more and more obvious that Salah is attracted to Sultana. He wants to take her to Algiers with him, to provide her with a safer environment. On the other hand, Vincent tries to tempt her with exotic escapism. He invites her to sail around the world with him, to traverse the desert. At the end of chapter 8, when Vincent is narrating, he describes Sultana's reaction to the suggestions of the two men: "Sultana nous observe l'un et l'autre, longtemps, un sourire figé sur les lèvres. Brusquement, elle éclate en sanglots. Elle pleure comme on pleure de joie, avec un visage radieux" (1993: 157). [Sultana looks at both of us for a long time. Suddenly she bursts into sobs. She cries as one cries for joy, with a radiant face] (Marcus 1998: 134). Her emotional outburst occurs after she has recounted her childhood to the two men. Two different realities stem from this moment and will alter Sultana's state: first, she has undergone a kind of purging. In her case, memory has helped to blur the lines between what is real and what is not. She has until now distanced herself from the trauma of her past and comes to terms with it here in front of her audience. Words and the act of remembering create reparation. Throughout her stay in Algeria, something has been broken; Sultana herself has been dismantled, or fragmented into small parts that fit together only with great difficulty. Now that she has faced up to that she feels a sense of relief and of comprehension that she could not feel while in France, avoiding her past.

Second, these two men have given her a *dual* solution—one is decidedly Western, while the other is Algerian. Vincent wants to explore, have adventures, much like the French colonizers. Salah wants to settle down and protect Sultana. She is once more faced with two worlds, two possibilities colliding. Her tears are joyous, because this is a familiar place for her to be, between two worlds. She is no longer that little girl who is being persecuted for her difference. While she struggles to embody the complex ideals of multiculturalism, she is still completely aware of the safety to be found in remaining dual. In the following chapter, when she becomes our narrator again, she asks herself why she suddenly feels so much happier:

> Qu'est-ce qui t'a fait changer d'avis? . . . L'émoi dû à la présence de deux hommes à aimer . . . ? Le projet du retour vers Montpellier? . . . Non, je ne crois pas. Tu es la dualité même et ne te préoccupes jamais de la provenance de ce qui t'assouvit dans l'instant. Car tout t'est éphémère et l'inquiétude ne semble t'assaillir que pour marquer le creux d'où jaillit et s'élance le rire décapant de ta dérision. . . . Forte du sentiment de ma complexité recomposée, je quitte la salle de bains. (1993: 160)
>
> [What made you change your mind? . . . The emotion due to the presence of two men to love . . . ? The plan to return to Montpellier? . . . No, I don't think so. You're duality itself, and you never worry about your source of satisfaction at any given moment. Because for you everything is ephemeral and worry doesn't seem to touch you except to mark the hollow from which the caustic laughter of your derision spurts in a rush. . . . Strengthened by the feeling of my recomposed complexity, I leave the bathroom.] (Marcus 1998: 136)

In order to function she is compelled to live *between*. She is neither in one place nor in the other. She does not look forward to making choices—it is not the joy of having options that she conveys here; rather, it is the state of duality in which she finds herself that gives her the will to go on with her life.

While Sultana and her dual, sometimes complex, nature takes center stage in Mokeddem's novel, there is another female character of importance. Until now we have focused almost exclusively on Sultana and her predicament. In order to emphasize that this is not a particular problem, one that is tied specifically to Sultana's unique situation, Mokeddem introduces the reader to a young Algerian girl, Dalila. It is Vincent who first meets Dalila, a solitary child, with whom he can converse in an almost surreal way. The words that Mokeddem places in the girl's mouth sometimes seem much too sophisticated or introspective for such a child; however, the underlying motivation for such a character seems to be twofold. First, Dalila is a child of contemporary Algeria, which means that any interactions she has with France will be purely *post*colonial. In other words, she is the epitome of the aftermath of contact between the two cultures. Second, in the eyes of Mokeddem, she is also a vision of what the future will hold for Algeria. Sultana has already been formed and molded by the relationships she has had with both nations; with Dalila we can witness "betweenness" in the making.

Before his death, the doctor, Yacine, had befriended this little girl. He had decided to encourage her and be involved in her life, much the same as the Challes had cared for Sultana. It is because of Yacine's death that Dalila meets Vincent and eventually Sultana. When Vincent first arrives at his hotel just outside of the village where Sultana is now living and working, he notices a young girl off in the distance, perched on a sand dune. Since, as we mentioned earlier, the one thing that Vincent is seeking in Algeria is human contact, he is immediately attracted to the curious sight of a small girl alone. During his first conversation with the child she is willing to speak to him because of his association with France. She remembers that her friend, Yacine, had been educated in France; therefore, she hopes there might be some sort of affinity between Vincent and Yacine. As she speaks with admiration of the now defunct doctor, Vincent grows more and more enthralled by the conversation. Dalila is obviously distraught by the fact that she has not seen Yacine, which is unlike him, especially since he promised to return to visit her again. When Vincent finally goes to the hospital and meets Sultana, he convinces her to come and visit the girl. Throughout their conversations with the child it becomes quite clear that she is already caught in the middle of two worlds: she attends school and spends much of her time with her schoolteacher, using books and knowledge as her escape from her life at home. She is the only daughter in a large family of boys whose futures appear dubious at best.

One of the most remarkable indicators of the "betweenness" of Dalila is her linguistic predicament. She lies between two languages, therefore embodying the *inter-dit(e)* of the novel's title: she is quite literally between two utterances, two things to be said. Due to her education and exposure to French, she uses it when she speaks to Vincent, for example. Since most of her practice in the language comes from school, she repeats things as she has heard them: "LaFrance" is all one word; "la versité" is the university; and "les migrés" are those who emigrate. In addition to her use of her own French words, her overall language is mixed. For her, interspersing Arabic and French remains totally normal. As a matter of fact, she delicately chastises Sultana for correcting her Arabic words into French:

> Tu fais comme le *roumi*, toi, tu me corriges les mots en algérien. . . . Nous, les vrais Algériens, on mélange toujours les mots. . . . Nous, les vrais, on mélange le français avec des mots algériens. Toi, tu es une vraie mélangée alors tu mélanges plus les mots. Quand tu étudies là-bas, tu deviens toujours une vraie mélangée. (1993: 93)
>
> [You, you do like the roumi, you correct the Algerian words. . . . Us, real Algerians, we're always mixing words. . . . Us, the real ones, we mix French with Algerian words. You, you're a real mix, so you don't mix words anymore. When you study over there, you become a real mix.] (Marcus 1998: 77)

Once again, Mokeddem is reminding us that Sultana does not fit into Algerian society anymore, because she is, as Dalila says, "une vraie mélangée." She is thus someone who has completely assimilated to the French way of life in the eyes of Dalila. In reality, as we have already seen, Sultana is not assimilated to the degree Dalila imagines (remember the passage in which Sultana describes the absence she feels from the French while in France— she describes it as a sort of pathology). Dalila's impression stems from an ever-present desire to delineate people into categories based on binary oppositions. For Dalila, Sultana must be one or the other; for Mokeddem Sultana should be neither one nor the other, because she embodies *L'Interdit(e)* of the title as well. She is that which falls between the two things said/dictated by binary oppositions. For Sultana herself the situation is not so clearly cut. Sometimes she feels she should be one or the other, but often she feels sectioned off into parts that incorporate different elements from both worlds. Significantly, in the words of Dalila we also witness a commentary about contemporary Algeria: a society that is still dealing with the confrontation of two worlds. Her bilingualism is a product of the history of her country and is impossible to avoid. She represents yet another phase in the ongoing attempt to achieve a movement of transculturation in the postcolonial world.

Kim Lefèvre is a French-Vietnamese author born in French-occupied Vietnam to a Vietnamese mother and a French father. Her body of work includes two novels written in French, *Métisse blanche* (1989) and *Retour à la saison des pluies* (1990), as well as several translations from Vietnamese into French. An autobiographical prose narrative, *Retour à la saison des pluies* delves into the author's desire to reconcile her contradictory self-perceptions, as both the colonized people and the colonizing power. Interpreting identity through a binary, and therefore oppositional, system, Lefèvre

begins this project believing that within herself she possesses two nationalities and two completely opposite world views: both that of the Vietnamese
subject and of the French *agent*. Raised by her mother and stepfather,
Lefèvre knows very little of her biological father, a French soldier who
abandoned her mother, leaving her pregnant and unmarried. Even this
man's name remains something of a mystery.[17] Thus, although she is
Eurasian, she describes a childhood full of incomprehension because she
felt herself to be entirely Vietnamese despite the reality of her paternity.
Hers is therefore an unresolved identity from the very beginning, bringing
confusion in the form of others constantly reminding her that she is physically different from her Vietnamese counterparts. Her face conveys a signi-
fying surface that others use to define her, but in reality, behind that face is
a "black hole" of subjectivity. This concept of the black hole comes from
Deleuze and Guattari's chapter entitled "Year Zero: Faciality" in *A Thousand Plateaus*. They posit that although in the West one is generally obsessed with the face as an identifying marker, there is in fact an entire realm
of subjectivity in the black hole behind it. We see examples of this in various works of fiction depicting encounters between East and West.[18]

In Amy Tan's 1989 novel, *The Joy Luck Club*, the author also explores the
concept of faciality. The story of four Chinese women who immigrate to the
United States and raise their four daughters as Americans, this narrative focuses upon the black hole of subjectivity behind the faces of these women.
During the opening chapter of the novel, we observe June, who is one of
the daughters, playing cards with her (now deceased) mother's three Chinese friends. The mothers are all astounded when June makes the comment that she is unsure as to whether or not she really *knew* her own
mother. In other words, (Western) June expresses her uncertainty of what
lies behind the faciality of her own (Eastern) mother. Throughout the
novel, and following this revelation, the other mothers attempt to reconcile
the two worlds—that of the mothers (or China) and that of the daughters
(America)—in order to be certain that their own daughters *know* them; or,
in Deleuze and Guattari's terminology, that their daughters are able to pen-
etrate the faciality and realize the subjectivity of the black hole beneath it.
This concept is explored in depth in the chapter entitled "Double Face,"
narrated by Lindo Jong (one of the mothers). She questions whether or not
it is possible to reconcile binary oppositions: those between herself and her
daughter, between China and America, but also between her experience as
an immigrant and her daughter's as a citizen: "I think about our two faces.
I think about my intentions. Which one is American? Which one is Chinese? Which one is better? If you show one, you must always sacrifice the

other" (Tan 1989: 266). We see the futility in attempting to belong to one or the other group: Lindo Jong's only solution out of this impasse is to shed the binarism of the two faces.

Another case in which we can read faciality as representative of a Western predilection for identity and, by extension, an expression of the East/West dichotomy, is Marguerite Duras's *L'Amant*. Recall, for instance, the opening lines of the novel:

> Un jour, j'étais âgée déjà, dans le hall d'un lieu public, un homme est venu vers moi. Il s'est fait connaître et il m'a dit: "Je vous connais depuis toujours. Tout le monde dit que vous étiez belle lorsque vous étiez jeune, je suis venu pour vous dire que pour moi je vous trouve plus belle maintenant que lorsque vous étiez jeune, j'aimais moins votre visage de jeune femme que celui que vous avez maintenant, dévasté." (1984: 9)
>
> [One day, I was already old, in the hall of a public place, a man came towards me. He introduced himself and told me: "I have always known you. Everyone says that you were beautiful when you were young, I came to tell you that for me I find you more beautiful now than when you were young, I liked your face of a young woman less than the one you have now, ravaged.]

Although it is safe to assume that Duras was not trying to connote a destroyed visage due to the East per se, the destruction apparent on her face is the result of her experiences in Indochina: the love affair and her family's numerous problems, including her mother's financial troubles and the loss of her brother. All of these events occur either in Indochina or as a direct result of her life there. She alludes to the shifting of her face again near the end of the novel when she describes a conversation with her Chinese lover in which he claims that the heat and sun of Indochina have transformed her: "Il dit que toutes ces années passées ici, à cette intolérable latitude, ont fait qu'elle est devenue une jeune fille de ce pays de l'Indochine" (1984: 120). [He says that all of these years spent here, at this intolerable latitude, have made it so that she has become a young girl from this country of Indochina.] He points out that she no longer resembles a French girl—she has become *Indochinoise*.[19]

This idea of sacrificing one face for another is evident in Lefèvre's search for understanding in *Retour à la saison des pluies*. Through the constructs of her novel, however, we will see that she tries to go beyond this in order to dismantle faciality as an identifying concept. In the beginning, during her writing of *Métisse blanche*, for example, she was still caught up in this system that expresses itself through binarism. She struggles throughout *Retour à la saison des pluies* to free herself of what she has always perceived to be a split. Unlike Mokeddem's depiction of Sultana in *L'Interdite* as someone struggling with binary oppositions and sometimes failing to overcome them, Lefèvre (the narrator) appears to be ultimately more successful in her attempt to achieve a transcultural comprehension of the postcolonial world.

Since her education took place in Vietnam within an elite French system, her initial language of written expression is French; however, in order to express herself in French, she is forcibly making a choice that places her in a unique position between two cultures. Thus, a normally impossible situation is created through her work: she is both colonizer and colonized at once. This echoes the predicament found in all four of the principal authors studied throughout this work (Yamina Mechakra, Ly Thu Ho, Malika Mokeddem, and Kim Lefèvre). What is specifically noteworthy in the case of Lefèvre is her contentious relationship with France as a result of her father's nationality. On one level, she is not only forced to divide herself between the language of the former oppressor and her indigenous cultural heritage, but on yet another more profound one, she is left to reconcile the choice to write in the paternal, unknown language, instead of the maternal, familiar one. From a psychological perspective, hers is a classic, if clichéd, divide between the mother and the father. Her mother does not speak or read French, but it is safe to assume that her father probably does. In selecting French as her vehicle of communication she is complicating her position between two worlds. Due to her status as *métisse,* she is in reality incapable of separating that which within her is French from that which is Vietnamese, but due to her status as an author, she must do this very thing.

An individual's existence between two languages is thematically represented in many postcolonial works. We have already seen an example of a similar predicament in the case of Dalila, the young girl in *L'Interdite*. The main difference, however, between Dalila's situation and that of Lefèvre resides in Lefèvre's psychological choice between the maternal and the paternal. Although not for the same reasons as Lefèvre, the Algerian author Assia Djebar also speaks of this split between the language of the mother and that of the father in *L'Amour, la fantasia*. Her father, who is an Algerian man, is also a French teacher who encourages her to go to school and sees to her education in French. Using the paternal language to carry on an amorous adolescent correspondence leads the narrator to an impasse when the father forbids it. She continues in secret: "La correspondance secrète se fait en français: ainsi, cette langue que m'a donnée le père me devient entremetteuse et mon initiation, dès lors, se place sous un signe double, contradictoire" (1995: 12). [The secret correspondence happened

in French: thus, this language that my father gave me becomes the inter-
mediary, and my initiation, from that point on, is found under a double,
contradictory sign.]

This contradictory nature of the French language is apparent in both
Lefèvre and Djebar, who as writers of the French language epitomize one of
the main characteristics of what Deleuze and Guattari would label a "minor
literature" in *Kafka: Toward a Minor Literature*.[20] According to them, a minor
literature must come from a major language in spite of the doubtless contradictions and numerous difficulties inherent in such an enterprise: "A minor literature doesn't come from a minor language; it is rather that which a minority
constructs within a major language" (1986: 16). To paraphrase Deleuze and
Guattari, this literature is something "impossible." These authors cannot *not*
write; they cannot write in *French*, but they cannot write *otherwise*. Both Djebar explicitly and Lefèvre implicitly demonstrate this impossibility but neces-
sity of choosing to write in a major language. They create works that are inevitably political due to the history of colonialism, relations between their
countries and metropolitan France, and the subjects about which they choose
to write. Even more political is the mere act of writing in French.

Further complicating matters in *Retour* is the fact that the narrator now
lives in France in a self-imposed exile, which has distanced her from her
past in Vietnam. Her narrative is a confrontation with her dual identity, one
that epitomizes the ambiguous dilemma of the postcolonial subject in general and the *métisse* in particular. This identity is one that has been forged
in the most literal sense by the "processes of imperialism" (Mishra and
Hodge 1994: 276–90). Her entire existence is a product of the colonial
domination of Vietnam. The complexity of the situation creates a prose narrative that is tied to geographical and national boundaries, fragmented
memory, and a severe *décalage* between reality and the imagined.

In 1990, following her successful autobiographical *récit*[21] *Métisse blanche*,
Kim Lefèvre published *Retour à la saison des pluies*, which is both a continuation of her story and a narrative that stands alone. In her first novel,
Métisse blanche, she recounts her childhood in Vietnam under French colonial rule and all of the difficulties that she had adapting to life in Vietnam.
She speaks of blatant and veiled discrimination, for which her solution is ultimately fleeing to France. Initially a supposedly temporary yet practical decision (she received a scholarship), it will eventually become a permanent
one. As she is preparing to leave Vietnam she is fairly certain that she will return one day, although she senses that perhaps she may not. This strangely
paradoxical thought is echoed by her mother and repeated throughout the
novel.[22] In the end, it is not until *Retour à la saison des pluies*, some thirty

years after her initial departure from Vietnam, that Lefèvre actually does go back. The story in *Retour* describes both her decision to return and the actual reconciliation with her country, family, and her past.

Retour à la saison des pluies is divided into two distinct parts that the author entitles *Le Passé resurgi* and *Le Retour*. In the first part of the text, the narrator takes us on the virtual journey she undergoes following her decision to return to Vietnam, an involuntary reaction to her appearance on Bernard Pivot's celebrated television show *Apostrophes*. During her interview with Pivot, Lefèvre is asked whether or not she intends to return to Vietnam, and without much forethought, she responds in the affirmative. Although she has evoked the possibility of her return many times before, she says that "Curieusement, et sans doute à cause du caractère théâtral de la situation, j'eus, cette fois-là, le sentiment d'avoir fait un serment solennel. C'était comme si j'avais levé la main devant un juge et prononcé les mots: 'Je le jure'" (Lefèvre 1990: 16–17). [Curiously, and undoubtedly because of the theatrical character of the situation, I had, at the time, the feeling that I had made a solemn oath. It was as if I had raised my hand in front of a judge and pronounced the words: "I swear it."] Having spoken the words, she makes the conscious decision to face her past and reunite with her mother (1990: 17). This decision, however, is made with a nagging feeling of reluctance, because the idea of a return has not ever truly been a consideration: "J'étais partie pour toujours, il n'y avait pas à revenir là-dessus" (1990: 116). [I had left for good, there was no turning back on that.] It is interesting to note that Lefèvre credits her interview on *Apostrophes* as the catalyst in her decision-making process. Pivot's television program, according to Stephen Heath, "actualizes and authenticates" books (1994: 1055), but in this instance it goes even beyond the text to actualize and authenticate the author's discourse. Furthermore, *Apostrophes* firmly enshrines Lefèvre within the French culture; yet it is at the moment of this enshrinement that she paradoxically reconnects with Vietnam. According to Heath's article, "Pivot and his 'Apostrophes' fit reassuringly in a France that is, profoundly, culturally and politically traditional while socially and economically modernizing itself according to the usual tenets of contemporary capitalism. The values of 'Literature' and 'French' are there intact, taken for granted and defended" (1994: 1060). Perhaps Lefèvre's *Métisse blanche* is, therefore, French, while *Retour à la saison des pluies* does not take this "Frenchness" for granted and instills a stronger Vietnamese element to unconsciously counteract the consecration of her first novel.[23]

In the meantime, while she is working at coming to terms with her decision to return to Vietnam, the protective shell in which she has encased her present (so as to avoid the past), suddenly cracks. Through the popularity of *Métisse blanche* and the appearance on *Apostrophes*, she is thrust into the spotlight. Suddenly old acquaintances who are now in Paris begin to resurface. In short, as the title of this first part of her text, *Le Passé resurgi*, indicates, her past comes to the forefront and begins to reinsert itself into her life. The confrontation is not voluntary, which she confirms at various moments throughout the text. Take, for example, her first encounter with an old acquaintance. Not long after her television appearance, a former student arrives unexpectedly at her front door. Lefèvre's surprise at the unanticipated meeting is something she deems familiar and reminiscent of Vietnam, but not entirely pleasant:

> [Au Viêt-Nam]. . . la plupart des événements heureux qui m'arrivaient semblaient tomber du ciel. Je reconnus la griffe du hasard, du moins de ce que j'ai toujours dénommé hasard. Et parce que ce hasard me reportait dans le climat d'autrefois, j'eus l'impression de me retrouver à nouveau au Viêt-Nam, ou plutôt que le Viêt-Nam recommençait à faire irruption dans ma vie, ce qui revenait au même. (1990: 21)
>
> [[In Vietnam] . . . most happy events that happened to me seemed to fall from the sky. I recognized the mark of chance, at least what I had always called chance. And because this chance carried me back to the long-ago atmosphere, I had the impression of finding myself once more in Vietnam, or rather that Vietnam was beginning again to erupt into my life, which was the same thing.]

Although she classifies the event as *heureux* (happy), she nonetheless characterizes it as the result of *la griffe du hasard* (the mark of chance). While *"griffe"* can indicate a signature or mark, its foremost meaning is that of a claw or a talon. Lefèvre therefore selects a metaphor that conjures up a possible weapon that can inflict pain. She goes on to explain that "ce hasard me reportait dans le climat d'autrefois" [this chance carried me back to the long-ago atmosphere]. Chance has played its tricks upon her before, and she is capable of recognizing it today. It is a phenomenon that she irrevocably associates with Vietnam. Thus, this meeting with a former student of hers from Vietnam allows her past to erupt in her life because of the memories the student triggers, but also because of the reintroduction of chance into her life. Inextricably linked to Vietnam is this feeling of pain, which she herself qualifies as one in which Vietnam actually imposes itself unto her life. The unexpected meeting reacquaints her with chance, a phenomenon that she readily associates with "the long-ago atmosphere" of Vietnam. It is her first moment of reconnection with the past.

The sudden reconnection with Vietnam is difficult for the narrator herself to comprehend. She has made such a concerted effort to distance herself geographically that renewing ties with former Vietnamese acquaintances while still in Paris already represents a step backwards, toward the past. Childhood friends who now live in France begin to contact her much to her surprise. During a conversation with one such person, the narrator finds herself to be completely incapable of explaining both her thirty-year break with the past and her evasion of the Asian quarter of the city. In her opinion, her predicament is far too complex for her friend to understand, because her status as *métisse* is unique to the postcolonial world (1990: 54). The *métisse* is unique in her embodiment of the extreme possibilities of colonial domination, but she also manages to represent the entire drama that is/was colonial occupation.

As Lefèvre begins to search out her past more consciously, she takes small yet significant steps closer to Vietnam. One of the most important is her decision to begin shopping in the thirteenth arrondissement, the Asian district of Paris, a place that she has avoided until now. Her willingness to reconnect with the Vietnamese part of her identity while still in Paris represents a step away from the French self that she has become and a step towards the Vietnamese self that she once was. During one trip to an Asian market she allows her senses to transport her back to her childhood through the sight and smell of fruits and vegetables she had completely forgotten, the sounds of a language that she once spoke fluently, and the touch of everything around her. In one sense the market is very familiar to her; in yet another, she is singled out as a stranger. She cannot remember the name of a fruit and asks a young girl who replies: "Nous, on l'appelle Gâc, mais le nom en français, on ne le connaît pas" (1990: 40). [We call it *Gâc*, but we don't know the name in French.] The narrator immediately notices that she is the "other," an outsider here. The girl looks at her and sees someone who is not part of the Vietnamese "us" she uses in her explanation of the fruit's name. She also instantaneously assumes that the narrator is searching for the name of the fruit in French and that she will not recognize the name in Vietnamese. The young girl's thoughts become readily apparent to Lefèvre, further illustrating the effort she will have to make in order to reconnect with this part of herself. Her endeavor remains ambiguous and painful because she still rests outside due to the way she looks, the language she now speaks, and the years that separate her from Vietnam.

In a moving chapter, where Lefèvre shares her mother's letters with the reader, she comes to a new understanding of her mother's life and as a result, her own. She also realizes that she has unknowingly always linked her life to that of her mother's, as she demonstrates in the following passage:

> Dans mon esprit se déroulent, comme dans une projection ciné-matographique, deux séquences presque identiques où l'on voit, parallèle-ment et dans le même décor, deux fillettes, l'une courant, l'autre assise. La première, ma mère; la seconde, moi. Je les vois d'abord séparément, puis peu à peu elles se superposent, les deux fillettes devenant, dans un fondu en-chaîné, une seule et même image, et je suis alors incapable de dire si cette im-age était celle de ma mère ou la mienne. Je découvre soudain que je n'ai cessé de la confondre avec moi, que j'ai continuellement considéré son destin comme le mien propre. (1990: 72)
>
> [In my mind unfold, like in a cinematographic projection, two nearly iden-titcal sequences where one sees concurrently and in the same setting two girls, one running, the other seated. The first, my mother; the second, me. I see them first separately, then little by little they overlap, the two girls becoming, in a fading mix, a single, same image, and I am then incapable of saying if this image was that of my mother or mine. I discover suddenly that I have not stopped confusing her with me, that I have continually considered her fate as my own.]

This confusion of destiny, implied in the superimposing of two images—mother and daughter—also recollects the cover photographs of both *Métisse blanche* and *Retour à la saison des pluies*. Remarkably, Lefèvre chooses a photograph of her mother to grace the cover of *Métisse blanche*, a work that is ostensibly the story of her own childhood, while the front cover of *Retour* bears a photograph of the author. The choice of cover pho-tographs seems to emphasize this intertwining destiny between the two women, a fact that she admits she never recognized before the moment cited above. She begins to see her return to Vietnam as an opportunity to demystify this interwoven destiny between her mother and herself: "Il me semble aussi qu'il est temps de confronter le souvenir que je garde d'elle avec son être réel, de distinguer enfin sa destinée de la mienne, afin que je puisse l'aimer sans éprouver par la même occasion la culpabilité d'avoir été la cause de son échec" (1990: 122). [It also seems to me that it is time to confront the memory that I have kept of her with her true being, to finally distinguish her destiny from mine, so that I can love her without feeling at the same time guilt for having been the cause of her failure.] By confronting her memories and in particular the image she has maintained of her mother, the narrator will be able to realize the differences between the two women. She speaks of a guilt that has forever linked her to her mother's fate. She must let go of this guilt and in so doing she will release part of the power that the past has had over her life. It is perhaps then completely logical that Lefèvre chooses her own portrait to serve as the cover of this text, because in the end, it is about her reconciliation with herself. In *Métisse blanche* she recounts her childhood, but it is solely as the product of her mother's relationship with a French soldier. In *Retour* she is a grown woman whose life is no longer determined by biological factors.

It would seem that the first part in this process of reconciliation is achieved by confronting her past through the act of writing. Thus, the power of the written word is of primary importance in Lefèvre's text. In the opening epigraph of *Retour*, she quotes Mesa Selimovic, a Serbian author: "Ce qu'on n'a pas écrit n'existe pas; la mort l'a emporté." [What has not been written does not exist; death has carried it away.] The quotation, from Selimovic's novel entitled *La Forteresse*, seems particularly significant given the overall theme of his work and *Retour*'s emphasis on the act of writing. In *La Forteresse* the ultimate question is one of destiny and how to face it. Selimovic's narrator utters the quoted sentence on the first page of the novel, expressing his desire to forget the past or at least to put it to rest. His is a past filled with violence, horror and sadness. However, he believes that if he does not give voice to this past through writing it will not and cannot exist (1981: 7). It becomes a part of reality only once it is documented as such. For Lefèvre's narrator, *Métisse blanche* was the act of writing that enabled her past to come into existence and therefore be part of a present reality. This acknowledgment of the past is depicted in *Retour*, where it has in fact re-emerged. By giving voice to it, she both creates it and then reincarnates it:

> Tout changea avec la parution du livre. En l'écrivant j'avais mis en marche, sans en avoir conscience, la machine à remonter le temps. Et les années-lumière que j'avais voulu jeter entre le Viêt-nam et moi, entre mon enfance et moi, comme un grand espace d'oubli, se retrouvèrent tout à coup abolies. (1990: 18)
>
> [Everything changed with the publication of the book. In writing it I had put into motion, without knowing it, the time machine. And the light years that I had wanted to cast between Vietnam and me, between my childhood and me, like a great space of oblivion, suddenly found themselves abolished.]

The written word thus dissolves the thirty years she has placed between Vietnam and herself. If during that time she has avoided contact with the Vietnamese part of herself, it is actually because she has denied its existence.

The reconciliation and subsequent destruction of binary divisions is the ultimate goal of *Retour*. Until now the narrator has in effect been split in two: past/Vietnamese and present/French. The geographical space in which the narrator has allowed herself to live is one that is strictly limited so as to avoid facing a duality that she sees as irreconcilable. Residing in Paris facilitates the distance necessary for her to separate herself from Vietnam and maintain a univocal identity. Through her initial refusal to return to Vietnam and through her gradual loss of contact with family and friends, she becomes more and more *singular* in the sense that her identity becomes irrevocably linked to France. She has used geography with its explicit and very divisive boundaries to create a perceived unity within herself. She has, in effect, become *French*, because she is now identifying with all that is French in her life. Nevertheless, in writing *Métisse blanche* she opened a door that suddenly makes it easier to transgress the boundaries she has created by thirty years of separation and by identifying solely with a French frame of reference.

In *Métisse blanche*, while the subject of the narrative is the childhood of a girl living in the middle of two opposing worlds, it is also a memoir of a past that no longer exists. Upon her arrival in France the narrator rejected her past, slowly but surely. She forced herself to make the choice between Vietnam and France. On both the practical level (where to live) and the more profound psychological level (where to belong), France won. Suddenly, with the resurgence of this past/Vietnam, she is forced to reconsider her choice and to face the possibility that she is not *one or the other*, but perhaps *both*. Indeed, it is a step toward an acceptance of a *transcultural* identity, which is the solution to the complex problem of identity. Françoise Lionnet writes: "The prefix 'trans-' suggests the act of journeying, or going through existing cultural territories" (1995: 13).

Given the title of the book, *Retour à la saison des pluies*, we expect the journey to Vietnam to be the focus of the text. While it is indeed the motivating factor behind its genesis, it is interesting to note that the first part of the narrative focuses upon the resurgent past, relegating the actual trip to a secondary role—it comes second in the novel and constitutes a significantly smaller portion of the text. Lefèvre devotes more time to discussing the past and its irruption into her present life, indicating that the textual space allotted to her return to the past is more significant than the actual voyage to Vietnam. The *Retour* itself does not completely dominate the *récit*, because she does not return permanently in either the literal sense or the figurative. In other words, she does not move back to Vietnam, nor does she *become Vietnamese*. This is where the transcultural element previously mentioned comes into play: there is a third space in which she will exist—between the two countries. While the purpose of her return has very complex reasoning, one of her reasons is *not* to reestablish herself as Vietnamese; thus, one of her greatest fears is destabilizing an equilibrium of identity that she has struggled to create. This is why she affirms that her return has nothing to do with a rediscovery of "her roots," because "je sais aujourd'hui que je n'en ai pas" (1990: 122). [I know today that I don't have any.] Her search for an origin is futile, because she realizes, as Deleuze and Guattari would indicate, that it is the rhizome, and not the root, for which she should strive. It is through the multiple lines of flight that pass through the rhizome that a person *becomes*. There is no fixed point in the end that defines an individual or creates an individual through filiation.[24] She goes on to characterize her personality as consisting of

> deux couches successives: vietnamienne pendant mon enfance, française par la suite. Parfois elles s'entremêlent mais la plupart du temps elles sont strictement cloisonnées, occultant la part vietnamienne que je porte en moi, du moins jusqu'à une date récente. (1990: 122)
> [two successive layers: Vietnamese during my childhood, French afterwards. Sometimes they intermix but most of the time they are strictly partitioned off, hiding the Vietnamese part that I carry inside of me, at least until recently.]

The eclipsing of one or the other of her identities is, as she explains, no longer necessary, because she realizes that the root system to which she thought she belonged is exclusionary. The partitioning between past/Vietnamese and present/French has become less predominant. Her conception of identity and what it means to be identified have entirely changed to the point that she believes in the peaceful coexistence of French and Vietnamese selves within her.

Before she can delve into the possibilities of a peaceably dual identity, the narrator needs to confront her memory—in other words, the gap between her imagined past and the reality of the present. This process will put into question the very memories that she has firmly cemented onto paper through the writing of *Métisse blanche*. The result will lead to the opening up of an "abyss," as she calls it,[25] between the present and the past. With the first letter from her mother and sisters she also receives a current photograph, one that compels her to face the nostalgic images she has maintained through the years. She realizes that in spite of herself she must recognize the ravages of time on her mother: "Non, je veux ignorer la destruction du temps, je veux ramener au jour sa splendeur d'autrefois" (1990: 68). [No, I want to ignore the destruction of time, I want to bring back to light her long-ago splendor.] As her mother's letters continue to come, she relearns her own childhood and recognizes the fact that her memory has not only fallen victim to nostalgia after thirty years, but it has also become selective: "Moi, je ne me souviens plus de ces jours terribles. Mon inconscient les a depuis longtemps relégués dans l'oubli et je lis ce qu'elle m'écrit avec curiosité et surprise" (1990: 91). [Me, I don't remember these terrible days. My subconscious relegated them to oblivion a long time ago and I read what she writes to me with curiosity and surprise.] Both of these textual examples demonstrate the function of writing as an enterprise in truth verification and re-presentation of the past not as a nostalgic stroll down memory lane, but as an explanation, an account of facts that will enable our narrator to incorporate them into her own project of identification.

Furthermore, the abyss dividing the present and the past emphasizes the narrator's fragmented, imperfect memory. Initially, it is through the descriptions in her mother's letters and her reactions to them that we sense this great divide, but eventually when she actually does return to Vietnam the gap widens even more. The fiction that she has created, which she calls "une réalité nouvelle" [a new reality] (1990: 157), must come face to face with reality: "Je dois faire l'effort d'apposer l'image que conserve ma mémoire à celle de la réalité" (1990: 157). [I must make the effort to affix the image that my memory conserves to that of reality.] The past that she has in fact reinvented for herself over the years is no longer valid; therefore, she relies on her family as well as documented proof in the form of photographs to help her bridge the past with the present (1990: 169).

However, as early as the first page of the book, this problem of fragmentation surfaces through both syntax on a formal level and content on an ideological level:

Les dés sont jetés, j'ai enfin pris la décision de retourner au Viêt-nam. Après trente ans d'absence.

Trente ans, c'est une mesure, une quantité. Mais pour moi, c'est une plage qui s'étend entre mes vingt ans et aujourd'hui.

C'est une vie.

Ma vie. Menée ailleurs que sur le sol vietnamien, flottant à des milles de l'endroit où j'ai pris ma source. Comme un long fleuve dont l'amont serait si éloigné qu'il me paraît à présent enveloppé de brume. Et lorsque ma mémoire s'y reporte, il m'arrive de douter de sa réalité. (1990: 13)

[The die have been cast, I have finally made the decision to return to Vietnam. After thirty years of absence.

Thirty years, it's a measurement, a quantity. But for me, it is a beach that extends between my twenty years and today.

It's a life.

My life. Led away from the Vietnamese soil, floating miles away from the place where I got my start. Like a long river where upriver waters would be so far that it seems to me now that they are enveloped by fog. And when my memory goes back there, I begin to doubt its reality.]

Textually, sentences are incomplete; separations come via marks of punctuation that appear to have been placed in the middle of a full thought. Take, for example, the first two lines of the text. Obviously the narrator wants to emphasize several aspects essential to our understanding of her dilemma: First, it has been thirty years since she has confronted her past face to face in Vietnam. That is undoubtedly the most important point; therefore, she has disrupted syntactical norms to get our attention. In addition, she cleverly combines two concepts: chance and will. In one breath she is telling us that she has thrown the dice, she has taken the risk—it's a gamble for her to return to Vietnam, and there is no turning back. Why? It is the unknown, the past, a past that she has in a way reconstructed thanks to the effects of time—in this case, the thirty years.

She begins the second paragraph insisting again on the thirty years. Not only does she focus on the passage of time, but she also uses the metaphor of a beach to illustrate it, a metaphor that calls to mind both the geographical boundaries, which we have already discussed, and the image of water, which recurs throughout he first page of the text: Water seems to be an element that she links to Vietnam and to her childhood; her life is a beach and a long river, emanating from the source, Vietnam. She also later recalls certain memories visually related to water, in the form of puddles covering the rice fields or steam floating out from a pot of boiling water. All of these images indicate the fluid nature of memory, which she exploits when she equates her birth to the "source" of the river that has flowed on through time and led her to France. The distance that this river has traversed is so great that it leads her to wonder if her memory is really correct and whether or not the passage of time has corrupted her ability to recall Vietnam and the "source" from which she came.

In addition, the rich metaphorical implication of the river provides us with yet another glimpse of Lefèvre's multiple cultural identity. In geography we learn that rivers have a source, but in reality, a river can have many different, sometimes changing sources. Various tributaries link up to form one river, to which we assign one name and look at as a homogeneous body of water. However, a river is in fact a creation out of a mix of waters—it is rhizomatic. Lefèvre's insistence upon the water metaphor, and in particular, the river, implies a relationship to her own cultural identity. Like the river

about which she speaks, she is the product of a heterogeneous mix of
"sources." Multiple peoples, nations, and civilizations have led to her creation. Just as a river does not really possess a unique source—only arbitrar-
ily speaking, because we know, in fact, that a river can have many different
sources—so, too, does the narrator.

On this first page she is also contrasting the concrete nature of measurement with her own more abstract definition of time. It cannot merely be a
quantity, a number, because it has a sensory value that goes beyond scientific analysis. This is the reason that the third paragraph of the text is nothing more than one line. Another fragment begins the fourth paragraph. This
statement, "Ma vie," with its brevity, conveys a poignancy that further de-
velops her definition of time. The years that have passed have created for
her a new life, *her* own life. The past/Vietnam is therefore as distant tem-
porally as it is geographically.

In the second part of the novel when the narrator actually makes the trip
to Vietnam, therefore disintegrating the geographical boundaries, she is
faced with the difficult task of attempting to shrink the temporal distance
to which she alludes in those first pages of the text. Various encounters with
places that were important in her past lead the narrator to feel as if the
sanctity of her memories has been lost forever. For example, she returns to
the Couvent des Oiseaux, the boarding school she attended as a young girl
in Dalat. In contemporary Vietnam, however, she is surprised to find the
school dilapidated, sectioned off for other uses, and empty of the life that
she remembers. When she leaves, she states: "Je quitte ce lieu avec le sentiment d'avoir à jamais perdu quelque chose de précieux" (1990: 202). [I am
leaving this place with the feeling that I have forever lost something precious.] The moments she recalls from her youth, the nostalgic ones that allowed her to write years later, have altered with time and become relics of
the past. The time that she described as a river on the first page of this novel
has eroded the solid ground upon which her memory was based. Colonial
Vietnam bears little resemblance to its postcolonial vestiges. The mix of waters now present in the river is no longer the same as it was in her childhood, because the "sources" of the river are ever-changing, multiplying, and
growing rhizomatically.

She speaks of her past as a broken mirror (1990: 212) but does not re-
nounce her plan to visit all of the places she mentions in her first book. In
a way, then, the narrator is coming to terms with her past, refusing to rely
on her memory, allowing herself to witness the present. As Jack Yeager explains: "She must break the silence, tear the veil that hides the past, expose
it, examine it closely, speak and write" (1993: 54). In writing she exposes the

reader to the duality that she had tried so desperately to deny for thirty years in France. She recognizes and embraces the Vietnam of today, all the while realizing that she will forever be tied to it: "Dans cette remontée vers l'amont où presque rien de ce qui fut ne subsiste, ma famille est mon point de repère, le cordon qui m'attache à ce pays où je suis née. Elle est mon passé vivant, le trait d'union entre ce que j'étais et ce que je suis" (1990: 221). [In this climb upstream where almost nothing of what was exists, my family is my landmark, the cord that attaches me to this country where I was born.]

This "*trait d'union*," this hyphen, is the indication of the transcultural identity about which Lionnet speaks. In fact, the word *Viêt-Nam* contains a hyphen in French, uniting the words that in Vietnamese are separately written. Therefore, Lefèvre's statement that the hyphen unites what she was with what she is can be visually depicted with the hyphenation of the word in French. It unites both the French and the Vietnamese in a literal fashion, just as Lefèvre unites the two cultures within herself. Lefèvre's coming to terms with her past is more than just a unification of past and present; it is also, and more importantly, a realization of the dual nature of the postcolonial subject. In the introduction to this study on Lefèvre's book, I said that she is at once both the *subject* and the *agent* of colonization and that her struggle is one to unite the two and to find her own identity. In fact, the complexity of her identity embodies much more than that fight between two opposing forces. She is not merely the colonized *subject*, a Vietnamese woman defined by her nationality, by geographical or national boundaries, or by race. Describing her in only that limited way would inaccurately imply an acceptance on our part of the belief that national borders define culture, and that one's identity stems from one's culture alone. This narrow interpretation of identity is an isolationist viewpoint that preaches difference on which an "overemphasis . . . is likely to lead from racial and biographical determinism into an essentialist impasse" (Lionnet 1995: 14). Equally restrictive is the belief that Lefèvre's virtually autobiographical narrator is merely the *agent*, the colonizer, a French woman defined by her bloodline, by her established residence in Paris, by her refusal to speak Vietnamese.

It is the narrator herself who points out to us that both definitions of identity are far too restrictive. In trying to reconcile two seemingly opposing traditions and backgrounds, she comes to the realization that she need not choose between two cultures, because her culture is indeed both Vietnamese and French, along with the myriad cultures within each of those two. Her new definition of culture is one that transcends national boundaries previously imposed by colonialism. The "*trait d'union*" that comes at the end of the novel is the "*trait d'union*" between the past and the present, between reality and the imagined, and most importantly between Vietnam and France. In other words, cultural identity is not located within the boundaries of either country. For Kim Lefèvre, to be Vietnamese in this postcolonial world is also to be, in part, French. This does not mean that she has been assimilated to the French culture; rather, it shows that French cultural identity has become a part of her. She is no longer a victim of colonization any more than she is a product of Vietnam.

This phenomenon of "transculturalism" is, as she states, something that implies a more active role than assimilation or acculturation. The narrator actively and independently chooses to incorporate the two identities originally imposed upon her (either by her biological or national roots) and which, until now, have conflicted within and around her. She demonstrates the resolution she has obtained on the final page of the novel. As she writes about her mother's pain in seeing her leave again for Paris: "Ne te tourmente pas, ma mère. Maintenant que nous nous sommes retrouvées, tu ne me perdras jamais plus" (1990: 222) [Don't torment yourself, mother. Now that we have found one another again, you will never again lose me], she acknowledges that her acceptance and reintegration of her mother, her family, and Vietnam will not be forgotten once she is back in Paris. She will not lose the Vietnamese part of herself, for she has actively taken it back, replaced it within her.

In the final paragraph of the novel, however, she speaks about leaving Vietnam without leaving a trace of herself behind—this trace is of her past life. She has returned to the Vietnam of the present, has faced her past, and is now willing and able to accept herself as *métisse* in the postcolonial world. Her new life, the one that she has led for the past thirty years in Paris, is the one to which she will return without leaving any part of herself in Vietnam. She is *taking* the present-day Vietnam *with her*. As Yeager explains in the conclusion to his article: "Reconstructing the past, then, becomes a struggle against silence and death" (1993: 56). *Retour à la saison des pluies* marks Lefèvre's final struggle with that past. It is a past that she reconstructed through *Métisse blanche* and slowly faced thanks to pivotal moments in its success, in particular the Pivot interview. *Retour* becomes her final attempt at reconstruction through memories and nostalgia, which by extension, then, creates her last confrontation with colonialism. Hers is a narrative that asks the beleaguered question of how. How does one integrate and live with a dual/hybrid identity? The answer is this text, her solution.

As we have seen in this chapter, both Malika Mokeddem and Kim Lefèvre place their narrators in a setting that is clearly defined by geographical boundaries that have led to self-imposed exile. The initial reasons for exile are due to educational opportunities in France. As grandchildren of the colonial system, these women are living out the remnants of the *mission civilisatrice*. Although the Algeria and Vietnam of these two novels are no longer French colonies, the hope of a French education remains. Because of the degradation of the indigenous systems a French education has maintained a certain level of prestige.[26]

However, in both cases, rejection by their compatriots became the defining reason for their exile. Both women are victims of their bloodlines (Sultana's cursed family and Lefèvre's mixed blood) and were therefore forced to search for inclusion elsewhere. What is important to realize in these two similarities is the postcolonial nature of such a situation. The French colonial presence in both Algeria and Vietnam *created* the situation in which these women could not be accepted. They are representative of a second generation of survivors of colonialism. Due to their ties to France, both Sultana and Lefèvre are forced to live out their lives there because they are considered traitors to their recently independent nations. Obviously, this predicament would not have existed had it not been for the initial presence of French colonizers in both Algeria and Vietnam. In order to best resolve the situation, these women choose to take up residence in France, which, as the former dominant power, has little problem accepting that a former subject reside there.[27] However, as former subjects sympathetic in some way to the formerly dominant power, these French-educated women find residence in their native countries nearly impossible. This is one factor that creates the internal split referred to in this study as fragmentation.

In *L'Interdite*, Mokeddem employs a fictional depiction of duality tied to narrative devices (the two narrators of Sultana and Vincent) to implant the idea of postcolonial fragmentation. Lefèvre's technique in *Retour* depicts the great divide between memory and reality along with directly addressing the problem of fragmentation itself. While the tools used by both authors may differ, the result is the same. We are left with an image of a woman whose identity appears to be sectioned off. Both Sultana and Lefèvre are searching for a way through which to join the pieces of themselves. In order to attempt this reconciliation with two different worlds, they return to the source of their trauma: Algeria for Sultana and Vietnam for Lefèvre. Neither one is immediately at home in the land of her birth, nor does she want to be. Both texts end with a look to the future and a hope of further reconciliation that does not force the denial of one or the other part of their identities. In the end, Sultana and Lefèvre opt neither for a French identity nor for an Algerian or Vietnamese one respectively. Rather than this, they select a third space, which does not force them to choose between France and Algeria or Vietnam. They create a transcultural identity for themselves that is not defined within the parameters of nationality.

Finally, in traditionally patriarchal societies, both Sultana and Lefèvre represent Westernized women who are categorically repelled by their male peers. Sultana undergoes violent retaliations led by the men in Aïn Nekhla. Symptomatic of a certain fear of powerlessness, the same fear realized under years of colonial domination, the men refuse to allow Sultana to peacefully exist in their world.[28] The town mayor and his supporters terrorize her through vandalism and vicious slander. Sultana falls victim to obvious and forceful rejections by Algerian men, but Lefèvre witnesses much subtler humiliations. Her apprehension at meeting the Vietnamese men who are her sisters' husbands stems from years of being reminded that no Vietnamese man would want to marry her because she was of mixed blood and would therefore produce children who would suffer the same fate. Moreover, her mother warned her to be extra vigilant in protecting her virginity, because she always had to try and be better than a "pure" Vietnamese in order to get any kind of respect.

Neither of these women appears to be indicting the men or traditions of their societies; rather, they are depicting a unique predicament of the postcolonial female subjects in these two texts. The singularity of such an experience, however, transcends national barriers, therefore acknowledging a similar situation in both Algeria and Vietnam. Ultimately these two texts bring up many of the same issues and in examining them, we arrive at the conclusion that a postcolonial female subject does in fact exist who is *not* defined by her nationality; rather, she is the product of circumstances that are common across borders.

NOTES

1. For examples of this, see chapter 1.

2. In addition to Françoise Lionnet's work, I will draw upon the work of Gilles Deleuze and Félix Guattari to aid in my analysis. Here, my conception of difference as a marker defining identity is taken from Deleuze's work in *Différence et Répétition*.

3. Christopher Miller's introduction to *Nationalists and Nomads* points out one of the logical fallacies of any argument against difference as a defining factor: "Exclusionary underpinnings appear to be inherent to attempts at nonexclusionary thinking (from the moment that you want to 'exclude' that which is exclusionary, you are caught in a dilemma). The contradiction does not invalidate hybrid or nomad thought, but awareness of this problem should be part of a broader process of

analysis that recognizes and tolerates particularisms" (1998: 7). This is the same cautionary note I highlighted in chapter 1 of the present study.

4. Nephrology is the scientific study of kidneys.

5. For a powerful look at the killings of artists and intellectuals in Algeria, see Assia Djebar's *Le Blanc de l'Algérie*.

6. The dedication reads as follows: "À Tahar Djaout, Interdit de vie à cause de ses écrits."

7. Although Sultana and Vincent share almost equal narrative time, the text undoubtedly focuses on Sultana and her plight; therefore, one can safely assume that she should be considered the main character of the novel.

8. Since this study is about the literary representation of women by women, the actual roles that women play in Islamic societies will not be discussed at great length herein; however, for an excellent explanation and probing analysis of the issue, see the following two different studies: Fatima Mernissi, *Beyond the Veil: Male-Female Dynamics in Modern Muslim Society*; and Marnia Lazreg, *The Eloquence of Silence*.

9. See Fatima Mernissi's discussion of this throughout her book, *Beyond the Veil: Male-Female Dynamics in Modern Muslim Society*.

10. This is the same kind of revolt against nomenclature that we see in Yamina Mechakra's *La Grotte éclatée*, in which the narrator asserts her nonidentity. See chapter 3 of this study for more details.

11. In the three categories listed in the Robert, Christians, Muslims, and Jews can all be Arabs, but it is interesting to note that those who live in the Near East or in North Africa but do not speak Arabic would not, according to the third explanation, be classified as Arabs.

12. In the original French text, the much more technical word "infarctus" is employed here. In English we could translate this as an infarction, which is the medical terminology used to describe a heart attack, which manifests itself through the dead tissue resulting from loss of blood supply.

13. Note that Flaubert's Orientalist discourse will relegate women in the East to the monolithic Oriental Woman, which parallels the already refuted notion of the equally monolithic Algerian Woman found in *L'Interdite*.

14. One needs only to peruse works that deal with France's history in Algeria to find references to all of these terms. They have become irrevocably linked with French presence there, and their mere invocation by Vincent calls to mind colonial discourses. See, in particular, works by Charles-Robert Ageron, David Prochaska, and Benjamin Stora.

15. For more on French colonial policy, see Raymond Betts, *Assimilation and Association in French Colonial Theory, 1890–1914*.

16. I am taking the liberty of assimilating Flaubert's thoughts to the words and reactions of the king in Hérodias. I think this is justifiably the case given what critics such as Saïd have cited to be Flaubert's personal correspondence on the subject of Oriental Women. See, in particular, pages 186–88 in *Orientalism*.

17. Before her trip to Vietnam, the narrator receives letters from her mother, retelling the story of her affair with the French soldier, but his name is never mentioned, leaving Lefèvre to wonder whether or not the family name of the man is the one she always believed (1990: 79). As for his first name, that too remains unclear (1990: 183). This is an interesting commentary on naming, which is a theme that recurs in *L'Interdite* and in chapter 3's study on *La Grotte éclatée*. What we see, in effect, is the desire of individuals to pinpoint and name people so as to confirm or deny an identity. In the end, Mokeddem, Mechakra, and as we will see here, Lefèvre, all realize the ambivalence inherent in naming.

18. For more on faciality and on Deleuze and Guattari's theory applied to works of fiction depicting encounters between East and West, return to chapter 2 of the present study, particularly the section dealing with Kateb Yacine's play, *L'homme aux sandales de caoutchouc*.

19. Duras, as an Indochinoise, is certainly not an uncommon theme. See Pierre Assouline's article "Duras, L'Indochinoise" and Laure Adler's biography, *Marguerite Duras*, for further references to this idea.

20. It could without a doubt be argued that both Djebar and Lefèvre demonstrate all of the necessary qualifications for a minor literature, but for the purposes of this specific point, I am focusing only on the linguistic criterion that is suggested in *Kafka: Toward a Minor Literature*.

21. For a discussion on the ambiguous nature of autobiography and fiction with regard to Lefèvre's work, see Jack Yeager, "Kim Lefèvre's *Retour à la saison des pluies*: Rediscovering the Landscapes of Childhood," specifically page 48.

22. In her interview with Bernard Pivot on *Apostrophes*, Kim Lefèvre comments that her mother thought she would go to France, marry a Frenchman, and never come home again. Lefèvre adds that part of her felt this was a ridiculous thought, but another part also felt that she would be away for a very long time.

23. It is interesting to note that following her consecration into French literary circles (thanks to Pivot), Lefèvre's autobiographical voice echoes that of Marguerite Duras and Nathalie Sarraute. As mentioned in chapter 1 of this study, both authors utilize fragmentation as the major technique in recounting their own versions of autobiography. Coincidentally, Duras is a child of Indochinese colonization, and Sarraute is a Russian immigrant. All three women's experiences could therefore be said to question the "Self versus Other" paradigm. While not mirror images of one another, their use of fragmentation serves to manifest the similarities in postcolonial French-language fiction.

24. See *A Thousand Plateaus*, specifically "Introduction: Rhizome" and "1730: Becoming-Intense, Becoming-Animal, Becoming-Imperceptible . . . "

25. In speaking about the changes acted out upon her mother over time, which are apparent in comparing past and present photographs, the narrator says "Entre ces deux femmes: un abîme" [Between these two women: an abyss] (1990: 68).

26. The colonial system promoted its own schools both in the countries themselves and at home, which meant that indigenous schools, if they existed, were se-

verely neglected. The problem has led to various levels of disregard for schooling in both Vietnam and Algeria. For the history of this problem and of the education of colonial subjects in metropolitan France and abroad, see Scott McConnell's book, *Leftward Journey: The Education of Vietnamese Students in France 1919–1939,* and David W. Mize's study, *Algeria: A Study of the Educational System of Algeria and a Guide to the Academic Placement of Students in Educational Institutions of the United States.*

27. Here I do not mean on a purely political level, because recently the French government has adopted a forced expatriation policy for North African immigrants in France. On a philosophical level, the problem appears much less controversial for a previously dominant country than a previously dominated one.

28. For an understanding of the way in which women empower men in Islamic societies, see Fatima Mernissi, *Le Harem politique.*

AFTERWORD

Through four chapters of this study, I have shown the parallels that can be drawn across vast geopolitical, cultural, and linguistic borders among four women writers, Yamina Mechakra, Ly Thu Ho, Malika Mokeddem, and Kim Lefèvre, and their works. The bond that they achieve is seen through themes, such as changing women's roles in society; narrative techniques, such as fragmentation; and finally, the unifying use of French. Along with the unification that is a product of their shared colonial history and subsequent struggles for independence, they also go beyond mimetic literary productions. While the French literary traditions and techniques appear in their work, as we have seen, they manifest their own multiple origins, authorities, and identities. Binary oppositions and an understanding of the self in reference to the other occasionally resurface in these works, but they ultimately serve as moments of transition. The métissage that Françoise Lionnet describes in *Postcolonial Representations* takes place in these four novels: *La Grotte éclatée*, *Le Mirage de la paix*, *L'Interdite*, and *Retour à la saison des pluies* (Lionnet 1995: 5). The female protagonists depicted in these novels weave together various traditions, languages, and concepts of identity. Superficially contradictory, this braiding allows these women to exist in the in-betweenness that Deleuze and Guattari invoke in *A Thousand Plateaus* (1987: 293). The four authors, in explaining self-conception in this way, illustrate their belief that identity, especially in the context of the postcolonial female subject, is not determined by one of two cultures: the former colonizer's or the formerly colonized. They are envisioning new ways to think about women and their roles in Algeria and Vietnam.

Not surprisingly, women novelists from the two regions often choose to describe female characters' struggles in an ever-changing new world. Women's written representation of these changes takes the form of a sometimes multiple, often fragmented concept of personal identity. Nationality, language, even gender are alternately discarded and readopted to create a new postcolonial identity for these characters. While these four authors never give one clear definition of the postcolonial female subject, they explore various possibilities, expand upon them, and put them into question. Although the differences between Algeria and Vietnam are striking, it is through their connections to one another that we can foreground postcolonial gender issues. Whereas geographical boundaries and official nationalities serve as divisive classifications, the links between the works lead us to a much more engaging dialogue and ultimate understanding of postcolonial Francophone literature.

We have seen the historical and literary connections between Algeria and Vietnam and thus understand how a certain reciprocal relationship exists between the two. Due to these bonds, it is less surprising to consider that Francophone writers from Algeria and Vietnam often deal with similar topics in their work: these are manifested in chapters 3 and 4, where I did close analysis of the four novels, *La Grotte éclatée*, *Le Mirage de la paix*, *L'Interdite*, and *Retour à la saison des pluies*. In the case of these novels, the women writers each focus at least in part on issues of identity. This is not of course to say that Francophone women writers from Algeria and Vietnam monopolize the study of postcolonial identity; however, the frequency of this topic in their works indicates that it is a concern for all four of these women. Along with demonstrating how their characters strive to understand their own identity through the written word, Mechakra, Ly, Mokeddem, and Lefèvre also grapple with how to represent this predicament. Each of them has thus striven to use some form of fragmentation as a literary technique. As we have seen, employing fragmentation is nothing new in twentieth-century literature; however, it further reveals the commonalities between the two bodies of literature, and leaves us with the overwhelming evidence that the postcolonial Francophone female subject is defined not by her nationality, but by a commonly shared experience. In the ongoing French versus Francophone debate, specific examples of writers who are categorized in one way or another have not often led to comparative studies. One of my goals in this book has been to provide a unique comparative approach, introducing readers to the rich connections between Francophone Algerian and Vietnamese literature.

Furthermore, analyzing these four novels in comparison to one another allows for us to see them in a dialogic relationship. Each work appears to both ask and respond to a question about postcolonial women. In the end, the juxtaposition of Francophone Algerian and Vietnamese women, along with their work, opens a way toward understanding feminism in the post-colonial, globalized world. It allows us to consider what the future of this literature will be. Enough time has passed since the wars of independence that perhaps postcolonialism is no longer a relevant term. Anne McClintock, in her conclusion to *Imperial Leather*, notes that one of the pitfalls with having recourse to this term is that it condemns us to forever look to the past and not to envision the future (1995: 392). Thanks to the specific literary examples I have examined in this study, we notice the common bonds, which come from a shared history, but we also realize the particular ways the authors have chosen to convey their messages. Both groups are working from within French to introduce Western readers to the feminine condition in each specific instance, but they go beyond the mere referential and project new solutions for the future. With the portrayal of each female character's individual struggle, the monolithic "Third World Woman" diminishes in power. Ultimately, the destruction of the monolith allows for a new image of "Third World Feminism," feminism, and global understanding. Showing links between Third World nations in the postcolonial aftermath (because we are perhaps beyond postcolonial now) reminds us of the solidarity shown politically during the fights against the French, and later in the creation of the Afro-Asian Solidarity that Robert Mortimer discusses in his article (2003: 60–61).

Part of the purpose of this book is to draw connections between distant parts of the Francophone world in order to demonstrate how the common ground they share can lead to an overall understanding of the postcolonial Francophone female subject. The end result is of course much more universal, because the boundaries that these examples allow us to cross become less and less visible the world over. We are able to draw parallels between formerly colonized nations and to consider their future ties to one another.

The technique of fragmentation, the shared experience of French colonial domination, and the resulting similar transformation of women's roles in both Algeria and Vietnam link *La Grotte éclatée*, *Le Mirage de la paix*, *L'Interdite*, and *Retour à la saison des pluies*. These texts manifest role transformations as both positive and negative, but always either directly or indirectly as the result of the ruins of French colonialism. These are the remnants of the French empire in Algeria and Vietnam—women, words, and war.

BIBLIOGRAPHY

Achour, Christiane. "Kateb Yacine, La Dynamique d'une position dans le champ culturel." *Revue Celfan / Celfan Review* 3 (1986): 24–28.

———. *Le Dictionnaire des œuvres algériennes en langue française.* Paris: L'Harmattan, 1990.

———. *Le Dictionnaire des livres de la guerre d'Algérie.* Paris: L'Harmattan, 1996.

Adler, Laure. *Marguerite Duras.* Paris: Éditions Gallimard, 1998.

Ageron, Charles-Robert. *Histoire de l'Algérie contemporaine.* 9e édition. Paris: Presses Universitaires de France, 1990.

Alloula, Malek. *The Colonial Harem.* Trans. Myrna Godzich and Wlad Godzich. Minneapolis: University of Minnesota Press, 1986.

Altbach, Philip G., and Gail P. Kelly, eds. *Education and Colonialism.* New York: Longman, 1978.

———. *Education and the Colonial Experience.* 2d rev. ed. New York: Advent Books, Inc., 1991.

Amireh, Amal. "Writing the Difference: Feminists' Invention of the 'Arab Woman.'" In *Interventions: Feminist Dialogues on Third World Women's Literature and Film,* ed. Bishnupriya Ghosh and Brinda Bose, 185–211. New York: Garland, 1997.

Amrane, Djamila. *Les Femmes algériennes dans la guerre.* Paris: Plon, 1991.

Amrane-Minne, Danièle Djamila. *Des Femmes dans la guerre d'Algérie.* Paris: Éditions Karthala, 1994.

———. "Women and Politics in Algeria from the War of Independence to Our Day." *Research in African Literatures* 30, no. 3 (1999): 62–77.

Anderson, Benedict. *Imagined Communities.* rev. ed. London: Verso, 1991.

Apostrophes. Bernard Pivot interview with Kim Lefèvre, Antenne 2, Paris, 7 Apr. 1989.

Aresu, Bernard. *Counterhegemonic Discourse from the Maghreb: The Poetics of Kateb's Fiction*. Tübingen: Gunter Narr Verlag, 1993.

Arnaud, Jacqueline. *La Littérature maghrébine de langue française*. 2 vols. Paris: Publisud, 1986.

——. Introduction. *L'Œuvre en fragments* by Kateb Yacine, ed. Jacqueline Arnaud, 11–29. Paris: Éditions Sindbad, 1986.

Ashcroft, Bill, Gareth Griffiths, Helen Tiffin. *Key Concepts in Postcolonial Studies*. London: Routledge, 1998.

Assouline, Pierre. "Duras, L'Indochinoise." *L'Histoire* (Octobre 1996): 46–47.

Barry, Kathleen, ed. *Vietnam's Women in Transition*. New York: St. Martin's Press, 1996.

Barthes, Roland. *S/Z*. Paris: Éditions du Seuil, 1970.

Battle of Algiers. Dir. Gillo Pontecorvo. Casbah Films-Algiers, 1967.

Bensmaia, Réda. "On the Concept of Minor Literature: From Kafka to Kateb Yacine." In *Gilles Deleuze and the Theater of Philosophy*, ed. Constantin V. Boundas and Dorothea Olkowski, 213–28. New York: Routledge, 1994.

——. "The School of Independence." In *A New History of French Literature*, ed. Denis Hollier, 1018–22. Cambridge, MA: Harvard University Press, 1994.

Betts, Raymond. *Assimilation and Association in French Colonial Theory, 1890–1914*. New York: Columbia University Press, 1961.

Bhabha, Homi K. "DissemiNation: time, narrative, and the margins of the modern nation." In *Nation and Narration*, 291–322. London: Routledge, 1990.

Bouillon de Culture. "La Résistance algérienne," France 2, Paris, 18 Apr. 1997.

Bourqia, R., M. Charrad, N. Gallagher, eds. *Femmes, Culture et Société au Maghreb*. 2 vols. Casablanca: Afrique Orient, 1996.

Brocheux, Pierre. "Un Siècle de colonisation," *L'Histoire* 203 (Octobre 1996): 26–33.

Cao, Lan. *Monkey Bridge*. New York: Viking Penguin, 1997.

Caws, Mary Ann et al., eds. *Écritures de femmes: nouvelles cartographies*. New Haven, CT: Yale University Press, 1996.

Césaire, Aimé. *Cahier d'un retour au pays natal*. 1939. Paris: Présence Africaine, 1983.

——. *Discours sur le colonialisme*. Paris: Présence Africaine, 1955.

Chiem T. Keim, trans. *Women in Vietnam. Selected Articles from Vietnamese Periodicals, Saigon, Hanoi, 1957–1966*. Honolulu: Institute of Advanced Projects, East-West Center, 1967.

Clayton, Anthony. *The Wars of French Decolonization*. London: Longman, 1994.

Cooke, Miriam, and Angela Woollacott, eds. *Gendering War Talk*. Princeton, NJ: Princeton University Press, 1993.

Déjeux, Jean. *Littérature maghrébine de langue française*. Ottawa: Editions Naaman, 1973.

———. *Assia Djebar: romancière algérienne cinéaste arabe*. Québec: Éditions Naaman de Sherbrooke, 1984.

———. *La littérature féminine de langue française au Maghreb*. Paris: Karthala, 1994.

Deleuze, Gilles. *Difference and Repetition*. Trans. Paul Patton. New York: Columbia University Press, 1994.

Deleuze, Gilles, and Félix Guattari. *Kafka: Toward a Minor Literature*. Trans. Dana Polan. Minneapolis: University of Minnesota Press, 1986.

———. *A Thousand Plateaus: Capitalism and Schizophrenia*. Trans. Brian Massumi. Minneapolis: University of Minnesota Press, 1987.

Didier, Béatrice. *L'Écriture femme*. Paris: Presses Universitaires de France, 1981.

Djebar, Assia. *L'Amour, la fantasia*. Paris: Albin Michel, 1995.

———. *Le Blanc de l'Algérie*. Paris: Albin Michel, 1995.

———. *Oran, langue morte*. Paris: Actes sud, 1997.

———. *La Femme sans sépulture*. Paris: Albin Michel, 2002.

Donadey, Anne. *Recasting Postcolonialism*. Portsmouth, NH: Heinemann, 2001.

Dugas, Guy, ed. *Algérie: Un rêve de fraternité*. Paris: Omnibus, 1997.

Duiker, William J. *Ho Chi Minh*. New York: Hyperion, 2000.

Duong Thu Huong. *Paradise of the Blind*. Trans. Phan Huy Duong and Nina McPherson. New York: William Morrow and Company, Inc., 1993.

———. *Novel Without a Name*. Trans. Phan Huy Duong and Nina McPherson. New York: William Morrow and Company, Inc., 1995.

Duras, Claire de. *Ourika*. Ed. Joan DeJean and trans. John Fowles. New York: The Modern Language Association, 1994.

Duras, Marguerite. *L'Amant*. Paris: Editions de Minuit, 1984.

Eagleton, Terry. *Literary Theory: An Introduction*. Minneapolis: University of Minnesota Press, 1983.

Echenberg, Myron. *Colonial Conscripts: The Tirailleurs Sénégalais in French West Africa, 1857–1960*. Portsmouth, NH: Heinemann, 1991.

Eisen, Arlene. *Women and Revolution in Viet Nam*. London: Zed Books, 1984.

Elliott, Duong Van Mai. *The Sacred Willow: Four Generations in the Life of a Vietnamese Family*. New York: Oxford University Press, 1999.

Fanon, Frantz. *Peau noire, masques blancs*. Paris: Éditions du Seuil, 1952.

———. *The Wretched of the Earth*. Trans. Constance Farrington. New York: Grove Press, 1963.

———. *A Dying Colonialism*. Trans. Haakon Chevalier. London: Writers and Readers, 1980.

Feray, Pierre-Richard. *Le Viêt-Nam*. Paris: Presses Universitaires de France, 1984.

Fernea, Elizabeth Warnock. *Women and the Family in the Middle East: New Voices of Change*. Austin: University of Texas Press, 1985.

Flaubert, Gustave. "Hérodias." In *Trois Contes*, 111–52. Paris: Gallimard, 1966.

Gavronsky, Serge. "Linguistic Aspects of Francophone Literature," *French Review* 51, no. 6, (1978): 843–52.

Ghosh, Bishnupriya, and Brinda Bose, eds. *Interventions: Feminist Dialogues on Third World Women's Literature and Film*. New York: Garland, 1997.

Gilly, Adolfo. Introduction. Trans. Nell Salm. In *A Dying Colonialism*, by Frantz Fanon, trans. Haakon Chevalier, 1–21. New York: Grove Press, 1965.

Graffenried, Michael von. *Inside Algeria*. New York: Aperture Foundation, Inc., 1998.

Green, Mary Jean et al., eds. *Postcolonial Subjects: Francophone Women Writers*. Minneapolis: University of Minnesota Press, 1996.

Ha, Marie-Paule. *Figuring the East*. Albany: State University of New York Press, 2000.

Harrow, Kenneth W., ed. *The Marabout and the Muse: New Approaches to Islam in African Literature*. Portsmouth, NH: Heinemann, 1996.

———. *With Open Eyes: Women and African Cinema*. Amsterdam: Editions Rodopi, 1997.

Heath, Stephen. "Friday Night Books." In *A New History of French Literature*, ed. Denis Hollier, 1054–60. Cambridge, MA: Harvard University Press, 1994.

Heggoy, Alf Andrew. "Colonial Education in Algeria: Assimilation and Reaction." In Altbach and Kelly, *Education and the Colonial Experience*. 2d rev. ed., 97–116.

Hémery, Daniel. *Ho Chi Minh: De l'Indochine au Vietnam*. Collection Histoire. Paris: Découvertes Gallimard, 1990.

Hodgson, John. *The Uses of Drama*. London: Eyre Methuen Ltd, 1972.

Hollier, Denis, ed. *A New History of French Literature*. Cambridge, MA: Harvard University Press, 1994.

Holter, Karin. "Femmes d'Alger sortant de leur appartement." *Narcisse*, no. 9 (1989): 179–97.

Honderich, Ted, ed. *The Oxford Companion to Philosophy*. Oxford: Oxford University Press, 1995.

Huannou, Adrien. *La Question des littératures nationales*. Abidjan: CEDA, 1989.

Hubner, Zygmunt. *Theater and Politics*. Ed. and trans. Jadwiga Kosicka. Evanston, IL: Northwestern University Press, 1992.

Jamieson, Neil L. *Understanding Vietnam*. Berkeley: University of California Press, 1993.

Kahf, Mohja. *Western Representations of the Muslim Woman*. Austin: University of Texas Press, 1999.

Kandiyoti, Deniz. "Identity and Its Discontents: Women and the Nation." In *Colonial Discourse and Postcolonial Theory*, ed. Patrick Williams and Laura Chrisman, 376–91. New York: Columbia University Press, 1994.

Karnow, Stanley. *Vietnam: A History*. 1983. New York: Penguin Books, 1984.

Kateb, Yacine. *Nedjma*. 1956. Paris: Éditions du Seuil, 1996.

———. *L'Homme aux sandales de caoutchouc*. Paris: Éditions du Seuil, 1970.

———. Preface. In *La Grotte éclatée*. By Yamina Mechakra. Alger: Editions SNED, 1979.

———. *L'Œuvre en fragments*. Edited by Jacqueline Arnaud. Paris: Éditions Sindbad, 1986.

———. *Éclats de mémoire*. Edited by Olivier Corpet, Albert Dichy and Mireille Djaider. Paris: IMEC, 1994a.

———. *Le Poète comme un boxeur: Entretiens 1958–1989*. Edited by Gilles Carpentier. Paris: Editions du Seuil, 1994b.

———. *Boucherie de l'espérance*. Edited by Zebeida Chergui. Paris: Éditions du Seuil, 1999a.

———. *Minuit passé de douze heures: Écrits journalistiques 1947–1989*. Paris: Éditions du Seuil, 1999b.

Kaye, Jacqueline, and Abdelhamid Zoubir. *The Ambiguous Compromise: Language, Literature and National Identity in Algeria and Morocco*. London: Routledge, 1990.

Kelly, Gail P. "Colonial Schools in Vietnam: Policy and Practice." In *Education and Colonialism*, ed. Philip G. Altbach and Gail P. Kelly, 96–121. New York: Longman, 1978.

———. "Colonialism, Indigenous Society, and School Practices: French West Africa and Indochina, 1918–1938." In *Education and Colonialism*, ed. Philip G. Altbach and Gail P. Kelly, 9–32. New York: Longman, 1991.

Khatibi, Abdelkebir. "Incipits." In *Du Bilinguisme*, ed. Abdelkebir Khatibi, 172–195. Paris: Denoël, 1986.

Kingston, Maxine Hong. *The Woman Warrior*. New York: Alfred A. Knopf, 1994.

Lacoste, Camille, and Yves Lacoste. *L'État du Maghreb*. Paris: Éditions La Découverte, 1991.

Lanasri, Ahmed. *La Littérature algérienne de l'entre-deux guerres*. Paris: Publisud, 1995.

Landry, Donna, and Gerald Maclean, eds. *The Spivak Reader*. New York: Routledge, 1996.

Larsen, Wendy Wilder, and Tran Thi Nga. *Shallow Graves: Two Women and Vietnam*. New York: Random House, 1986.

Laroussi, Farid, and Christopher Miller, eds. *French and Francophone: The Challenge of Expanding Horizons*. New Haven, CT: Yale University Press, 2003.

Lazreg, Marnia. *The Eloquence of Silence*. New York: Routledge, 1994.

Lefèvre, Kim. *Métisse blanche*. Paris: Éditions Bernard Barrault, 1989.

———. *Retour à la saison des pluies*. Paris: Éditions Bernard Barrault, 1990.

———. Preface. In *Femmes du Vietnam: Visages d'hier & de demain*, ed. Christine Pictet, 13–20. Texte de Marie-France Briselance. Mane, France: Éditions de l'Envol, 1996.

Levenson, Michael, ed. *The Cambridge Companion to Modernism*. Cambridge: Cambridge University Press, 1999.

Lionnet, Françoise. *Postcolonial Representations: Women, Literature, Identity*. Ithaca, NY: Cornell University Press, 1995.

Louanchi, Denise. "Un essai de théâtre populaire: *L'Homme aux sandales de cautchouc*." In *Hommage à Kateb Yacine*, 187–204. Kalim 7: Langues et Littérature. Alger: Office des Publications Universitaires, 1987.

Lunn, Joe. *Memoirs of the Maelstrom: A Senegalese Oral History of the First World War*. Portsmouth, NH: Heinemann, 1999.

Ly Thu Ho. *Printemps inachevé*. Paris: J. Peyronnet et Cie, 1962.

———. *Au milieu du carrefour*. Paris: J. Peyronnet et Cie, 1969.

———. *Le Mirage de la paix*. Paris: Les Muses du Parnasse, 1986.

Mai Thu Vân, *Viêtnam: un peuple, des voix*. Paris: Pierre Horay Éditeur, 1983.

Malraux, André. *La Condition humaine*. Paris: Gallimard, 1946.

Mammeri, Mouloud. *L'Opium et le bâton*. 1965. Paris: Éditions La Découverte, Paris, 1992.

Marcus, K. Melissa, trans. Preface. In *The Forbidden Woman*, by Malika Mokeddem, vii–xiv. Lincoln: University of Nebraska Press, 1998.

Mariniello, Silvestra. Introduction. In *Gendered Agents: Women & Institutional Knowledge*, ed. Silvestra Mariniello and Paul A. Bové, 1–16. Durham, NC: Duke University Press, 1998.

Marr, David G. *Vietnamese Anticolonialism*. Berkeley: University of California Press, 1971.

Massu, Jacques. *La Vraie Bataille d'Alger*. Paris: Librairie Plon, 1971.

McClintock, Anne. "The Angel of Progress: Pitfalls of the Term 'Post-colonialism.'" In *Colonial Discourse and Post-Colonial Theory*, ed. Patrick Williams and Laura Chrisman, 291–304. New York: Columbia University Press, 1994.

———. *Imperial Leather: Race, Gender and Sexuality in the Colonial Contest*. New York: Routledge, 1995.

McConnell, Scott. *Leftward Journey: The Education of Vietnamese Students in France 1919–1939*. New Brunswick, NJ: Transaction Publishers, 1989.

Mechakra, Yamina. *La Grotte éclatée*. 2e édition. Alger: Entreprise nationale du livre, 1986.

———. "Arris: roman." *Algérie Littérature/Action* (September–October 1999): 5–91.

Mernissi, Fatima. *Beyond the Veil: Male-Female Dynamics in Modern Muslim Society*. Rev.ed. Indianapolis: Indiana University Press, 1987.

———. *Le Harem politique*. Paris: Albin Michel, 1987.

Messaoudi, Khalida. *Unbowed: An Algerian Woman Confronts Islamic Fundamentalism. Interviews with Elisabeth Schemla*. Trans. Anne C. Vila. Philadelphia: University of Pennsylvania Press, 1998.

Milkovitch-Rioux, Catherine. "Écritures féminines de la guerre/Feminine Representations of War." *L'Esprit Créateur* 40, no. 2 (2000): 3–8.

Miller, Christopher. *Theories of Africans*. Chicago: University of Chicago Press, 1990.

———. *Nationalists and Nomads*. Chicago: Chicago University Press, 1998.

Mishra, Vijay, and Bob Hodge. "What is Post(-)colonialism?" In *Colonial Discourse and Post-Colonial Theory*, ed. Patrick Williams and Laura Chrisman, 276–90. New York: Columbia University Press, 1994.

Mize, David W. *Algeria: A Study of the Educational System of Algeria and a Guide to the Academic Placement of Students in Educational Institutions of the United*

States. Washington, DC: American Association of Collegiate Registrars and Admissions Officers, 1978.

Mokeddem, Malika. *Les Hommes qui marchent*. 1990. Paris: Éditions Grasset et Fasquelle, 1997.

———. *Le Siècle des sauterelles*. Paris: Ramsay, 1992.

———. *L'Interdite*. Paris: Éditions Grasset et Fasquelle, 1993.

———. *Des Rêves et des assassins*. Paris: Éditions Grasset et Fasquelle, 1995.

———. *La Nuit de la lézarde*. Paris: Éditions Grasset et Fasquelle, 1998.

———. *N'zid*. Paris: Éditions du Seuil, 2001.

———. *La Transe des insoumis*. Paris: Éditions Grasset et Fasquelle, 2003.

Monego, Joan Phyllis. *Maghrebian Literature in French*. Boston: Twayne Publishers, 1984.

Mortimer, Mildred. *Journeys Through the French African Novel*. Portsmouth, NH: Heinemann, 1990.

Mortimer, Robert. "Algeria, Vietnam, and Afro-Asian Solidarity." *The Maghreb Review* 28, no. 1 (2003): 60–67.

Ngoc, Bich. "Opera of the Masses." *Vietnam Investment Review* 435 (February 14–20, 2000), at www.vir-vietnam.com/435vir/435tio00.htm.

Nguyen, Nathalie. "Across Colonial Borders: Patriarchal Constraints and Vietnamese Women in the Novels of Ly Thu Ho." In *Of Vietnam: Identities in Dialogue*. Ed. Jane Bradley Winston and Leakthina Chau-Pech Ollier, 193–209. New York: Palgrave, 2001.

———. *Vietnamese Voices: Gender and Cultural Identity in the Vietnamese Francophone Novel*. Dekalb, IL: Southeast Asia Publications, 2003.

Norindr, Panivong. *Phantasmatic Indochina: French Colonial Ideology in Architecture, Film, and Literature*. Durham, NC: Duke University Press, 1996.

Orlando, Valérie. *Nomadic Voices of Exile*. Athens: Ohio University Press, 1999.

———. *Of Suffocated Hearts and Tortured Souls: Seeking Subjecthood through Madness in Francophone Women's Writing of Africa and the Caribbean*. Lanham, MD: Lexington, 2002.

Parekh, Pushpa Naidu, and Sigma Fatima Jagne, eds. *Postcolonial African Writers: A Bio-Bibliographical Critical Source Book*. Westport, CT: Greenwood, 1998.

Pears, Pamela. "Kateb Yacine's Journey Beyond Algeria and Back." *Research in African Literatures* 34, no. 3 (2003): 100–114.

Pictet, Christine, ed. *Femmes du Vietnam: Visages d'hier et de demain*. Texte de Marie-France Briselance. Mane, France: Éditions de l'Envol, 1996.

Prochaska, David. *Making Algeria French: Colonialism in Bône, 1870–1920*. Cambridge: Cambridge University Press, 1990.

Rella, Franco. *The Myth of the Other: Lacan, Deleuze, Foucault, Bataille*. Trans. Nelson Moe. Washington, DC: Maisonneuve Press, 1994.

Rice, Laura. "Veiled Threats: Malek Alloula's *Colonial Harem*." In *Gendered Agents: Women & Institutional Knowledge*, ed. Silvestra Mariniello and Paul A. Bové, 144–58. Durham, NC: Duke University Press, 1998.

Roy, Jules. *La Guerre d'Algérie*. Paris: René Julliard, 1960.

Saïd, Edward W. *Orientalism*. New York: Random House, Vintage Books Edition, 1979.

———. *The World, the Text, and the Critic*. Cambridge, MA: Harvard University Press, 1983.

———. *Beginnings: Intention and Method*. New York: Columbia University Press. Morningside Ed., 1985.

———. *Culture and Imperialism*. New York: Random House, Inc. First Vintage Books Ed., 1994.

Salhi, Kamal. *The Politics and Aesthetics of Kateb Yacine: From Francophone Literature to Popular Theatre in Algeria and Outside*. Lewiston, NY: The Edwin Mellen Press, 1999.

Salhi, Zahia Smail. *Politics, Poetics and the Algerian Novel*. Lewiston, NY: The Edwin Mellen Press, 1999.

Sarraute, Nathalie. *Enfance*. Paris: Gallimard, 1983.

Sartre, Jean-Paul. "Les Damnés de la terre." In *Situations, V: Colonialisme et néo-colonialisme*, 167–93. Paris: Gallimard, 1964.

Schalk, David L. *War and the Ivory Tower: Algeria and Vietnam*. New York: Oxford University Press, 1991.

Schemla, Elisabeth. Glossary. In *Unbowed: An Algerian Woman Confronts Islamic Fundamentalism* by Khalida Messaoudi, 153–60. Trans. Anne C. Vila. Philadelphia: University of Pennsylvania Press, 1998.

Schipper, Mineke, ed. *Unheard Words: Women and Literature in Africa, the Arab World, Asia, the Caribbean and Latin America*. Trans. Barbara Potter Fasting. London: Allison and Busby, 1985.

Sebbar, Leïla. *Le Chinois vert d'Afrique*. Paris: Éditions Stock, 1984.

Segarra, Marta. *Leur pesant de poudre: romancières francophones du Maghreb*. Paris: L'Harmattan, 1997.

Selimovic, Mesa. *La Forteresse*. Trans. Jean Descat and Simone Meuris. Paris: Gallimard, 1981.

Sontag, Susan. *Illness as Metaphor*. New York: Farrar, Strauss and Giroux, 1978.

Sorum, Paul Clay. *Intellectuals and Decolonization in France*. Chapel Hill: The University of North Carolina Press, 1977.

Soucy, Alexander. "Vietnamese Warriors, Vietnamese Mothers: State Imperatives in the Portrayal of Women." *Canadian Woman Studies/Les Cahiers de la Femme* 19, no. 4 (2000): 121–26.

Spivak, Gayatri Chakravorty. "Can the Subaltern Speak?" In *Colonial Discourse and Post-Colonial Theory*, ed. Patrick Williams and Laura Chrisman, 66–111. New York: Columbia University Press, 1994.

Stone, Martin. *The Agony of Algeria*. New York: Columbia University Press, 1997.

Stora, Benjamin. *Histoire de l'Algérie coloniale*. Paris: Éditions La Découverte 1991.

———. *Imaginaires de guerre: Algérie-Viêt-nam, en France et aux Etats-Unis*. Paris: Éditions la Découverte, 1997.

———. *Algérie, Formation d'une nation*. Biarritz: Atlantica, 1998.

Suleiman, Susan Rubin. *Subversive Intent*. Cambridge, MA: Harvard University Press, 1990.

Tahon, Marie-Blanche. "Women Novelists and Women in the Struggle for Algeria's National Liberation (1957–1980)." *Research in African Literatures* 23, no. 2 (1992): 39–50.

Tan, Amy. *The Joy Luck Club*. New York: G. P. Putnam's Sons, 1989.

Taylor, Sandra C. *Vietnamese Women at War: Fighting for Ho Chi Minh and the Revolution*. Lawrence: University Press of Kansas, 1999.

Templer, Robert. *Shadows and Wind: A View of Modern Vietnam*. New York: Penguin Books, 1999.

Tétreault, Mary Ann, ed. *Women and Revolution in Africa, Asia, and the New World*. Columbia: University of South Carolina Press, 1994.

Trinh T. Minh-ha. *Cinema Interval*. New York: Routledge, 1999.

Turner, Karen Gottschang. *Even the Women Must Fight: Memories of War from North Vietnam*. New York: John Wiley and Sons, Inc., 1998.

Valensi, Lucette. "The Scheherazade Syndrome: Literature and Politics in Postcolonial Algeria." In *Algeria in Others' Languages*. Ed. Anne-Emmanuelle Berger, 139–53. Ithaca, NY: Cornell University Press, 2002.

Van Houwelingen, Flora. "Francophone Literatue in North Africa." In *Unheard Words: Women and Literature in Africa, the Arab World, Asia, the Caribbean and Latin America*. Ed. Mineke Schipper and trans. Barbara Potter Fasting, 102–13. London: Allison and Busby, 1985.

"Vietnam." Narrated by Daniel Zwerdling. *Weekend Edition Saturday*. National Public Radio. WDUQ, Pittsburgh. July 1, 2000.

Voogd de, Lourina. "Arabic Literature in North Africa." In *Unheard Words: Women and Literature in Africa, the Arab World, Asia, the Caribbean and Latin America*. Ed. Mineke Schipper and trans. Barbara Potter Fasting, 91–101. London: Allison and Busby, 1985.

Watts, Philip. "The Henri Martin Affair: A Forgotten *Cause Célèbre*." Paper presented at the Conference on Law and Literature, Emory University, Atlanta, GA, October 2000.

White, Christine Pelzer. "Vietnam: War, Socialism, and the Politics of Gender Relations." In *Promissory Notes*. Edited by Sonia Kruks, Rayna Rapp, and Marilyn B. Young, 172–92. New York: Monthly Review Press, 1989.

Williams, Patrick, and Laura Chrisman, eds. *Colonial Discourse and Postcolonial Theory: A Reader*. New York: Columbia University Press, 1994.

Wing-Tsit Chan, *A Source Book in Chinese Philosophy*. Princeton, NJ: Princeton, University Press, 1963.

Winston, Jane Bradley, and Leakthina Chau-Pech Ollier, eds. *Of Vietnam*. New York: Palgrave, 2001.

Woodhull, Winifred. "Unveiling Algeria." *Genders*, no. 10 (spring 1991): 113–31.
———. *Transfigurations of the Maghreb: Feminism, Decolonization, and Literatures*. Minneapolis: University of Minnesota Press, 1993.
Yeager, Jack A. *The Vietnamese Novel in French: A Literary Response to Colonialism*. Hanover, NH: University Press of New England, 1987.
———. "Blurring the Lines in Vietnamese Fiction in French: Kim Lefèvre's *Métisse blanche*." In *Postcolonial Subjects: Francophone Women Writers*. Ed. Mary Jean Green et al., 210–26. Minneapolis: University of Minnesota Press, 1996.
———. "Kim Lefèvre's *Retour à la saison des pluies*: Rediscovering the Landscapes of Childhood." *L'Esprit Créateur* 33, no. 2 (1993): 47–57.
Young, Iris Marion. *Justice and the Politics of Difference*. Princeton, NJ: Princeton University Press, 1990.

INDEX

ABOUT THE AUTHOR

Pamela A. Pears is Assistant Professor of French in the Department of Foreign Languages, Literatures, and Cultures at Washington College in Chestertown, Maryland. Her research interests include Algerian and Vietnamese writing in French, the impact of war on gender roles, the marketing of North African women writers, and the future of multiculturalism in France. She is also interested in both gender and postcolonial theory and how the two can be tied together.